The God of Human Blood

ISBN-10 1-59405-089-9
ISBN-13 978-1-59405-089-3
Design and cover, John Wayne Eastwood.

Published by N2Print.
Published and Printed in the United States of America.

This book is dedicated to my parents,
Ernest and Lorene Denney,
as well as to the
Denney sisters

. . .

and to all honorable cavemen everywhere.

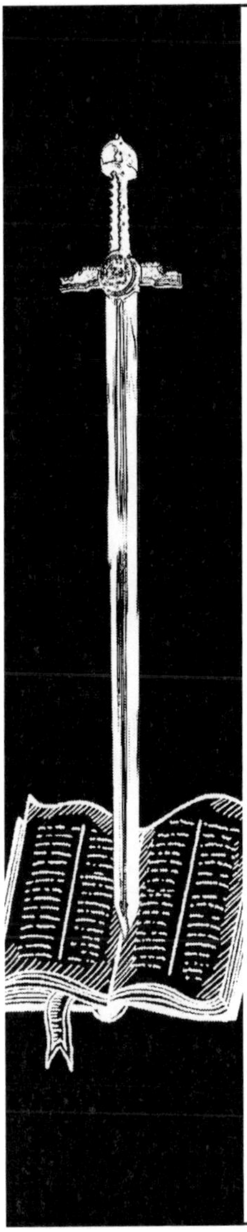

Table of Contents

Publisher's Preface xi
Preface. xvii
Chapter 1: Receipt of the Law .5
Chapter 2: Murders Prior to Mount Sinai 27
Chapter 3: Murder in the Wilderness 43
Interlude I: Israelites and God's Chosen People 55
Chapter 4: Murder in the Promised Land 61
Chapter 5: The Murderous Reign of King David 93
Chapter 6: Assassinations, Child Sacrifice and
Listening to the Prophets 117
Interlude II: Can God Commit Murder?. 135
Chapter 7: Chronicles (Killing Kin), Esther,
and Job 141
Chapter 8: Prophetic Murder. 153
Chapter 9: Judgment Against the Nations 165
Interlude III: Bibles, Dates, and Numbers 187
Chapter 10: Suicides and Assassinations Revisited . . 193
Chapter 11: Thy Will Be Dead. 201
Chapter 12: Psalms of Death and Proverbs
of Doom 217
Epilogue. 227
Exhibit A: Murders Prior to Mount Sinai. 235
Exhibit B: Attempted or Plotted Murder 241
Exhibit C: In the Wilderness. 245
Exhibit D: Conquering the Promised Land 251
Exhibit E: Settling the Promised Land 257
Exhibit F: Murderous Reign of King David 267
Exhibit G: Assassinations, Child Sacrifice,
and Prophets. 281
Exhibit H: Chronicles and Esther 295
Exhibit I: Prophetic Murder 301
Exhibit J: Final Numbers 305
Bibliography 309
Annotations 313

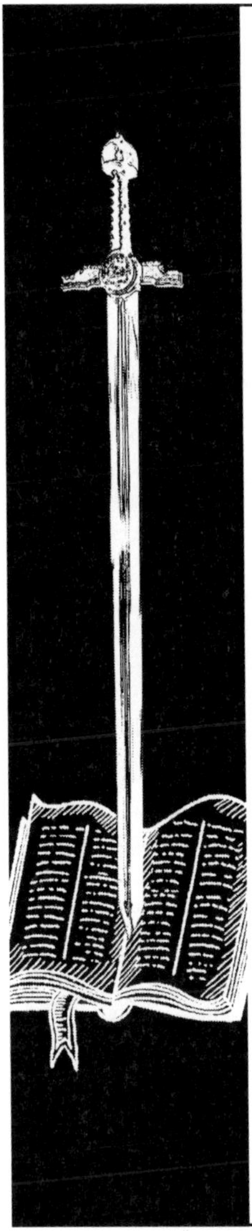

Publisher's Preface

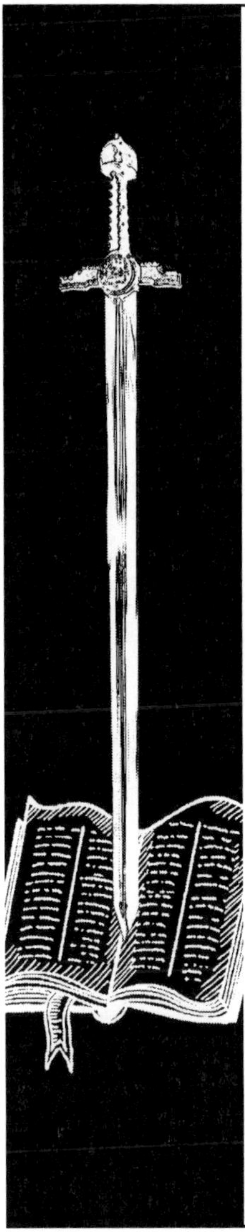

A bloody God - Different from all the rest?

Before reading this work, we believe some observations should be made. First, while we agree with the author's premise that the God of Israel and the Christians is with some justification conceived of as an avenging and spiteful God, a God that punishes iniquities to the nth generation; rationally speaking, we must state that the concept of such a God or gods is nothing more or less than the concretization of the national ideals and cultural sophistication of the peoples who venerated and believed in them.

Moreover, one is in danger of cursory and one-sided scholarship when one compares the gods of this formative time to those of our present conceptions, as most gods of that time were conceived by the peoples living in a more brutal and combative era than those views of our present era, hopefully!

Even so, the God of the Christians, who was conceived of by those who brought us the Inquisition, would be no less bloodthirsty and punitive — and this was only 400 to 500 years ago!

But, as stated earlier, every god must be viewed as the conception and embodiment of the world from which it sprang. That is, the gods of the war-like and constantly feuding Celts were no less bloodthirsty than the gods of the Norsemen—Thor with his hammer and Woden with his axe. Such was the level of culture in those times; and likewise, such

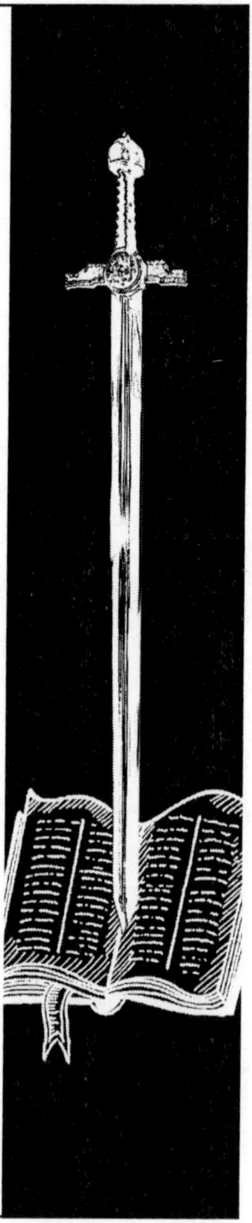

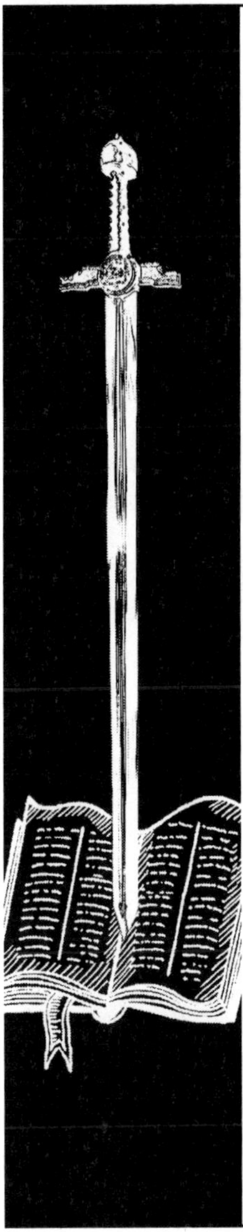

was the level of the Hebrews and Canaanites during the formative conception of their gods.

Unless one takes the culturally myopic and fundamentalist view of a one true God, these facts must be observed and stated here.

We believe this book makes a relevant point. The origin of the Hebrew god is more related to the volcano god of Sinai — mercurial, overflowing with hot flames and lava. However, we, as publishers, must state that the Jewish people are all too often held up to a separate standard distinct from every other group in the world. This is unfair, unjust, and can easily be motivated by a classic, formulaic European anti-Semitism.

The Jews, Hebrews, Canaanites, or whatever their origins may have been, were no more or no less bloodthirsty, than most every other group that dwelled in that far-distant period of time.

Therefore we believe that while the reader should understand the justification of the author's views, we wish to state that this "god" must not be seen as separate from any other god that was engendered by the mind of man at that time.

Still, the reader should be left with this one question: Was it the God of Christ, the God of love and understanding, who came up with the Inquisition, Auschwitz, Nagasaki, and Hiroshima? We will let the reader decide what progress has been made?

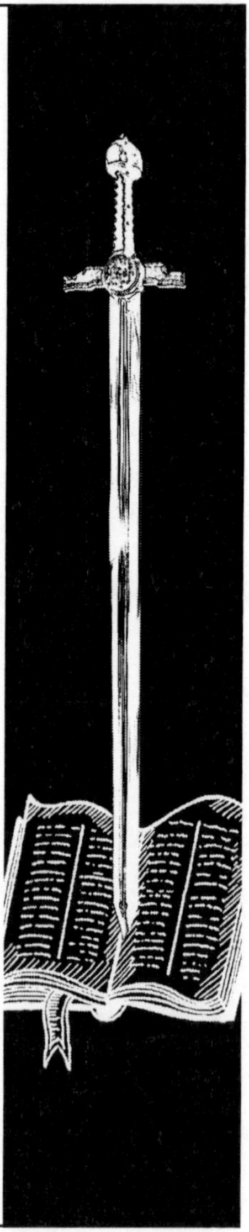

The Executive Editors,
New Age World Publishing

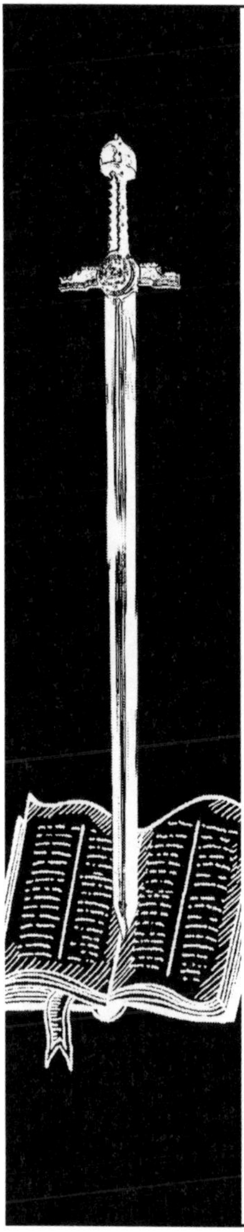

Preface

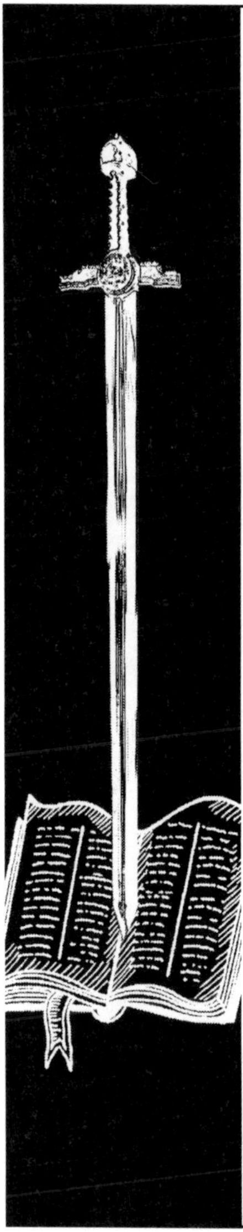

In the beginning, I assert that this book is not anti-Semitic.[1] Yes, it is a book that chronicles the Israelites' breaking of the Sixth Commandment, which declares: "Thou shalt not murder." But the fact that God's Chosen People were recognized as "Israelites" is not the issue or the focus.

For the purposes of this study, the Israelites could have been any nationality — Jordanians, Arabians, even Americans. The designation is secondary. The significant fact is that God's Chosen People of the Old Testament — by whatever name or title — were probably some of the greatest transgressors of the Sixth Commandment of all time.

I was reared as a Baptist and now attend the United Methodist Church. But any dedicated Christian knows that, although the New Testament inaugurated the life and teachings of Jesus Christ, the New Testament does not in any shape or form supplant the Old Testament. Indeed, knowledge and analysis of the Old Testament only heightens the Christian's appreciation for the Gospels and latter books. The first half of the Bible is as relevant to the Christian as a dictionary is to the wordsmith.

So what is the purpose of this book? What is to be gained by studying how God's Chosen People broke the Sixth Commandment, not once but *many* times over? Does it matter that He or His people were responsible for nearly 2.5 million deaths during

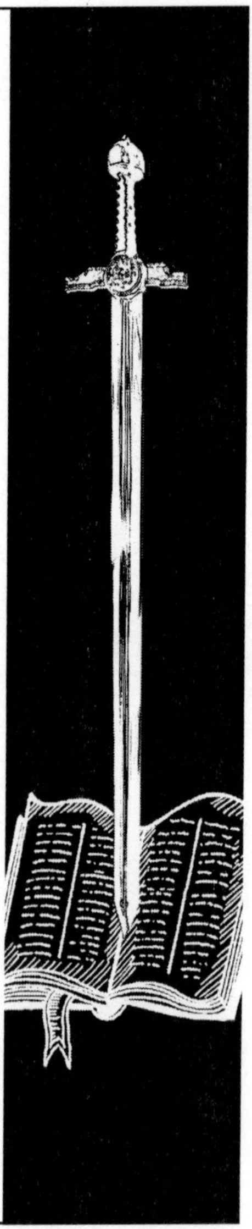

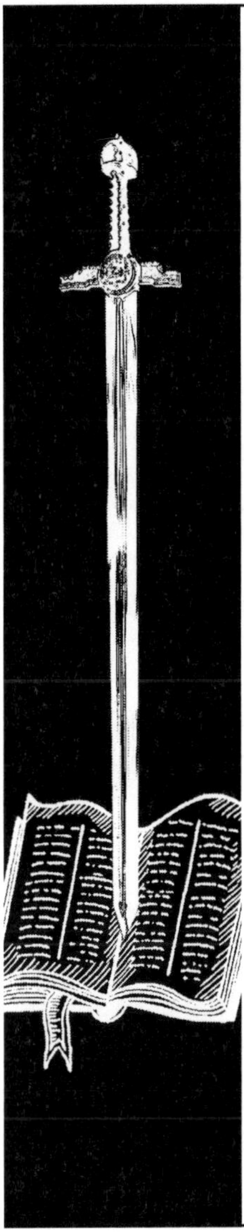

Old Testament times, not counting numerous instances of mass genocide? Is it relevant to today?

There is a term in the legal profession known as "black-letter law." In its most basic form, the concept means to look at the law (usually the statute or judicial decision) as written, without reading into it any personal or community interpretation. In other words, it says what it says and no more. The Sixth Commandment demands "Thou shalt not murder."[2] It does not say "thou shalt not murder unless you are killing in the name of God" or "thou shalt not murder unless you are acting in self-defense." The four words, by the black-letter law, speak for themselves — Thou Shalt Not Murder — period.

The purpose of this book, then, is to inspect — indeed stare at —

the black-letter law of the Old Testament and how its people transgressed that very law. The Old Testament, also known as the Hebrew Bible (or *Tanakh*), has survived for nearly three thousand years and is *the* sacred text for Christians and Jews, two of the world's most populous religions.[3] It is vitally important, therefore, to know exactly what the Old Testament says, not just the edited version that most of us were taught in Sunday School.

For example, even most secular persons know the story of how Moses went up onto Mount Sinai and received the Ten Commandments from the Lord. Coming down the mountain, Moses sees that the people have cast a golden calf in his absence. Moses, his anger burning hot, throws down and breaks the tablets on which

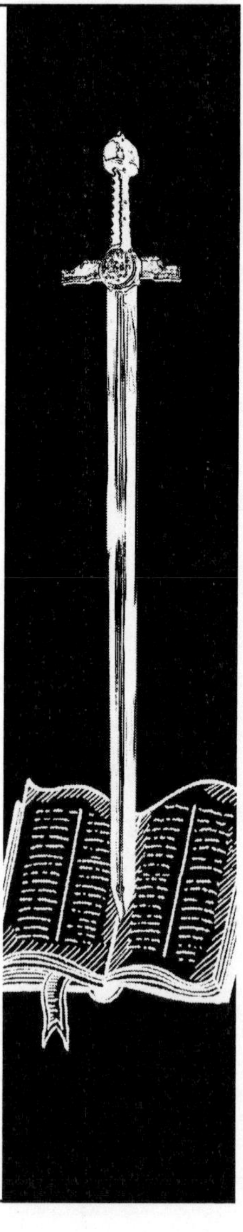

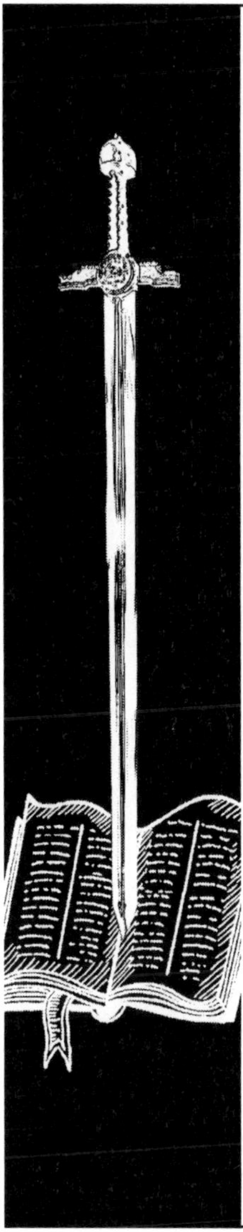

the Lord has written the Commandments.

But the story does not end there. Within hours (possibly minutes) of receiving the Sixth Commandment, "Thou Shalt Not Murder," Exodus 32:26–28 continues:

◆ ◆ ◆

[T]hen Moses stood in the gate of the camp, and said, "Who is on the Lord's side? Come to me!" And all the sons of Levi gathered around him. He said to them, "Thus says the Lord, the God of Israel, 'Put your sword on your side each of you! Go back and forth from gate to gate throughout the camp, and each of you kill your brother, your friend, and your neighbor.'" The sons of Levi did as Moses commanded, and about three thousand of the people fell on that day.

◆ ◆ ◆

Moses has just ordered, in God's name, the summary murder of fellow Israelites. Moreover, there appears no hesitation on the part of the Levites to carry out Moses' judgment of execution. The Sixth Commandment thus stands as one of the first commandments broken, 3,000 times, after Moses' descent from the mountain.

Moses' descent with the Ten Commandments then is a critical juncture in the biblical story. The argument is persuasive that prior to Mount Sinai, any transgression of the Sixth Commandment cannot be counted against God's people as they would have been unaware of God's commandments. This book, therefore, chronologically divides violations as occurring either before or after Moses' receipt of the tablets — with one

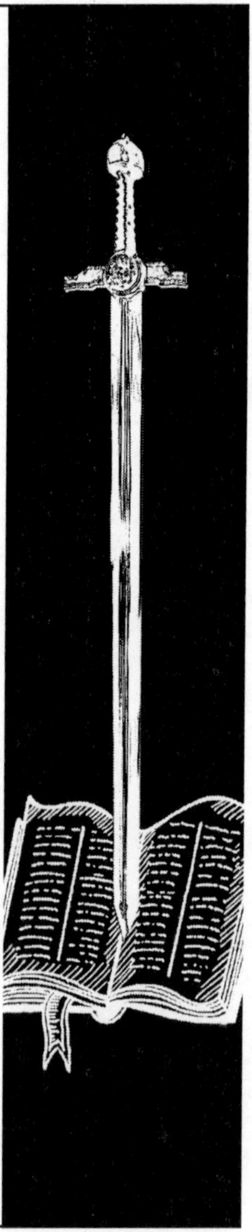

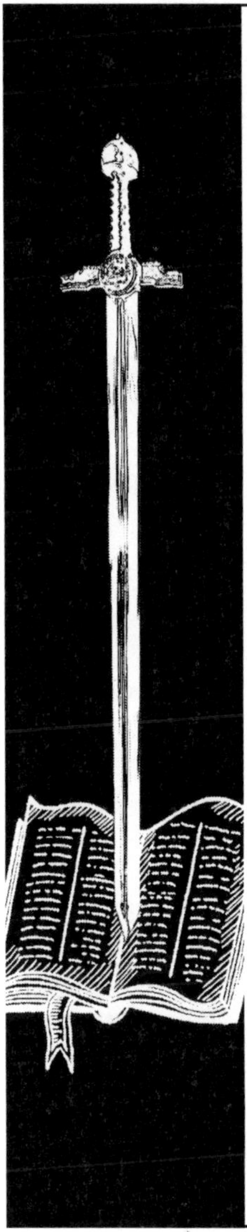

exception. In Genesis 9:5–6a, God states:

◆ ◆ ◆

For [man's] own lifeblood I will surely require a reckoning: from every animal I will require it and from human beings, each one for the blood of another, I will require a reckoning for human life. Whoever sheds the blood of a human, by a human shall that person's blood be shed.

◆ ◆ ◆

The prohibition against murder (and the concept of capital punishment) thus occurs very early in Scripture.

Whether a killing should be counted as a trespass against God's law, either after the Genesis decree or only after Mount Sinai, is a decision I leave to the individual reader.

Finally, hopefully to whet your appetite for the following pages, I bring you a story straight from the Old Testament. The facts are accurately recorded, although the groups have been re-named to accord with present-day circumstances.

I use Christian denominations also to underscore the fact that the designation of God's Chosen People in the Old Testament as either "Israelites" or "Jews" is not the issue.

◆ ◆ ◆

Once upon a time, there were twelve denominations of Christians: Baptists, Methodists, Lutherans, Episcopalians, Roman Catholics, etc. A Baptist preacher and his mistress were on a journey and stopped at a friend's house to stay the night. Some perverse men in the town, from the Meth-

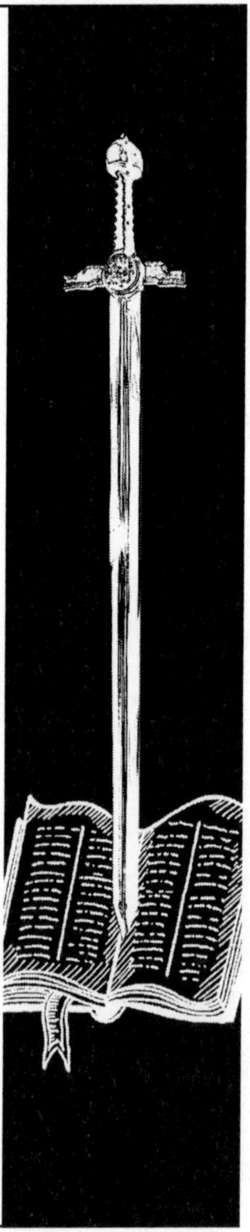

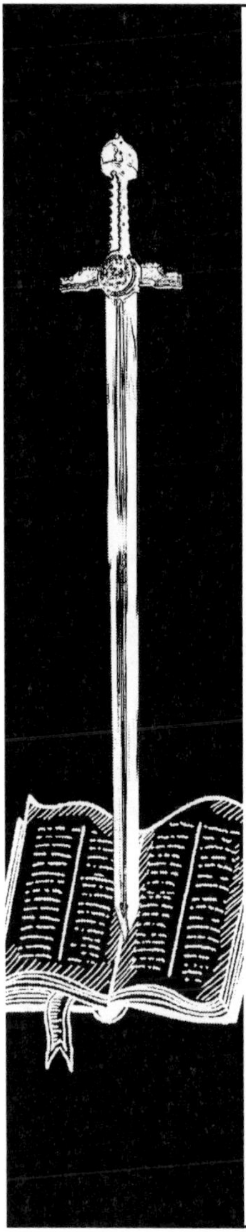

odist denomination, come to the friend's house and demand that the Baptist preacher be brought out so they can have homosexual relations with him. The friend refuses, offering the men instead his own virgin daughter as well as the Baptist preacher's mistress.

The Methodists refuse, but the Baptist preacher sends out his mistress anyway. The Methodist men then proceed to rape and abuse the mistress all through the night until the next morning.

When they finally let her go, she makes it to the doorstep of the friend's house before dying on the threshold. The Baptist preacher takes home his dead mistress, cuts her up into eleven pieces, and sends a piece to each of the other eleven denominations to show what the Methodists have done.

Groups from each of the eleven denominations meet and then decide to avenge the Baptist preacher by going to war against the Methodists. On the first three days of battle, 40,030 men from the eleven denominations are killed.

On the third day, however, the tide turns and the eleven dominations kill 25,100 Methodist men, as well as all the Methodist wives. After all is said and done, only 600 Methodist men survive.

Oops.

The eleven denominations now realize that since all the Methodist wives have been killed, the Methodist denomination may die out. Not wanting this to happen, the eleven denominations devise two strategies to find new wives for the remaining 600 Methodist men.

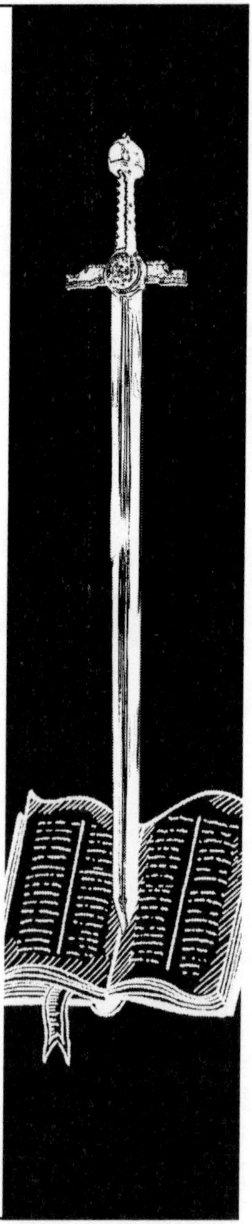

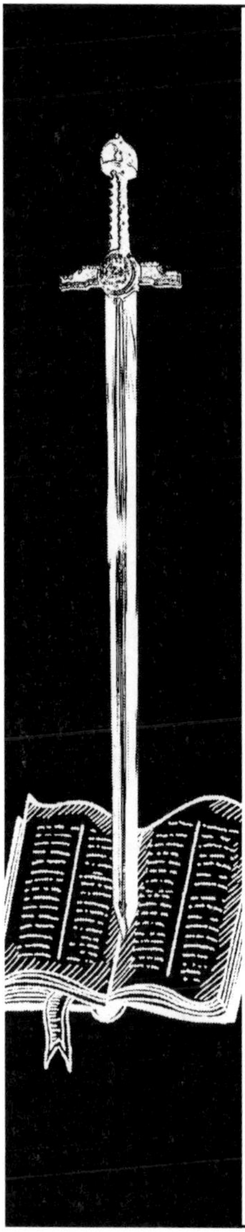

First, the eleven denominations go to a city of Lutherans who did not participate in the initial war against the Methodists. As punishment, the eleven denominations kill all the males and non-virgin women in the city. The 400 virgin women are then taken to the Methodist men to be their wives.

The second strategy involves going to a city that is having a dancing festival. Men from the eleven denominations proceed to abduct some women dancers to be additional wives for the Methodist men.[4]

* * *

True story.

Only the names are changed.

Read on . . .

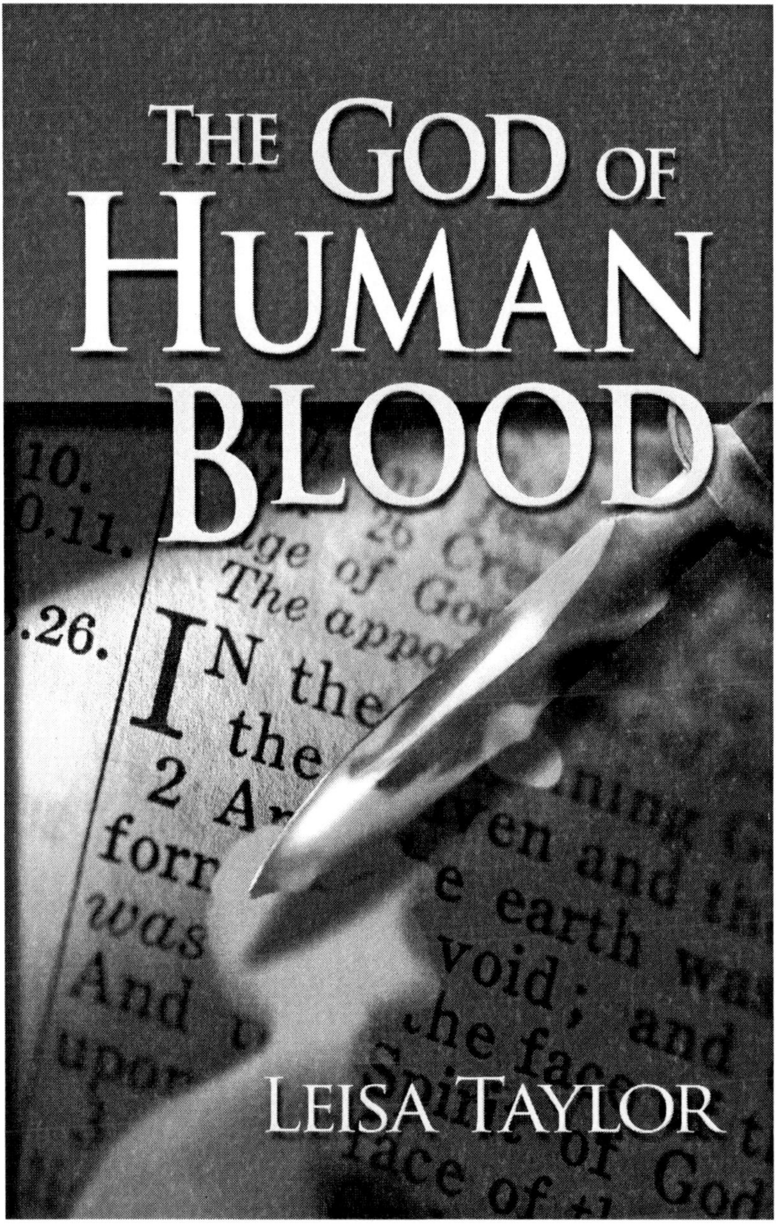
THE GOD OF
HUMAN
BLOOD
LEISA TAYLOR

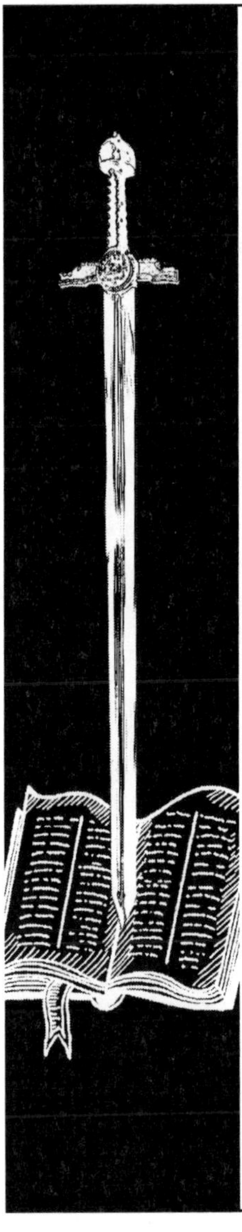

Chapter One

Receipt of the Law

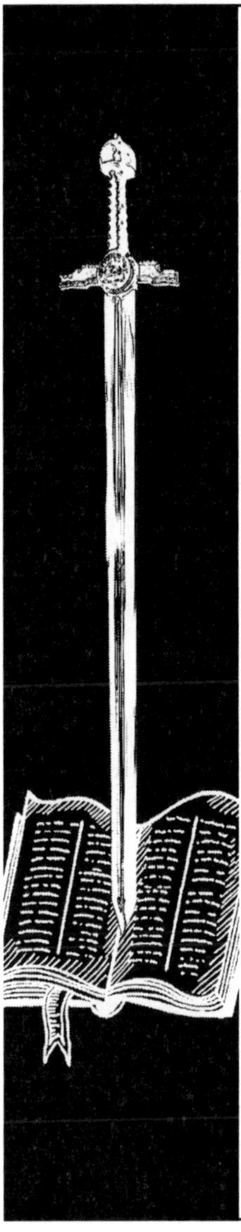

Much has already occurred by the time Moses receives the Ten Commandments from the Lord on Mount Sinai:

God has created the world in six days; Adam and Eve[1] have been expelled from the Garden of Eden; Cain has murdered Abel; Noah has rescued a remnant of mankind and the animals from God's worldwide flood; and the people have been scattered from the Tower of Babel.

Sodom and Gomorrah have been destroyed; Abraham has received the call from God and almost sacrifices his son; and Joseph ends up in Egypt after being sold by his jealous brothers. As the reader can see, the book of

Genesis is, if nothing else, an action-packed narrative.

Exodus opens with the story of the oppression of the Israelites in Egypt and Moses' famous call to "let my people go."[2] Pharaoh's heart is hardened so that God may display his miraculous powers through the ten plagues, ending with the wholesale slaughter of every firstborn in Egypt — "from the firstborn of Pharaoh who sits on his throne to the firstborn of the female slave who is behind the handmill, and all the firstborn of the livestock."[3]

The Israelites' firstborns are saved by the angel of death "passing over" any doorpost marked with the sacrificial blood of a year-old, unblemished male lamb.

Psalms 78:49–51 commemorates this final and virulent plague:

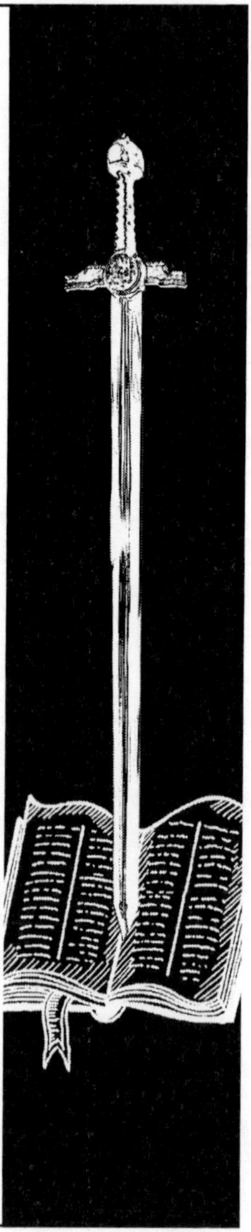

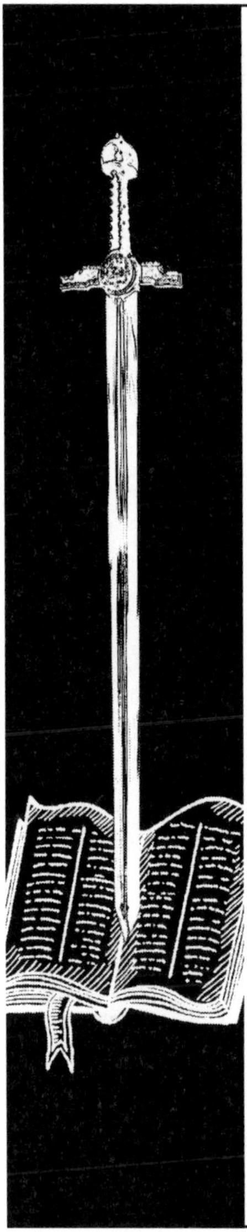

◆ ◆ ◆

[God] let loose on [the Egyptians] his fierce anger, wrath, indignation, and distress, a company of destroying angels.

He made a path for his anger; he did not spare them from death, but gave their lives over to the plague.

He struck all the firstborn in Egypt, the issue of their strength in the tents of Ham.

◆ ◆ ◆

Yet even the plagues and firstborn carnage prove insufficient to display God's potency. God has one more miracle up his sleeve — parting the Red Sea[4] — before the Israelites begin their sojourn in the wilderness.

In Exodus 15:7–8, Moses and the Israelites sing a victory hymn to the Lord:

◆ ◆ ◆

In the greatness of your majesty, you overthrew your adversaries;

You sent out your fury, it consumed them like stubble.

At the blast of your nostrils the waters piled up, the floods stood up in a heap;

The deeps congealed in the heart of the sea.

◆ ◆ ◆

Exodus 19:1 transports the Israelites into the wilderness of Sinai on the third new moon after leaving the land of Egypt. It is on the Israelites' third day of encampment that Scripture, Exodus 20, begins to swell with imagery and suspense.

First, there is thunder and lightning, a thick cloud on Mount Sinai, and a trumpet blast so loud that all the people tremble. Smoke descends on the mountain, which

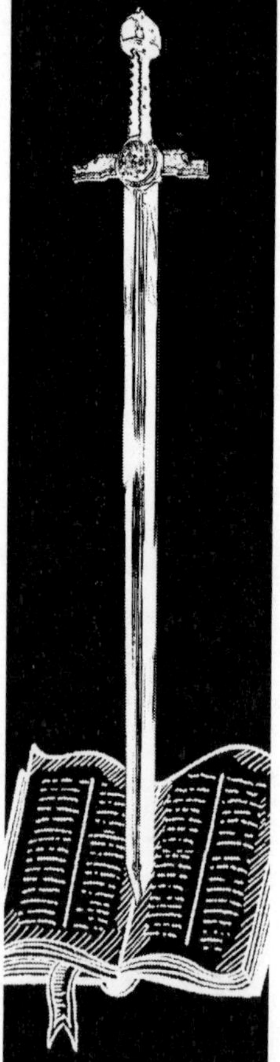

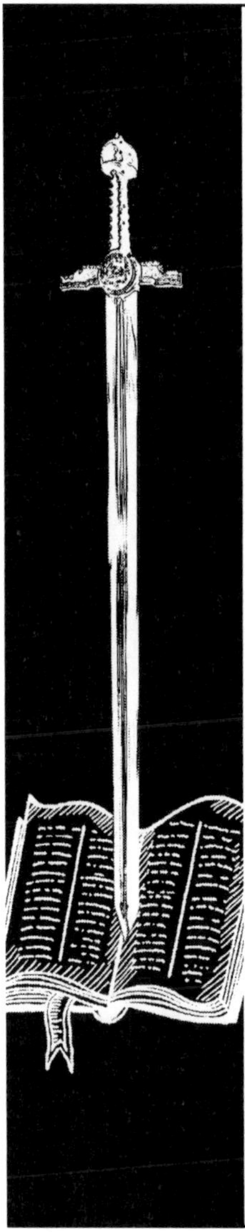

shakes violently, and when Moses speaks, God answers him in thunder.

The Lord descends to the top of Mount Sinai, whereupon Moses is summoned to ascend for their first meeting.[5] It is at this initial encounter that Moses verbally receives the Ten Commandments and thereafter relays them to the people.

Moses ascends Mount Sinai for a second time in Exodus 24, where the Ten Commandments are actually written by God on the stone tablets. Exodus 20, however, is where the Israelites first learn of their new laws.

The Christian Old Testament and the *Tanakh* (the Hebrew Bible) vary slightly in their interpretation of the first two commandments. The difference does not affect the import of the commandments, but for the sake of accuracy, it should be identified for the reader.

The Book of Exodus Chapter 20, verses 1–5a taken from the *Tanakh* read:

◆ ◆ ◆

God spoke all these words, saying: I the Lord am your God who brought you out of the land of Egypt, the house of bondage: You shall have no other gods besides Me.

You shall not make for yourself a sculptured image, or any likeness of what is in the heavens above, or on the earth below, or in the waters under the earth. You shall not bow down to them or serve them.

◆ ◆ ◆

The slight variance between the Christian and Jewish traditions can be summarized as follows:

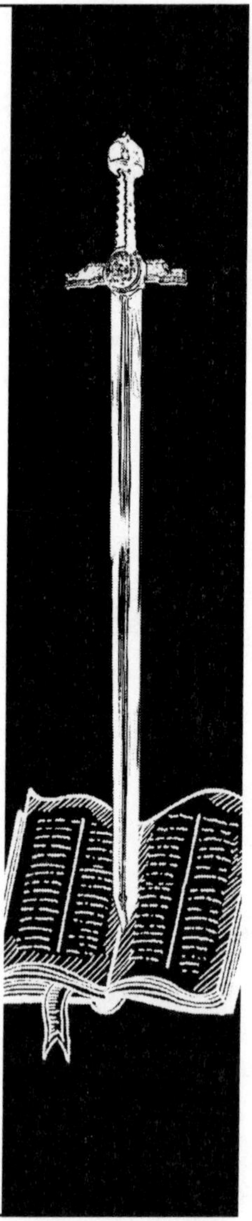

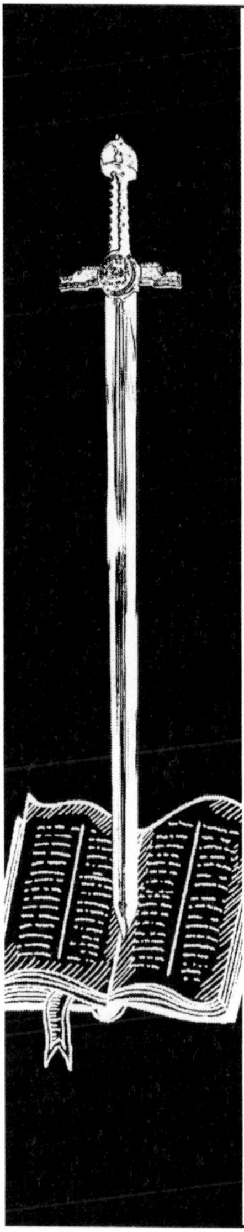

Hebrew First Commandment—I the Lord am your God. Second—No other gods besides the Lord. No graven images. Christian First Commandment—No other gods besides Lord. Second—No graven images.

The difference is slight, being basically a matter of how the paragraphs are constructed. And for the purposes of this book, the variation is inconsequential as both versions agree in meaning.

The final eight commandments are the same in both Bibles:

Third: You shall not swear falsely by the name of the Lord.

Fourth: Remember the Sabbath and keep it holy.

Fifth: Honor your father and mother.

Sixth: You shall not murder.

Seventh: You shall not commit adultery.

Eighth: You shall not steal.

Ninth: You shall not bear false witness.

Tenth: You shall not covet.

◆ ◆ ◆

Although the Ten Commandments represent the pinnacle of God's decrees, the book of Exodus and its follow-up, Leviticus, are rife with other rules, restrictions, and ordinances.[6] Everything from sacrificial offerings of animals to forbidden sexual relations is covered, often several times over.

Leviticus in particular demonstrates both the scope and specificity of the biblical instructions. For example, Leviticus 12:2–8 dictates in detail the purification ritual of a woman after childbirth:

◆ ◆ ◆

If a woman conceives and bears a male child, she shall be

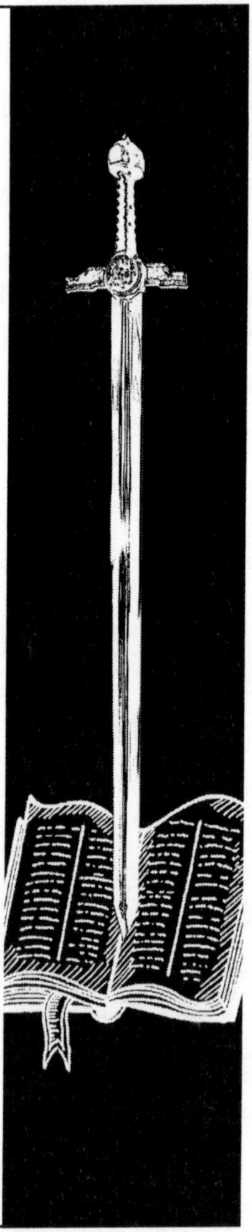

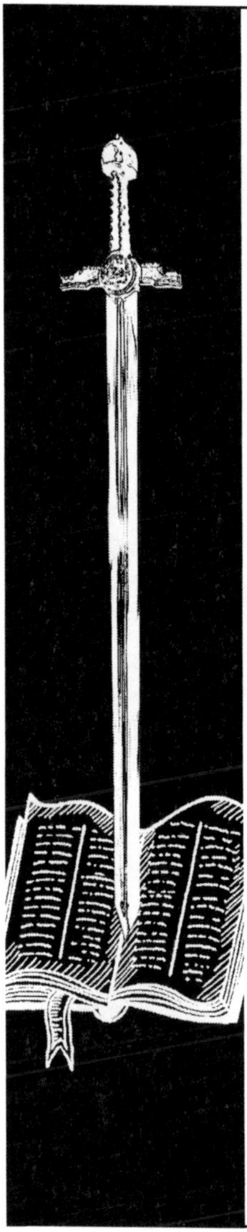

ceremonially unclean for seven days; as at the time of her menstruation, she shall be unclean . . . Her time of blood purification shall be thirty-three days; she shall not touch any holy thing, or come into the sanctuary, until the days of her purification are over. If she bears a female child, she shall be unclean two weeks, as in her menstruation; her time of blood purification shall be sixty-six days. When the days of her purification are completed, whether for a son or for a daughter, she shall bring to the priest at the entrance of the tent of meeting a lamb in its first year for a burnt offering, and a pigeon and a turtledove for a sin offering . . . If she cannot afford a sheep, she shall take two turtledoves and two pigeons . . .

◆ ◆ ◆

As evident, dictates about the intimate details of life, like a woman's giving birth and menstruation, are passed on to the people through Moses. Even a man's bodily discharges are regulated, as Leviticus 15:2–5 provides:

◆ ◆ ◆

When any man has a discharge from his member, his discharge makes him ceremonially unclean. The uncleanness is this: whether his member flows with his discharge, or his member is stopped from discharging, it is uncleanness for him. Every bed on which the one with the discharge lies shall be unclean; and everything on which he sits shall be unclean. Anyone who touches his bed shall wash his clothes, and bathe in water, and be unclean until the evening.

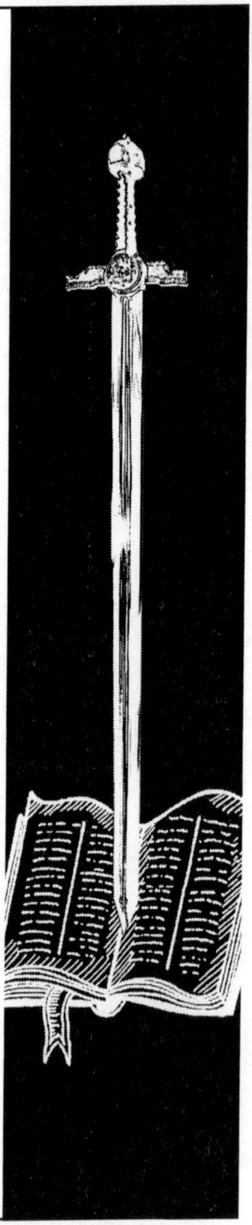

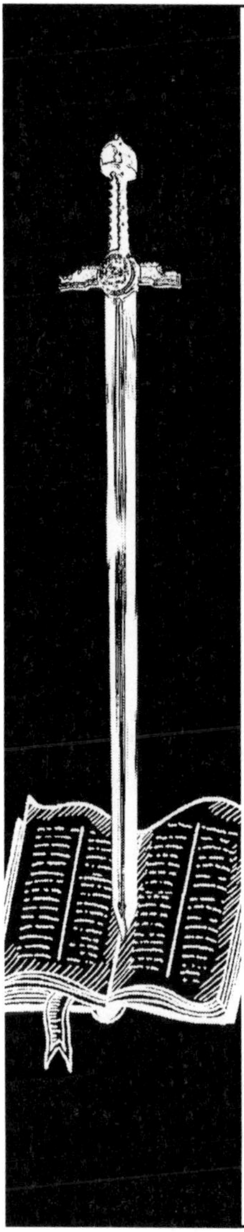

• • •

The laws and statutes regarding a man's bodily emissions actually continue for another thirteen verses, but the reader gets the point. Exodus and Leviticus may be sometimes tedious and repetitive reading, but they are certainly fascinating for their breadth and detail — definitely *not* bedtime material.

Wading in this sea of comprehensive and often perplexing regulations, one must always return to the first rules given by God through Moses to the Israelites: the Ten Commandments. They are interesting not only for what they include, but also for what they don't. Modern-day evils such as pedophilia, pornography, and terrorism don't make the list. Nor do kidnapping, prostitution, or slavery.

Forced labor was prevalent in the Old Testament, as was slavery. Although it was not permissible for Israelites to enslave fellow Israelites, Leviticus 25:44–46 permitted the Israelites to acquire male and female slaves from other nations.

Moreover, slaves were considered property and would be inherited by one's children as property. Taking children as slaves was also legal (Exodus 21:7; 2 Kings 4:1).

The Ten Commandments are just that — commands. No specific punishments are included, although God states in Exodus 20:5a that He will punish children for the iniquity of their parents, to the third and fourth generations. Not punishing the actual sinner but the sinner's children instead was actually quite common in the Old Testament.

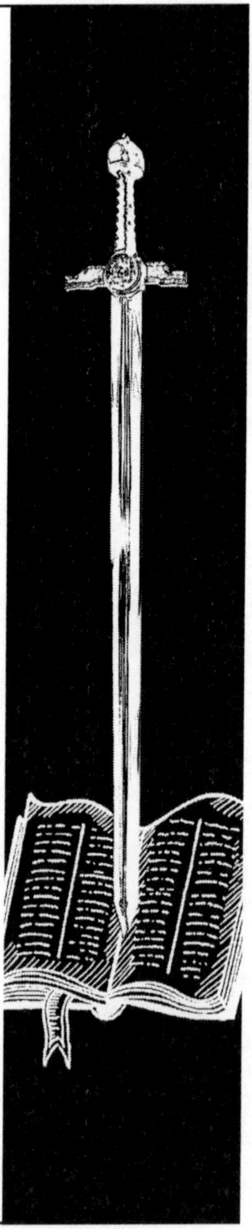

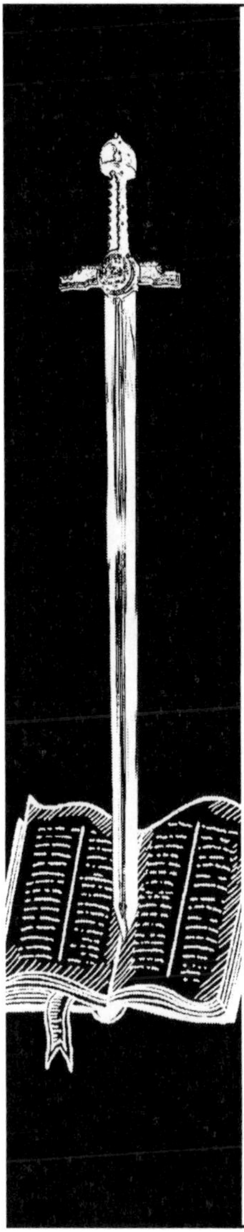

Details of this practice, as well as its questionable morality, are beyond the scope of this study. Suffice it to say that by the eighteenth chapter of Ezekiel (the twenty-sixth of the thirty-nine books of Old Testament), the notion of individual responsibility has entered the scene.

If the Ten Commandments themselves do not prescribe any punishments for failure to keep them, Leviticus and Deuteronomy fill in the gaps. Remembering that the people of the time were hunters and gatherers, rewards and punishments were often tied to the land.

For example, Leviticus 26:20 promises that disobedience will result in the land not yielding its produce and the trees not yielding their fruit. Lack of rain is also a common threat.

One school of thought propounds that obedience to God's laws was not motivated by fear of punishment, but rather by God's absolute authority and the people's desire to live in accordance with His will.[7] God had established His authority by delivering His people out of Egypt.

But the people's desire to live in accordance with His will cannot be divorced from their fear of punishment. Scripture repeatedly guarantees disastrous consequences for failure to follow the Lord's decrees. Leviticus 26 and Deuteronomy 28 contain a litany of punishing ills from the Lord, including:

1. terror and pestilence, panic, disaster, destruction and death;
2. consumption and fever that waste the eyes and cause life to pine away;

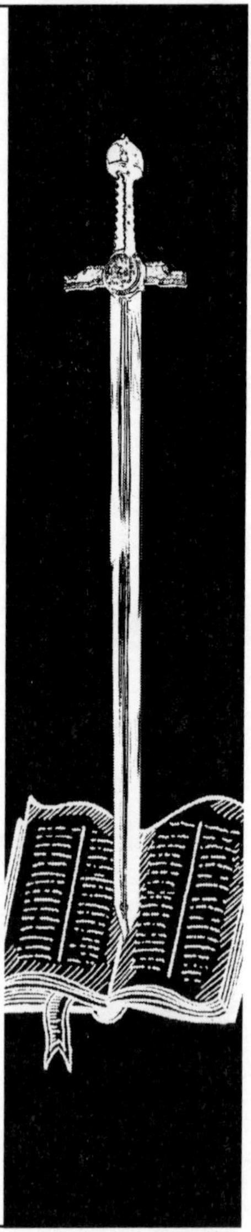

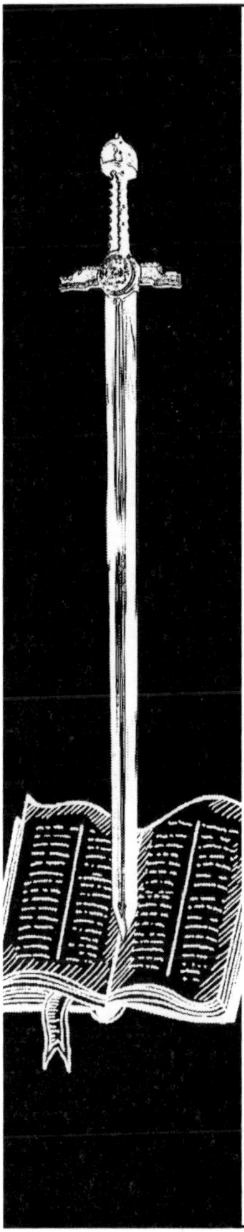

3. striking down or deliverance into enemy hands;
4. wild animals that destroy children and livestock;
5. vengeance by the sword of the Lord;
6. heaping of the Israelites' carcasses upon their idols;
7. waste of their cities and devastation of the land;
8. inflammation, fiery heat, drought, blight, and mildew;
9. Israelite corpses as food for the birds and animals;
10. ulcers, scurvy, and itching which cannot be healed;
11. madness, blindness, and confusion of the mind;
12. abuse and theft without anyone to help;
13. adultery by the woman to whom a man is engaged;
14. sons and daughters given to other people or captured;

15. grievous boils from sole of foot to crown of head;
16. an iron yoke on the neck until destroyed;
17. severe and lasting afflictions and grievous and lasting maladies; and
18. all the diseases of Egypt.

◆ ◆ ◆

Perhaps most disturbing are the passages in Deuteronomy 28:53 and 57:

◆ ◆ ◆

In the desperate straits to which the enemy siege reduces [the sinner], you will eat the fruit of your womb, the flesh of your own sons and daughters . . . [the woman] begrudging even the afterbirth that comes out from between her thighs, and the children that she bears, because she is eating them in secret for lack of anything else. . . .

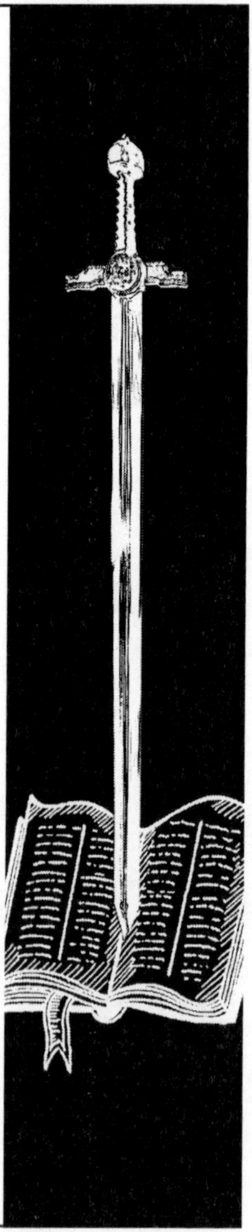

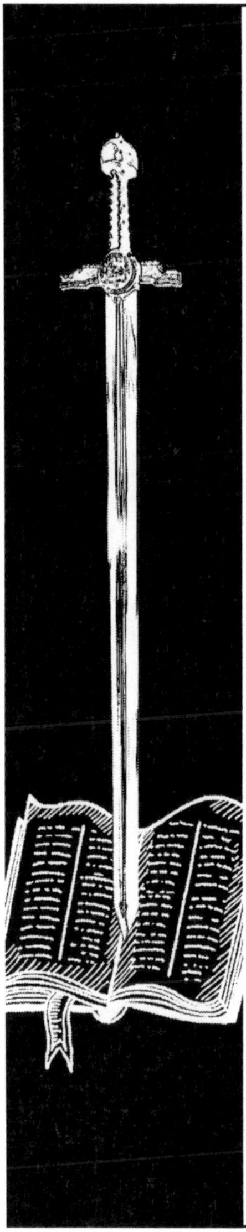

◆ ◆ ◆

Finally, the Lord promises in verses 45–46 that:

◆ ◆ ◆

All these curses shall come upon you, pursuing and overtaking you until you are destroyed, because you did not obey the Lord your God, by observing the commandments and the decrees that he commanded you. They shall be among you and your descendants as a sign and a portent forever.

◆ ◆ ◆

No wonder Psalms 18:26 proclaims that with the crooked, the Lord shows himself perverse![8] And no wonder the Israelites desired to live in accordance with God's will!

Indeed, the Israelites' choice — between obedience and disobedience — is ultimately a decision between either life and prosperity or death and adversity, as plainly avowed in Deuteronomy 30:15.

Verse 19 of the same chapter reiterates the choice: either life and blessings or death and curses. But did the Israelites *really* have a choice in the matter?

Ezekiel was an Israelite priest in the late 500s BCE and, as stated above, the book that bears his name is twenty-sixth in the total of thirty-nine Old Testament books. Speaking directly to the Israelites in Ezekiel 20:25–26, the prophet quotes the Lord:

◆ ◆ ◆

I gave [the Israelites] statutes that were not good and ordinances by which they could not live. I defiled them through their very gifts, in their offering up all their firstborn, in order that I might horrify them, so

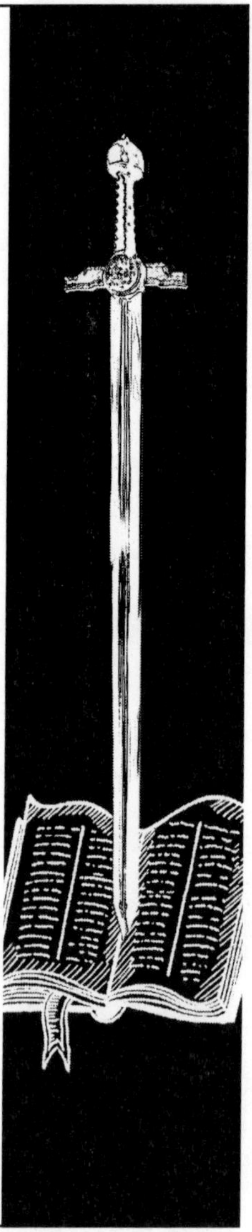

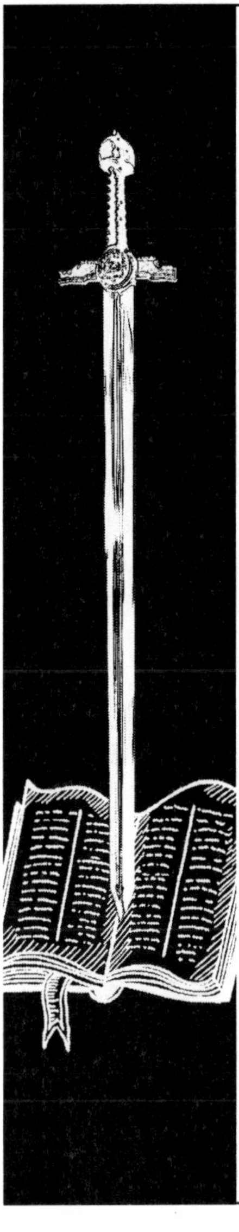

that they might know that I am the Lord.

◆ ◆ ◆

Does this mean that God *intentionally* decreed too-stringent rules for the Israelites, and thereby masterminded their disobedience so that He could "teach them a lesson" and display His (often terrifying) magnificence? Would a just and righteous Lord devise such a seemingly un-godlike scenario?

Admittedly, the above-cited Scripture from the book of Ezekiel seems to be in direct contradiction to the often quoted maxim that says mankind possesses free will, but the text and its implication remain extremely troubling.

In Exodus, didn't God harden the Egyptian Pharaoh's heart so that He could display His wondrous powers?

Is the psalmist too intuitive when he announces:

Our God is in the heavens;
He does whatever he pleases.

in Psalms 115:3?

Is Isaiah, who was one of the most renowned prophets of all the Old Testament, so totally off-base when he cries in Isaiah 63:17a:

Why, O Lord, do you make us stray from your ways and harden our heart . . . ?

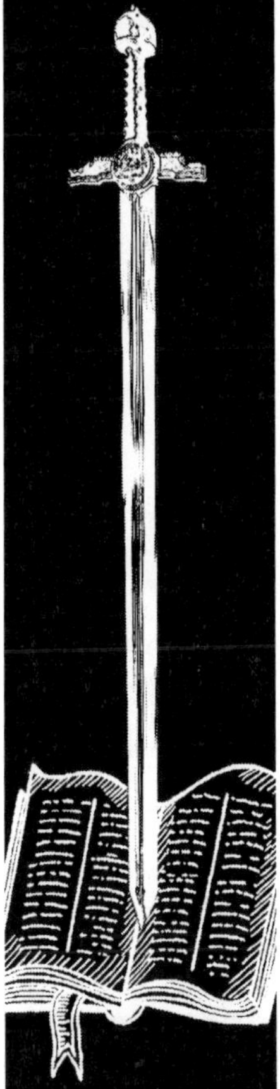

Chapter Two

Murders Prior to Mount Sinai

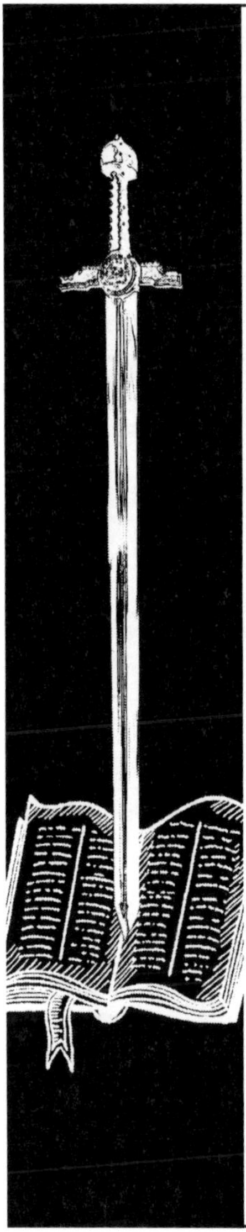

Who doesn't know the familiar phrase: "For everything there is a season, and a time for every matter under heaven"? Ecclesiastes 3:1 is lyrically beautiful; verse 3 is downright prophetic: *A Time to Kill.*

Perhaps no other commandment is more controversial than the Sixth: THOU SHALT NOT MURDER. The decree is anchored by statements such as "the Lord abhors the bloodthirsty" in Psalms 5:6 and "the Lord . . . hates the lover of violence" at 11:5. But the Old Testament is awash with human blood. From Cain's murder of Abel to the final word of its concluding book, the Old Testament gorges itself on death, destruction, mass murder, genocide, and the widespread annihilation of peoples.

But before jumping into the fray, four preliminaries are in order. First, this book records only killings by either God (see Interlude II) or the Israelites, to whom the Sixth Commandment is directed. The Egyptian Pharaoh's murder of the firstborns, therefore, is not included in the list. Nor are killings by other peoples of the Old Testament.[1] For example, this study does not address the breaking of the Sixth Commandment by the Philistines when they kill 4,000 Israelites in 1 Samuel 4:3. Although Israelites died, the killing was not at the hand of either God or fellow Israelites.

Secondly, where actual numbers of the dead are provided in Scripture, those numbers are re-

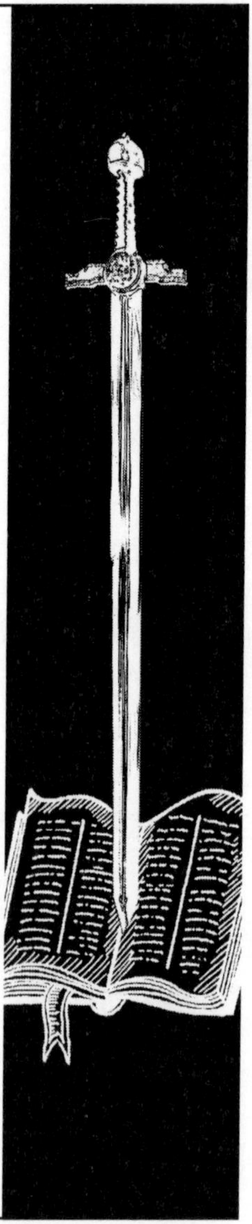

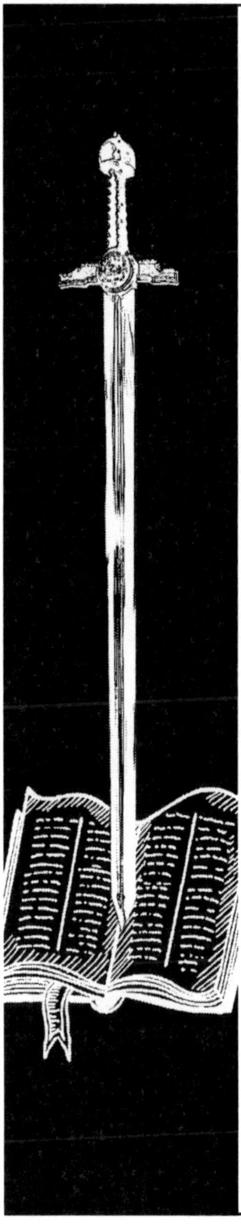

corded and entered for the final tally. Seemingly too often, however, Scripture relates a scene of "mass slaughter" or the "utter destruction" of every person, and no official count is supplied. When numbers are not given in these instances, the occurrence is tallied as a *massacre*.

Third, unless Scripture clearly states that a person or persons were killed, no assumption has been made otherwise.

For example, Genesis 14:14–16 states that Abraham routed and defeated the people that had captured his nephew, Lot. No bloodshed is mentioned, so no bloodshed is recorded. In numerous instances, however, although the Scripture does not specify a killing or murder, the text can indicate such: for example, by recording the burial of the dead or pronouncing that "not a single survivor was left." In these instances, a killing can be safely assumed. Any assumptions other than the foregoing will be addressed in context.

Finally, an apology to the reader: the initial goal of this study was a completely narrative book for a smooth flow of information and ease of reading. However, due to the overwhelming source material of the Sixth Commandment, a majority of the information had to be reduced to chart format. This writer dislikes charts — perhaps a throwback to the teenage years when the weight always outstripped the height. But a strictly narrative rendition of all the killings is unfeasible, as the reader will quickly discover!

If God created the world "in the beginning," then murder reared

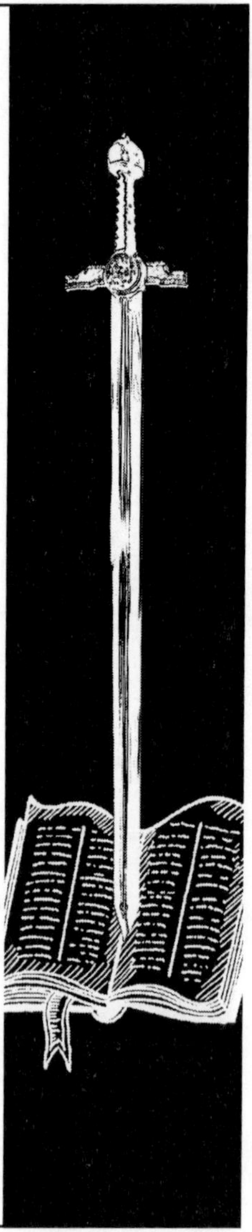

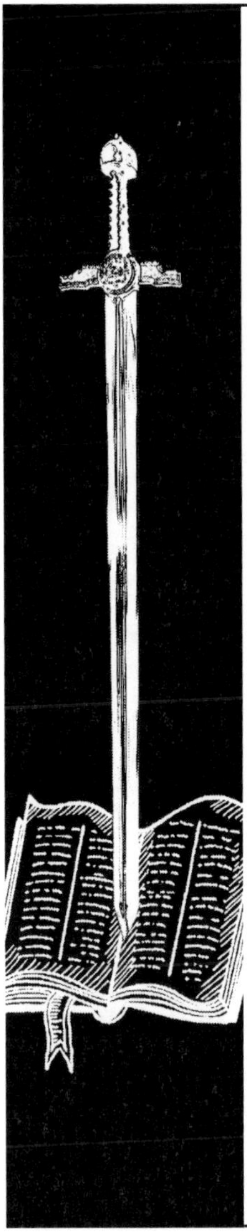

its ugly head shortly thereafter. By the fourth book of Genesis, the first two brothers of the new creation are already at odds.

We learn in verse 2 that Abel is a keeper of sheep while Cain is a tiller of the ground. Their two different ways of life — farmer vs. semi-nomad — produce two different kinds of offering to the Lord: Abel brings to the Lord the firstlings of his flock, while Cain offers the fruit of the ground.

Today's health-conscious environment would extol Cain, but God, some 4,000 years ago, didn't see it that way. Verse 4 states that:

. . . the Lord had regard for Abel and his offering, but for Cain and his offering he had no regard.

No expressed reason is given for the Lord's preference, and Cain is angry. He lures his brother out into the field and kills him. When questioned by God, Cain delivers one of the famous biblical one-liners in Genesis 4:9: "Am I my brother's keeper?"

Tally: one.

Exhibit A - Murders Prior to Mount Sinai records 606 killings and at least four instances of a massacre, three of these committed by the Lord himself. Genesis chapters 6–9 commemorate Noah and describe the worldwide flood at the hand of God. Genesis 6:5–6 dispenses the reason:[2]

◆ ◆ ◆

The Lord saw that the wickedness of humankind was great in the earth, and that every inclination of the thoughts of their hearts was only evil continually.

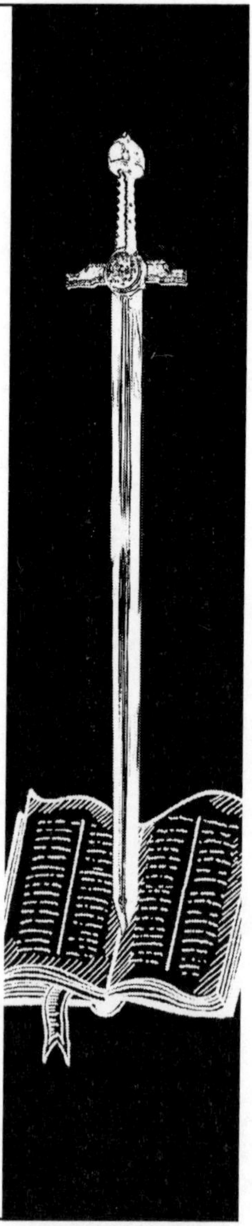

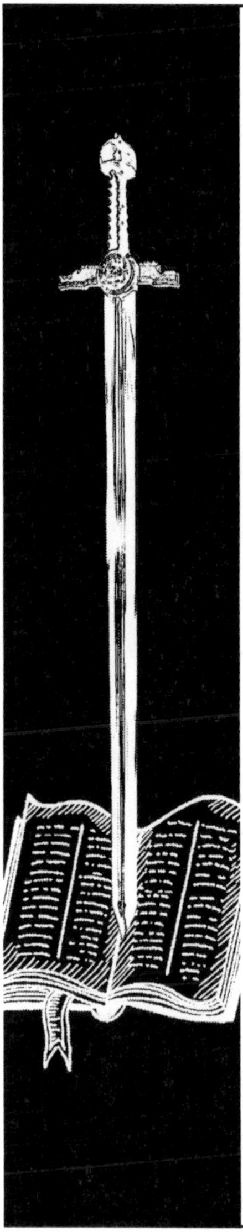

And the Lord was sorry that he had made humankind on the earth, and it grieved him to his heart.

◆ ◆ ◆

If God was grieving, he didn't grieve very long. By 7:17, the waters commence, and God's purpose is achieved in verses 21–23:

◆ ◆ ◆

And all flesh died that moved on the earth, birds, domestic animals, wild animals, all swarming creatures that swarm on the earth, and all human beings; everything on dry land in whose nostrils was the breath of life died.

He blotted out every living thing that was on the face of the ground, human beings and animals and creeping things and birds of the air; they were blotted out from the earth. Only

Noah was left, and those that were with him in the ark.

◆ ◆ ◆

The pun *is* intended: Thank God for Noah.

The first instance of a massacre by God's Chosen People comes in Genesis 34. Because the story involves a large cast of characters and several sub-plots, the reader is referred to the actual text for a full account of the events. The nutshell here is this:

◆ ◆ ◆

Two sons of Jacob and Leah believe that their younger sister, Dinah, has been raped by an uncircumcised male named Shechem. When Shechem thereafter asks for Dinah's hand in marriage, the sons of Jacob (Dinah's brothers) say that they will consent, but only if Shechem and all the other males in his city are first cir-

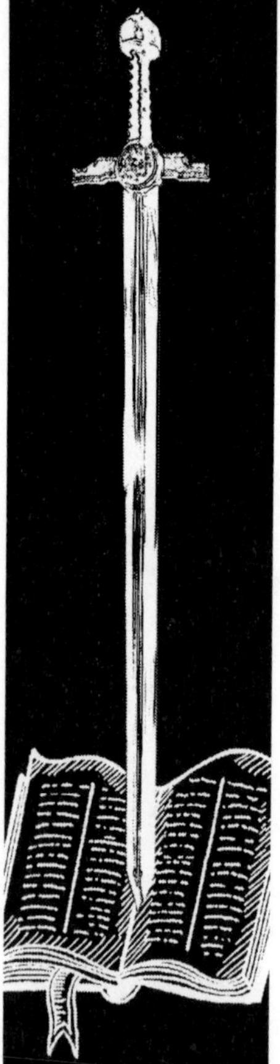

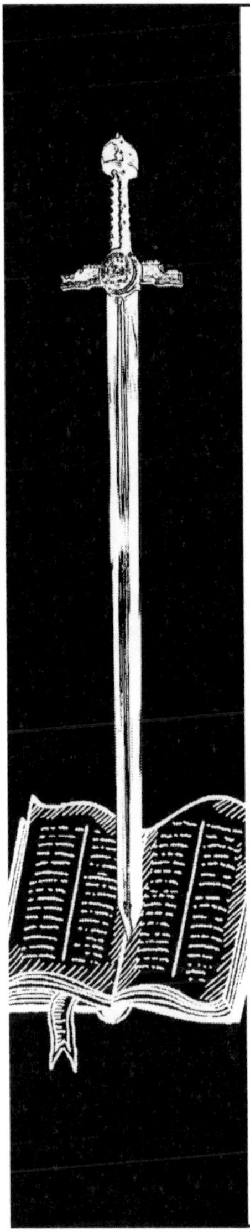

cumcised. Shechem agrees, has the circumcision, as does every other male in Shechem's hometown. Just one more name to be remembered: Hamor, who is Shechem's father and prince of the region.

◆ ◆ ◆

Verses 25–29 resume the story as Shechem and the males are still in pain from the circumcision:

◆ ◆ ◆

On the third day, when they were still in pain, two of the sons of Jacob . . . took their swords and came against the city unawares, and killed all the males. They killed Hamor and his son Shechem with the sword and took Dinah out of Shechem's house, and went away. And the other sons of Jacob came upon the slain, and plundered the city, because their sister had been defiled. They took their flocks and their herds, their donkeys, and whatever was in the city and in the field. All their wealth, all their little ones and their wives, all that was in the houses, they captured and made their prey.

◆ ◆ ◆

The biblical duty of brothers-in-law also arises in Genesis. According to ancient custom, if one's married brother died without leaving any descendants, the duty of a surviving brother was to bear a male descendant with the brother's widow, thus perpetuating the deceased brother's name and inheritance.[3]

In Genesis 38:1–10, Er, the firstborn of Judah (the son of Jacob and Leah), is married to Tamar. Er does what is wicked in the sight of the Lord, and the Lord

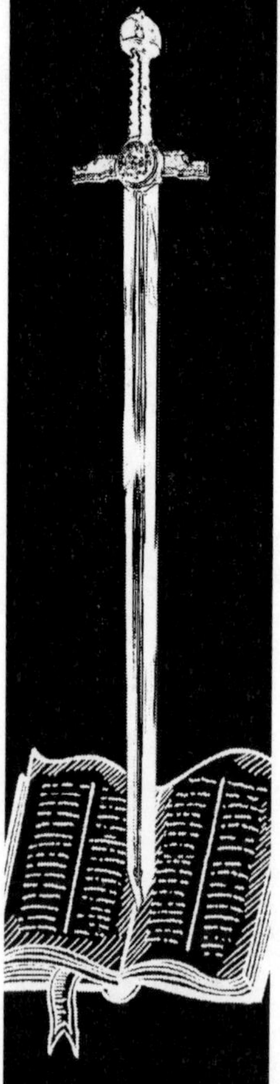

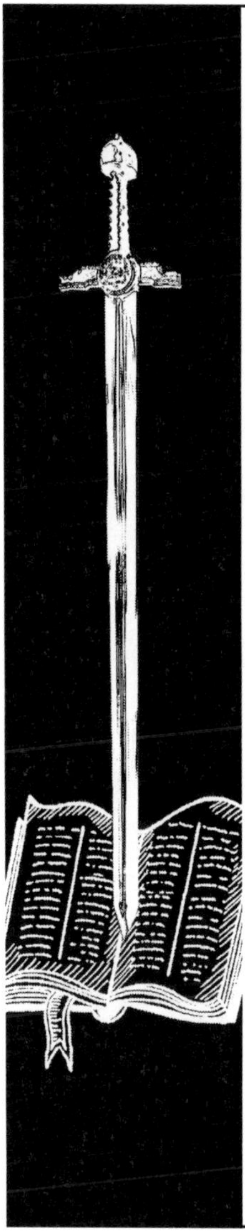

puts Er to death. Judah then commands Er's younger brother, Onan, to have sexual relations with Er's widow, Tamar.

Scripture relates:

◆ ◆ ◆

But since Onan knew that the offspring would not be his, he spilled his semen on the ground whenever he went in to his brother's wife, so that he would not give offspring to his brother. What he did was displeasing in the sight of the Lord, and he put him to death also.

◆ ◆ ◆

Exhibit B presents five cases of either attempted or plotted murder. The most famous is Abraham's near sacrifice of his son, Isaac.[4] Perhaps the least well-known occurs at Exodus 4:24–26. The setting is after Moses' experience with the burning bush, where God commands Moses to return to Egypt and deliver the Israelites from oppression.

By this time, Moses is married to Zipporah and they have a son, Gershom. Moses is journeying to Egypt with his family to fulfill God's mandate when, out of nowhere, the three verses declare:

◆ ◆ ◆

On the way, at a place where they spent the night, the Lord met him and tried to kill him. But Zipporah took a flint and cut off her son's foreskin, and touched Moses' feet with it, and said, "Truly you are a bridegroom of blood to me!" So he let him alone. It was then she said, "A bridegroom of blood by circumcision."

◆ ◆ ◆

A reader definitely needs annotations to explain this! The *Jew-*

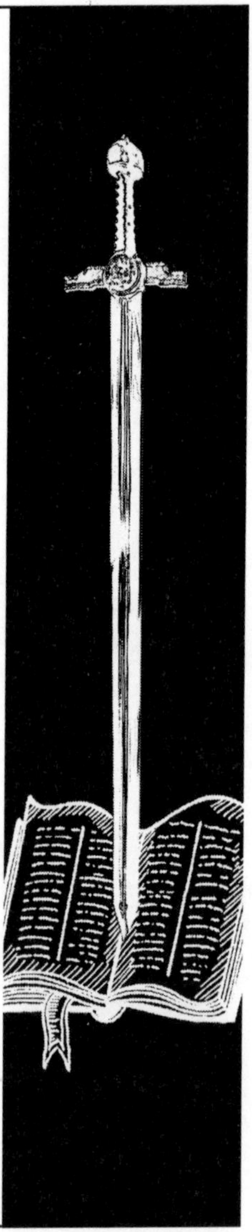

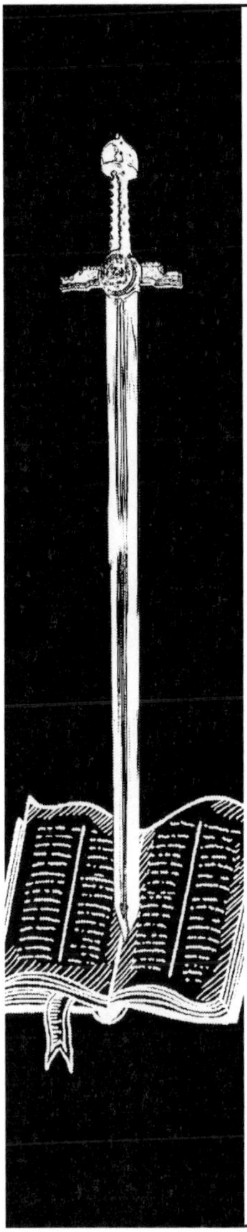

ish Study Bible concurs that this episode is extremely puzzling because the motive for God's attack is unclear, the pronouns are ambiguous, and Zipporah's remarks are enigmatic. Further, the circumcision seems to have protective power, and by touching her son's foreskin to Moses' "legs" (which some interpret as his genitals), Zipporah saved him. Finally, the term translated "bridegroom" can mean "to protect" in Akkadian and Arabic and "to circumcise" in Arabic.[5]

The *New Oxford Annotated Bible* agrees that God's attack was warded off by the timely performance of a rite. It adds that the circumcision of the son was apparently effective for Moses, who was evidently uncircumcised. "Feet," it concludes, is a euphemism for the genitals.[6]

However the incident is interpreted and analyzed, verse 24 seems clear: the Lord tried to kill Moses. But he didn't. And as the saying goes, "All's well that ends well."

Until, that is, the murders resurface (or rather explode) after Moses' experience at Mount Sinai.

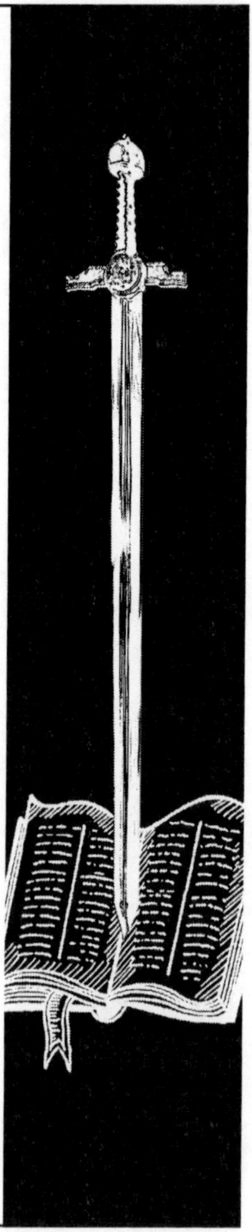

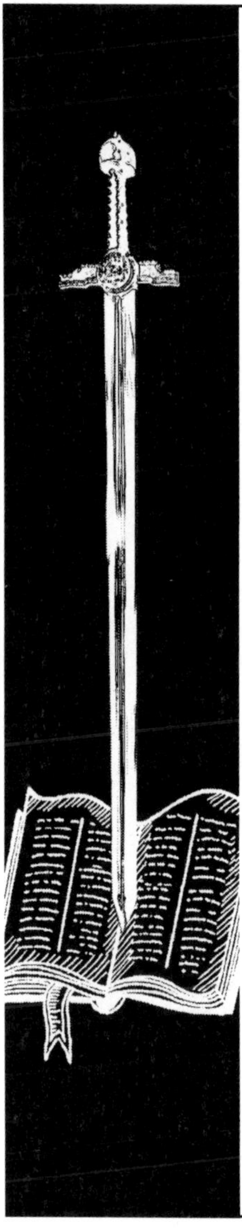

Chapter Three

Murder in the Wilderness

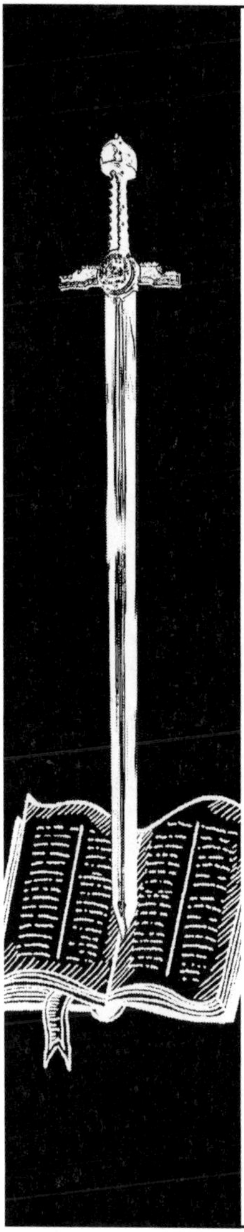

There are no excuses now, no "I didn't know." Moses has descended from his mountaintop experience and verbally instructed the Israelites of God's premier laws.

As noted in Chapter One, Moses ascends and descends the mountain a second time, and the Ten Commandments are literally set in stone. The Preface introduced the first murders after Mount Sinai — when the Israelite priests kill 3,000 of their kinsmen for the golden calf incident — that occur shortly after they receive the Sixth Commandment: THOU SHALT NOT MURDER. There is actually more to this story, however.

Exodus 32:35 reveals that as further punishment for the golden calf, the Lord inflicts a plague upon the people. Scripture does not mention, however, the type of plague it is or whether anyone else is killed. Moses' prayer at verses 7, 9 and 11 of Psalm 90 capture the heat of God's ire:

◆ ◆ ◆

For we are consumed by your anger; by your wrath we are overwhelmed.

For all our days pass away under your wrath; our years come to an end like a sigh.

Who considers the power of your anger?

Your wrath is as great as the fear that is due you.

◆ ◆ ◆

Indeed, Deuteronomy 9:8–21 indicates that the Lord's wrath was so provoked that He was prepared to destroy all the Israelites until Moses intervened and plead-

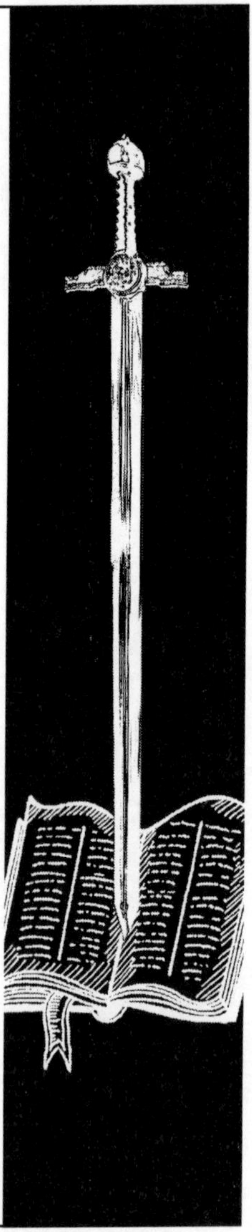

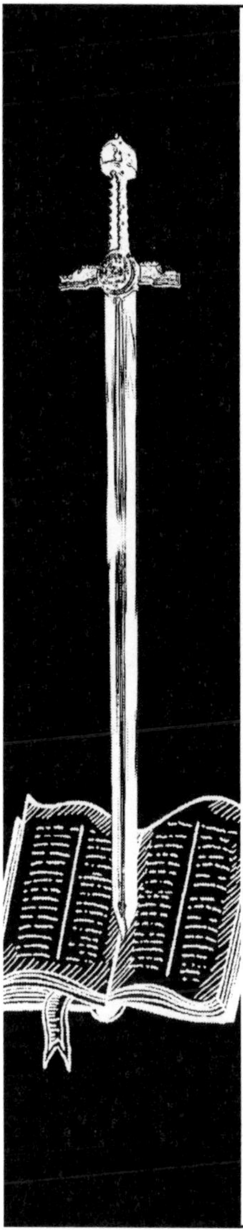

ed on their behalf.[1] Psalms 106:23 supports the Deuteronomy text:

Therefore [the Lord] said he would destroy them — had not Moses, his chosen one, stood in the breach before him, to turn away his wrath from destroying them.

This time, thank God for Moses.

The next round of slaying, while the Israelites wander around in the wilderness, is chronicled in Leviticus and Numbers, the third and fourth books of the Old Testament. These books also introduce the reader to new instruments of death: fire, stones, plagues, a hole in the earth, a spear, and poisonous snakes.

Leviticus 10:1–2 exemplifies the phrase "an eye for an eye," or more accurately, fire for fire. While in the wilderness, Aaron is Moses' right-hand man. Aaron's two sons, Nadab and Abihu, offer "unholy fire"[2] before the Lord. Biblical interpretations vary and are complex on what exactly constituted "unholy fire," but for purposes of this study, the two sons were offering fire that had not been commanded by the Lord.

Verse 2:

◆ ◆ ◆

And fire came out from the presence of the Lord and consumed them, and they died before the Lord.

◆ ◆ ◆

Verse 3b concludes that Aaron (the father) was silent.

◆ ◆ ◆

Stoning is the Lord's mode of execution for a blasphemer in Leviticus 24:10–23. The incident

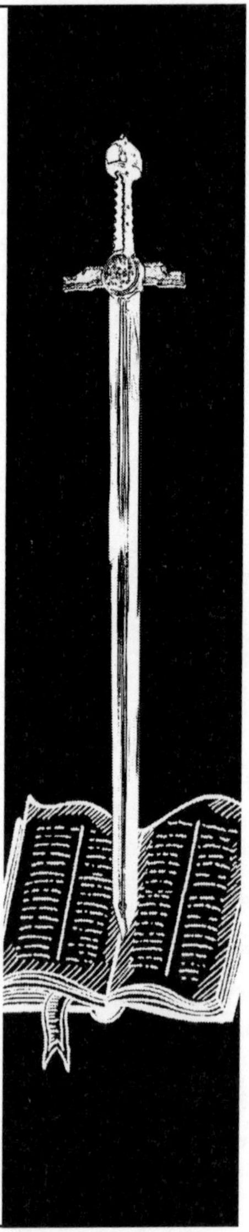

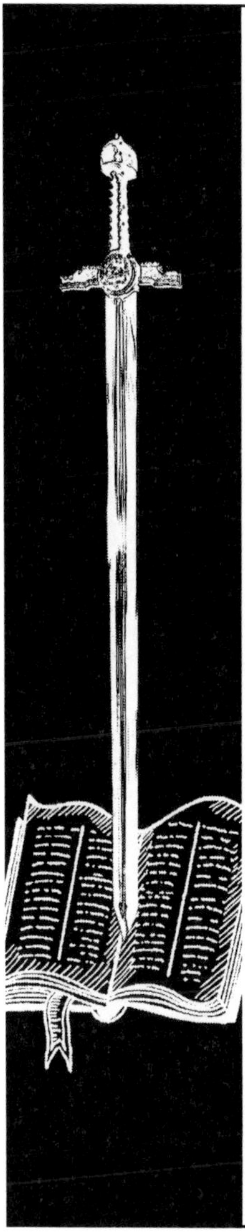

occurs between two Israelites, and the Lord instructs Moses to take the blasphemer outside the camp so the whole congregation can stone him. And they do.

But what is fascinating are verses 16 and 17 of the Scripture. Verse 16 decrees that anyone who blasphemes the name of the Lord shall be put to death. Verse 17 then immediately declares "anyone who kills a human being shall be put to death." Didn't the whole congregation of Israelites just put to death a human being? So should they be put to death too?

While on the subject of stoning, Numbers 15:32–36 reveals why one should keep the Sabbath holy, even in the wilderness, as demanded by the Fifth Commandment. When an Israelite man is found gathering sticks on the Sabbath, he, too, is stoned to death by his peers.

Two instances implicating the Sixth Commandment occur when the Israelites complain about the food situation in the wilderness. In Numbers 11:1–34 and again at 21:4–9, the people grumble about the lack of adequate food and water.

The first time, the Lord strikes them with a very great plague, and the second time, God sends poisonous serpents. The Israelites do not complain a third time.

Chapter 16 of Numbers relates two instances where the people challenge Moses. In verses 1–35, 250 Israelite men confront Moses and charge him with exalting himself above the assembly of people. Verse 31b-33 spits out the punishment for the 250 challengers:

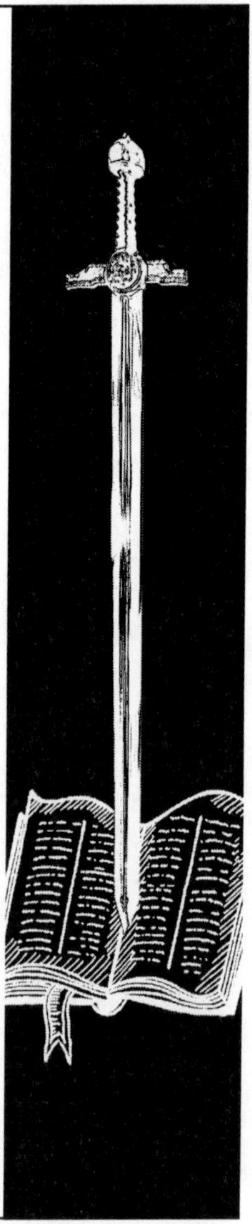

◆ ◆ ◆

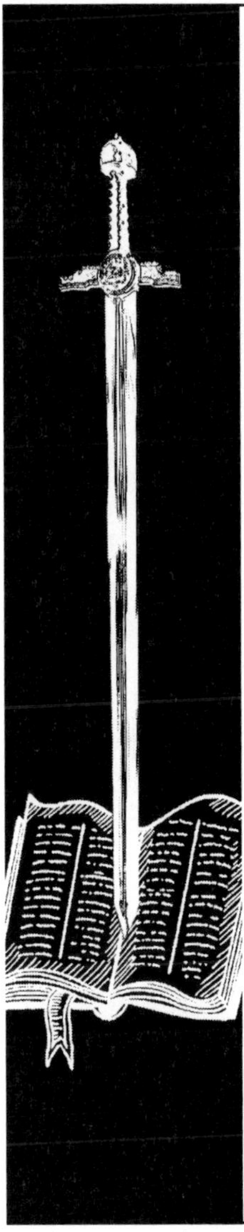

[T]he ground under them was split apart. The earth opened its mouth and swallowed them up, along with their households . . . So they with all that belonged to them went down alive to Sheol; the earth closed over them, and they perished from the midst of the assembly.

◆ ◆ ◆

Sheol is an Old Testament synonym for hell.[3] But the earth opening its mouth and swallowing the doubters must not have impressed the people. Numbers 16:41–50 discloses that on the very next day, the whole congregation of Israelites rebels against Moses and Aaron, blaming them for the prior day's deaths.

The Lord releases another plague on the people, which only relents when Aaron runs into the middle of the assembly and atones for the people. But not before the number having died by the plague is a staggering 14,700.

The Israelites are also tempted to intermix with the native peoples, a practice denounced by the Lord.[4]

In Numbers 25:1–9, Israelite men begin having sexual relations with a non-Israelite people called the Midianites. The Israelites then worship the Midianite gods. In retaliation, the Lord sends a plague on his people, and 24,000 die. The plague is finally stopped when a grandson of Aaron takes a spear and pierces through an Israelite man and one of the women apparently "in the act."

In Numbers 31, the Lord directs Moses to take revenge on the Midianites. Twelve thousand Israelite troops proceed to murder every Midianite male as well as the

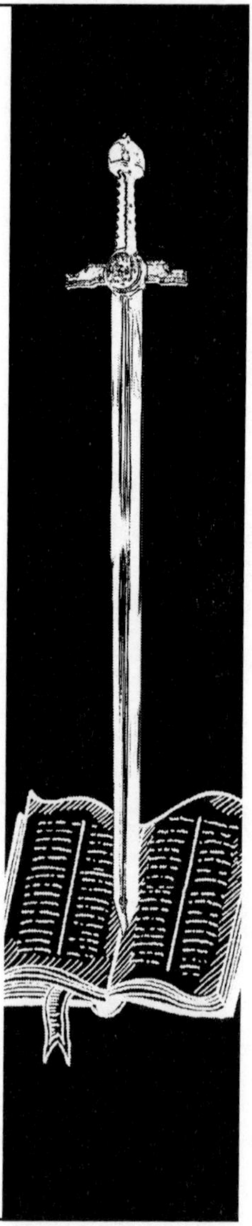

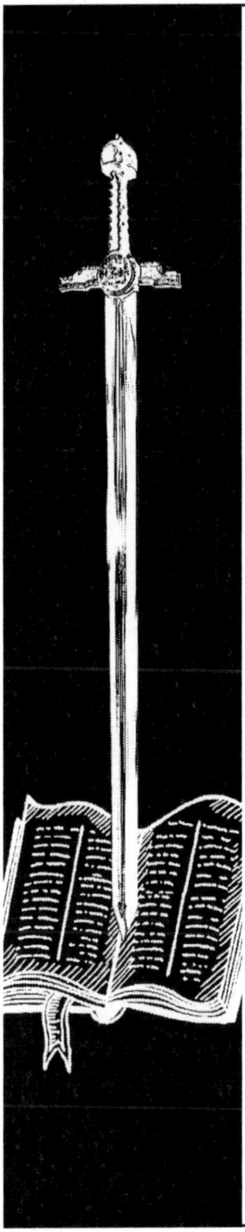

five Midianite kings. Scripture relates that the troops take as captives the women of Midian as well as their little ones, bringing them to Moses.

A disturbing passage follows in verses 15–18 when Moses speaks to his troops:

◆ ◆ ◆

Moses said to them, "Have you allowed all the women to live? These women here . . . made the Israelites act treacherously against the Lord . . . so that the plague came among the congregation of the Lord. Now therefore, kill every male among the little ones, and kill every woman who has known a man by sleeping with him. But all the young girls who have not known a man by sleeping with him, keep alive for yourselves.

◆ ◆ ◆

The overall carnage must have been huge because verse 35 informs that 32,000 women "who had not known a man by sleeping with him" were part of the spoil taken by the Israelite troops.

These and other episodes of murder in the wilderness are chronicled in Exhibit C.

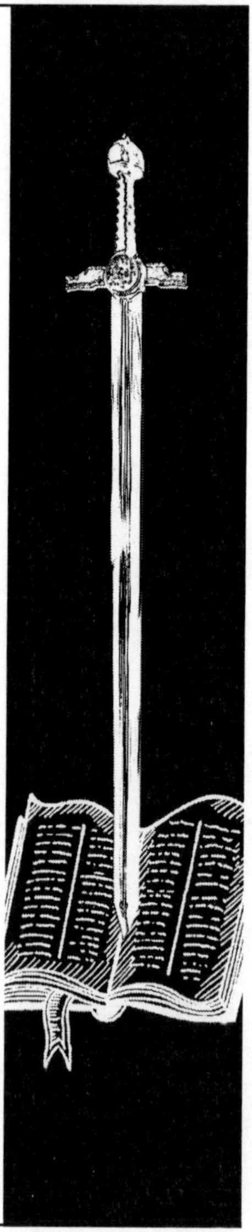

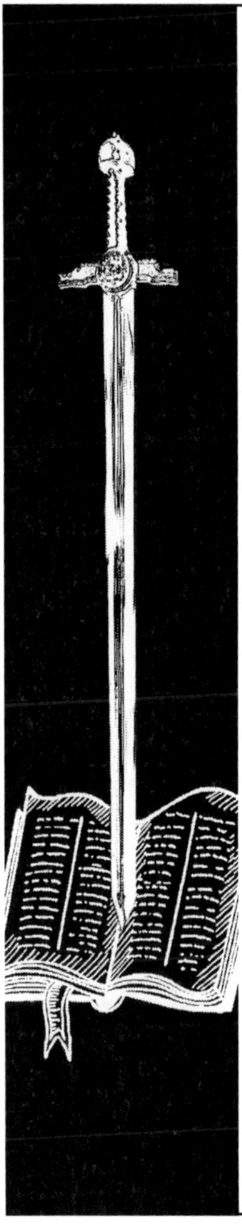

Interlude I

Israelites and God's Chosen People

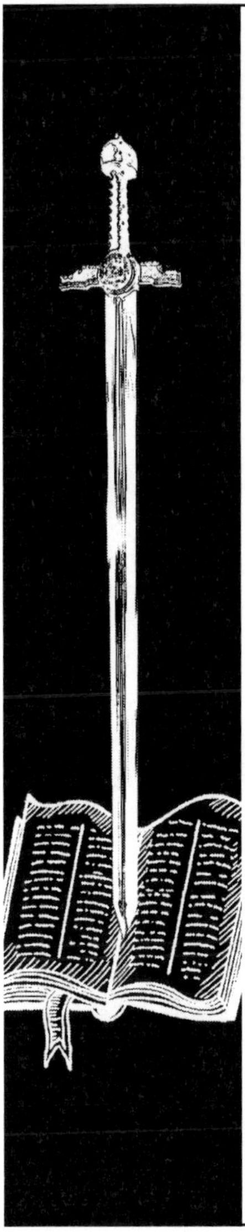

Throughout this study, the term "God's Chosen People" or "Israelites" are used interchangeably to refer to either:

1. those persons associated directly with the Lord; or
2. the people to whom God covenants the Promised Land.

With regard to the former, the descendants of Adam and Eve are considered part of God's Chosen People.

God created Adam and Eve in His image; therefore, their children and succeeding generations should behave in accordance with God's will. Transgressions, or more particularly murders, by these persons are included in the tally.

Abraham and his descendants are likewise considered God's Chosen People. When Abraham received the call from God, Abraham was living in Haran, in northwest Mesopotamia. But in Genesis 14:13, Abraham is referred to as a Hebrew, and his descendants were thereafter known as Hebrews. Abraham's grandson, Jacob, was renamed Israel[1] by the Lord, giving birth to the designation "Israel."

The term "Israelite" makes its debut in the Old Testament at Genesis 32:32, and "Israelite" becomes interchangeable with "Hebrew." When the monarchy under King David divides into the two nations of Israel and Judah, the term "Israelite" refers to Hebrews living in either kingdom.

Some people differentiate between the names "Israelite" and

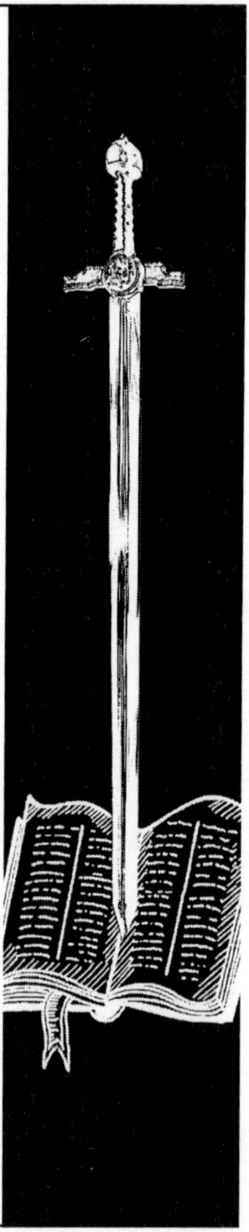

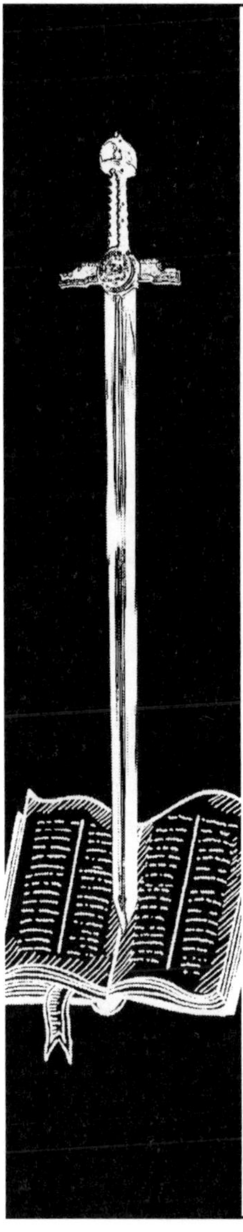

"Judahite," but this can be confusing.

For the sake of simplicity, "God's Chosen People" and "Israelites" mean the same group of people: those called by the Lord to obey Him and His commandments.

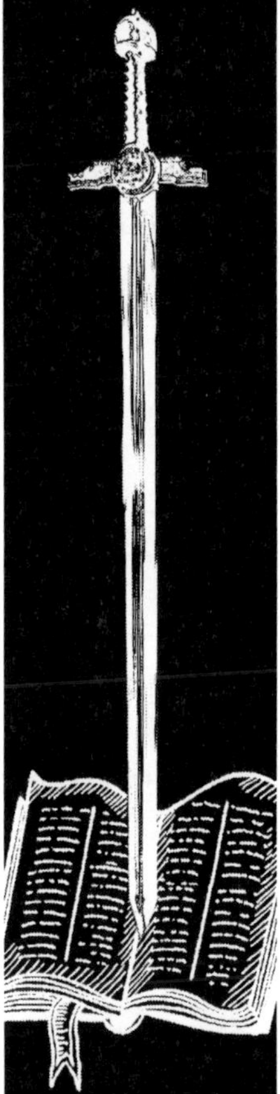

Chapter Four

Murder in the Promised Land

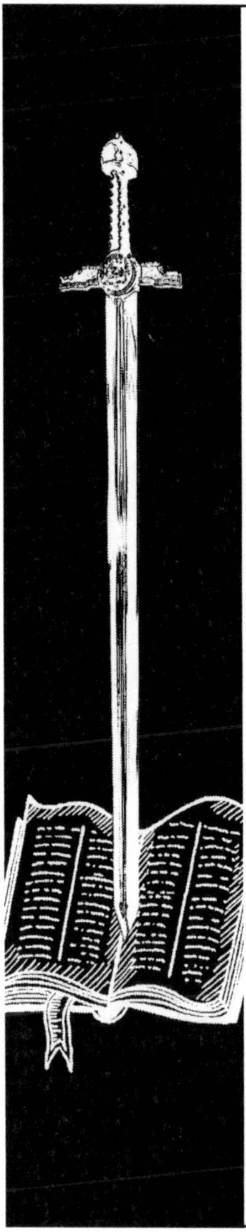

To describe the books of Joshua and Judges as disturbing is a gross understatement. Psalm 68:21–23 is a condensed version:

◆ ◆ ◆

God will shatter the heads of his enemies so that the Israelites may bathe their feet in blood.

◆ ◆ ◆

Or maybe 110:5–6:

◆ ◆ ◆

The Lord will fill the nations with corpses and shatter heads over the wide earth.

◆ ◆ ◆

After forty years in the wilderness, the Israelites prepare to enter the Promised Land, the land of Canaan, under the leadership of Joshua after Moses' death. The book of Joshua chronicles the Israelites' conquest[1] — or rather mass genocide[2] — of the peoples in the land.

The book of Judges continues the story of the conquest and depicts the settlement of the Israelites in Canaan.[3] The title of Judges springs from the leaders or rulers of the Israelites as they gradually inhabit the area, annihilating anyone in their path.

Death and destruction saturate these two books.[4] As God guides the Israelites throughout the land, the native inhabitants are seemingly eliminated without mercy or thought.[5]

Psalm 10:16:

◆ ◆ ◆

The Lord is king forever and ever; the nations shall perish from his land.

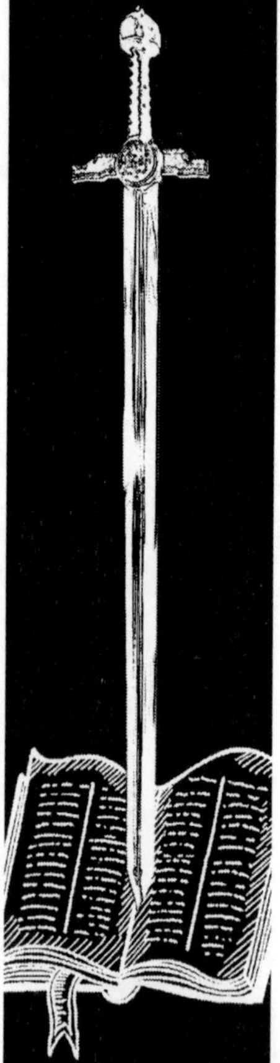

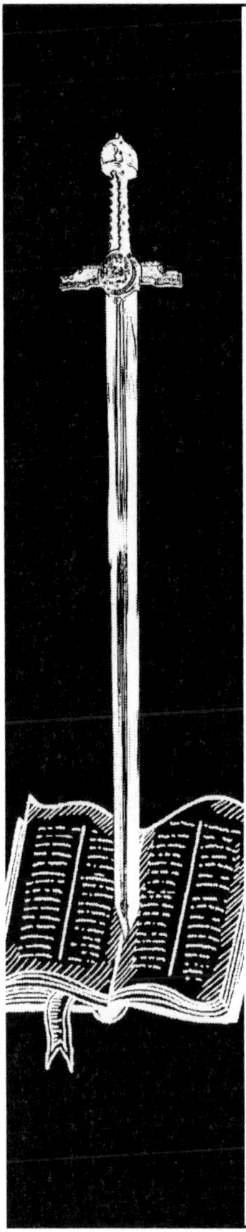

◆ ◆ ◆

But could there have been another approach? Could the Israelites have merely dispossessed the native peoples, driving them into another land? What about surrender and capture? Was widespread elimination the only option?[6]

Back in Deuteronomy 20:1–14, God delineates the rules for waging his holy wars:

◆ ◆ ◆

When you go to war against your enemies, and see horses and chariots, an army larger than your own, you shall not be afraid of them; for the Lord your God is with you . . . for it is the Lord your God who goes with you, to fight for you against your enemies, to give you victory. . . . When you draw near to a town to fight against it, offer it terms of peace. If it ac-

cepts your terms of peace and surrenders to you, then all the people in it shall serve you at forced labor.

If it does not submit to you peacefully, but makes war against you, then you shall besiege it; and when the Lord your God gives it into your hand, you shall put all its males to the sword. You may, however, take as your booty the women, the children, the livestock, and everything else in the town, all its spoil. You may enjoy the spoil of your enemies, which the Lord your God has given you.

◆ ◆ ◆

God does, therefore, address the concept of surrender. However, just two sentences later in verses 16–18, God commands:

◆ ◆ ◆

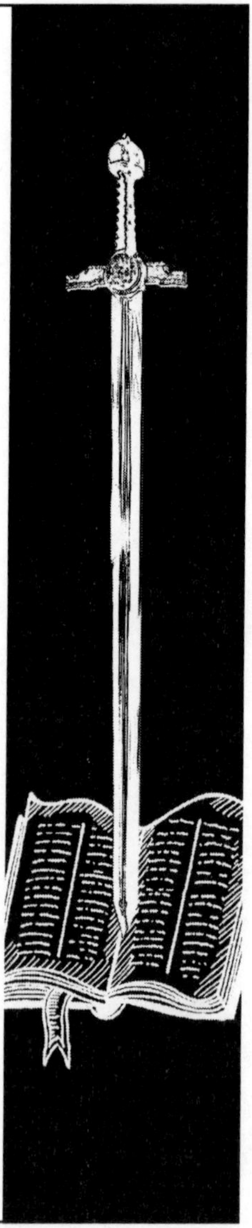

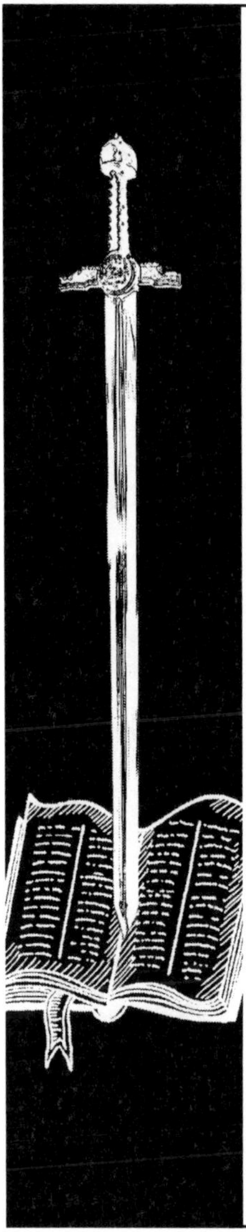

But as for the towns of these peoples that the Lord your God has given you as an inheritance, you must not let anything that breathes remain alive. You shall annihilate them — the Hittites and the Amorites, the Canaanites and the Perizzites, and the Hivites and the Jebusites — just as the Lord your God commanded, so that they may not teach you to do all the abhorrent things that they do for their gods, and you thus sin against the Lord your God.

◆ ◆ ◆

The reason for genocide is stated. The peoples in the land of Canaan worship other gods, and the Lord does not want the Israelites to be tempted by these "abhorrent things."

The earlier Deuteronomist's statement about surrender is

squarely contradicted in Deuteronomy 7:1–2:

◆ ◆ ◆

When the Lord your God brings you into the land that you are about to enter and occupy, and he clears away many nations before you . . . and when the Lord your God gives them over to you and you defeat them, then you must utterly destroy them. Make no covenant with them and show them no mercy.

◆ ◆ ◆

And again in verses 20-24:

◆ ◆ ◆

Moreover, the Lord your God will send the pestilence against them, until even the survivors and fugitives are destroyed . . . God will clear away these nations before you little by little; you will not

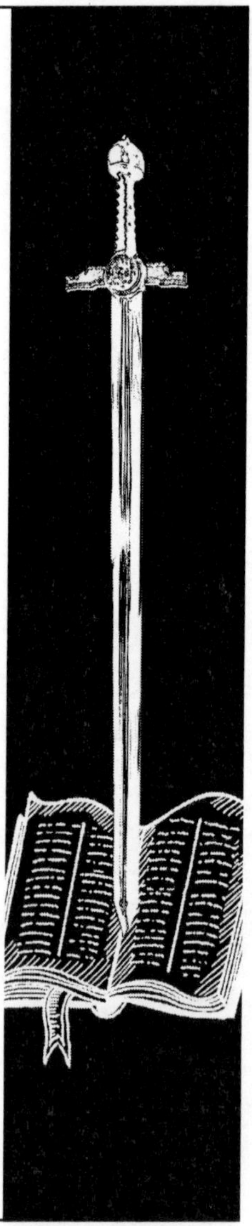

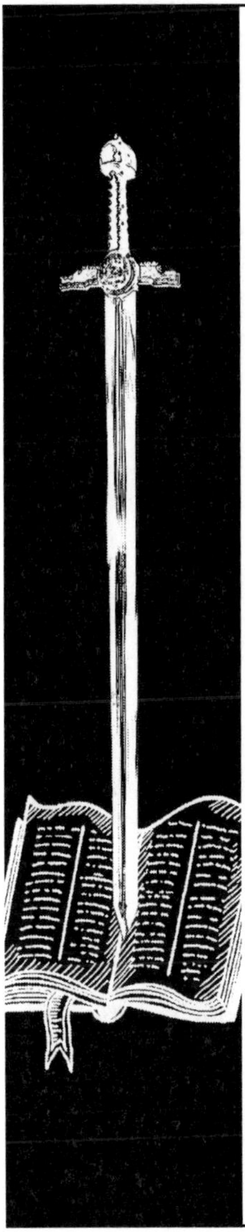

be able to make a quick end of them, otherwise the wild animals would become too numerous for you. But the Lord your God will give them over to you, and throw them into great panic, until they are destroyed. He will hand their kings over to you and you shall blot out their name from under heaven; no one will be able to stand against you, until you have destroyed them.

* * *

The Israelites' conquest of the Promised Land begins in the second chapter of Joshua with the siege of Jericho.[7]

Initially, Joshua sends two spies into Jericho to assess the situation. The spies enter the house of a prostitute named Rahab, spending the night there. When the king of Jericho gets wind of potential spies in the city, Rahab is questioned, but the prostitute lies to protect them. She also assists the spies in escaping from the city back to the Israelite camp.

The fall of Jericho is memorable for the marching of the Israelites around the city for six days, continually blowing their trumpets of rams' horns. Joshua 6:15–21 delivers the climax:

◆ ◆ ◆

On the seventh day [the Israelites] rose early, at dawn, and marched around the city in the same manner seven times. It was only on that day that they marched around the city seven times. And at the seventh time, when the priests had blown the trumpets, Joshua said to the people, "Shout. For the Lord has given you the city." . . . So the people shouted, and the

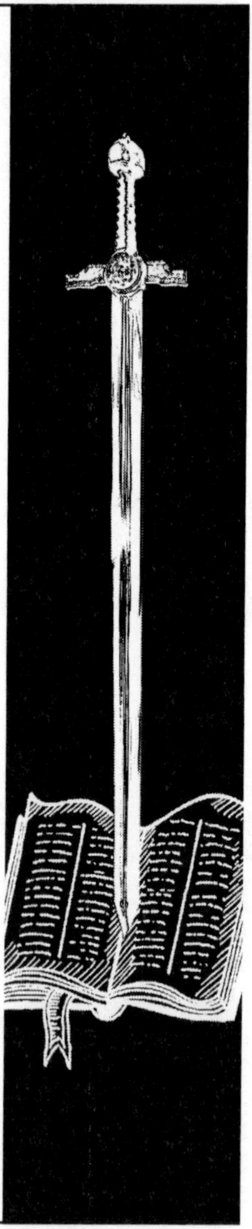

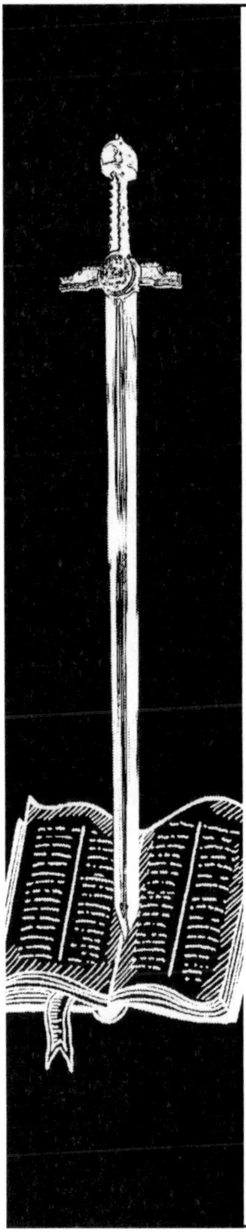

trumpets were blown. As soon as the people heard the sound of the trumpets, they raised a great shout, and the wall fell down flat; so the people charged straight ahead into the city and captured it. Then they devoted to destruction by the edge of the sword all in the city, both men and women, young and old, oxen, sheep and donkeys.

◆ ◆ ◆

The account does not indicate the number of people killed by the Israelites, but Joshua 4:13 states that about 40,000 Israelites are armed for war. Rahab and her household are spared and brought to the Israelites' camp just before they proceed to burn the city of Jericho.

In Joshua 6:18, Joshua had told the Israelites not to keep any of the items from the city of Jericho:

◆ ◆ ◆

Keep away from the things devoted to destruction, so as not to covet and take any of the devoted things and make the camp of Israel an object for destruction.

◆ ◆ ◆

But Scripture reveals that the Israelites break faith in regard to the things devoted for destruction. Specifically, an Israelite named Achan steals some of the devoted things, and Joshua 7:1 apprises that the anger of the Lord burns against the Israelites.

When thirty-six Israelites are killed in their next battle, the people realize that the Lord's wrath is upon them for transgressing his edict about the devoted things from Jericho. Achan finally con-

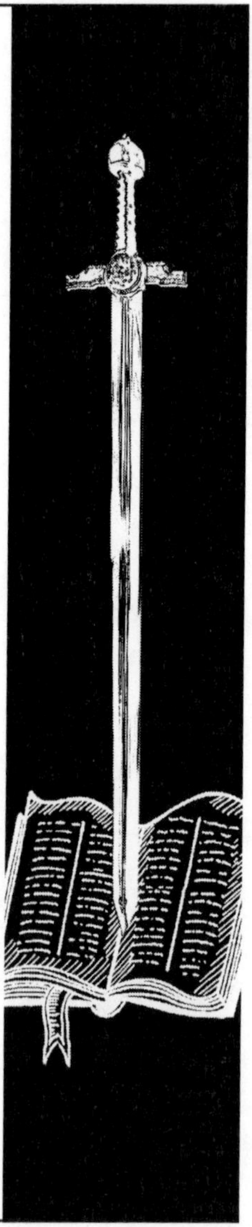

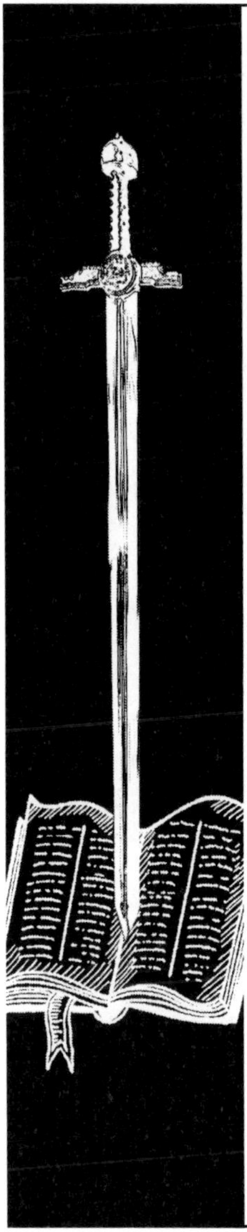

fesses his guilt, and Joshua 7:24–26a metes out the punishment:

◆ ◆ ◆

Then Joshua and all Israel with him took Achan . . . with his sons and daughters, with his oxen, donkeys, and sheep, and his tent and all that he had; and they brought them up to the Valley of Achor. Joshua said, "Why did you bring trouble on us? The Lord is bringing trouble on you today." And all Israel stoned him to death; they burned them with fire, cast stones on them, and raised over him a great heap of stones that remains to this day. Then the Lord turned from his burning anger.[8]

◆ ◆ ◆

The Israelites' massacre of native peoples in thirteen other battles in Joshua is summarized in Exhibit D.

Chapter 12 of the Book of Joshua lists at least fifteen other sieges and defeats of other peoples by the Israelites. Since there is no mention of death, however, no assumption has been made that any were killed as previously explained. Joshua 12:1–24 indicates that Joshua and the Israelites defeated thirty-three kings in all (two on east side of Jordan and thirty-one on west side).

The book of Judges continues the Israelites' campaign in Canaan, and the killings in this book are charted in Exhibit E. Judges introduces more instruments of death: an oxgoad, a tent peg, a millstone, and the fresh jawbone of a donkey. The book of Judges also discusses three famous Israelite warriors, Gideon, Jephthah, and Samson.

In Judges 3:31, an Israelite named Shamgar murders 600

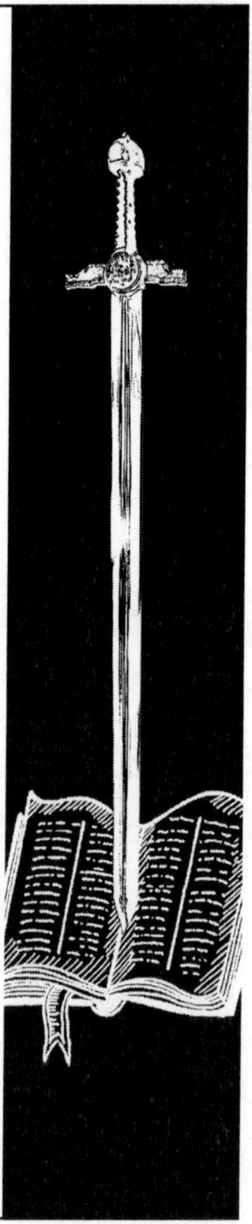

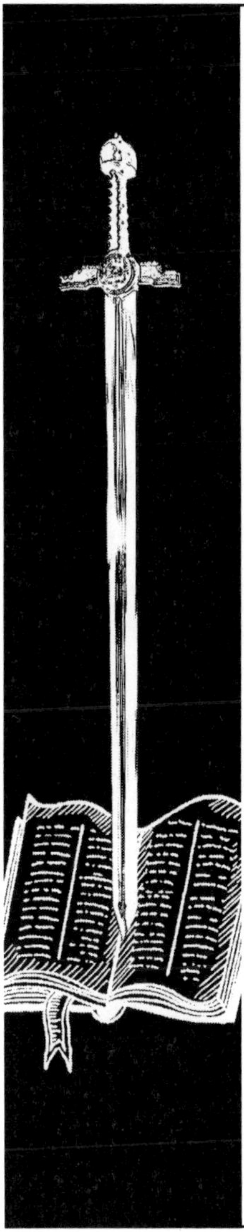

Philistines with an oxgoad.

A goad is a sharpened metal point on the end of long pole, and goads were used by farmers to prod animals to keep them moving. Ecclesiastes 12:11 notes that the wise instruction of a good teacher acts like a goad.

Shamgar's slaying of 600 Philistines consists of one verse. Shamgar is also briefly mentioned in the next incident, which introduces the first known female murderer, Deborah. By the time of Judges 4, the Israelites have been oppressed for twenty years by the non-Israelite Jabin, king of the city of Hazor in Canaan. Verse 1 reveals that the Lord had sold the Israelites into the hand of King Jabin because they had been unfaithful to Him.

Deborah, the fifth judge of Israel and the only female judge, instructs an Israelite named Barak to take 10,000 warriors and wage war against Sisera, the commander of King Jabin's army. The Lord throws Sisera's army into a panic, and "all the army of Sisera fell by the sword; no one was left."

Except Sisera himself. Verse 17 states that Sisera flees on foot to the tent of an Israelite woman named Jael, whom Sisera believes will hide him. Verses 21–22 prove him (deadly) wrong:

◆ ◆ ◆

But Jael . . . took a hammer in her hand, and went softly to him and drove the peg into his temple, until it went down into the ground — he was lying fast asleep from weariness — and he died.

Then, as Barak came in pursuit of Sisera, Jael went out to meet him, and said to him,

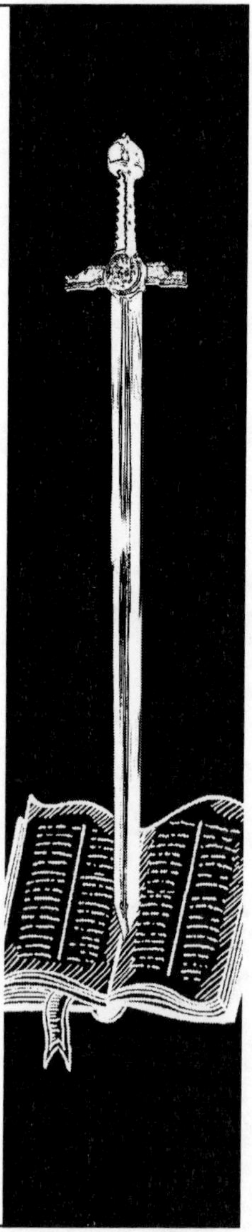

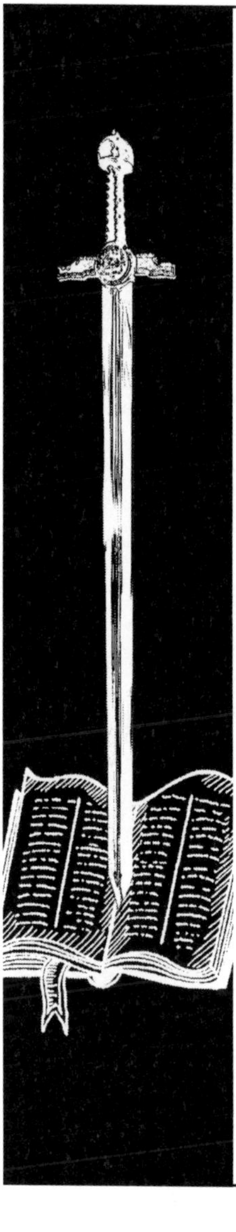

"Come and I will show you the man whom you are seeking." So he went into her tent; and there was Sisera lying dead, with the tent peg in his temple.

◆ ◆ ◆

The "Song of Deborah" follows in chapter five.[9] Verses 26–27 memorialize Jael:

◆ ◆ ◆

She put her hand to the tent peg and her right hand to the worker's mallet;
She struck Sisera a blow, she crushed his head, she shattered and pierced his temple.
He sank, he fell, he lay still at her feet;
At her feet he sank; he fell; where he sank, there he fell dead.

◆ ◆ ◆

Psalm 83:9–10 adds:

Sisera . . . became dung for the ground.

◆ ◆ ◆

Judges 6 introduces Gideon, a mighty Israelite warrior who wages war in the Israelites' continuing struggle for control of the land.

In Judges 6:1–8:21, Gideon and an army of 300 Israelites go to war against 135,000 Midianites, Amalekites, and other people of the east. The ratio is staggering: 450 to every one Israelite.

But the Lord is leading Gideon's army, and they slay 120,000. The text at 7:12 indicates that the remaining 15,000 are thrown into a panic.

As for the four Midianite kings, the heads of Oreb and Zeeb are

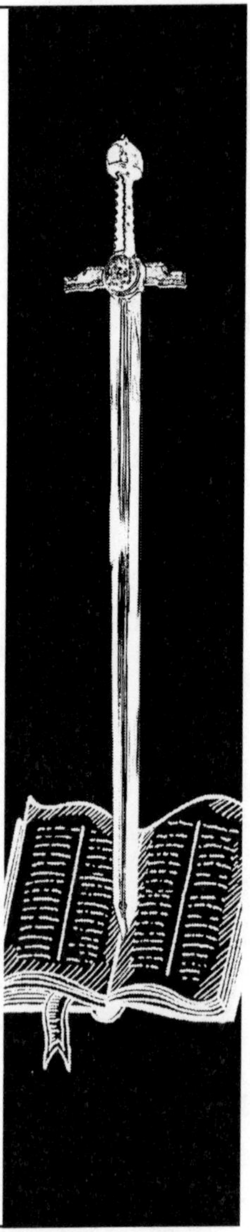

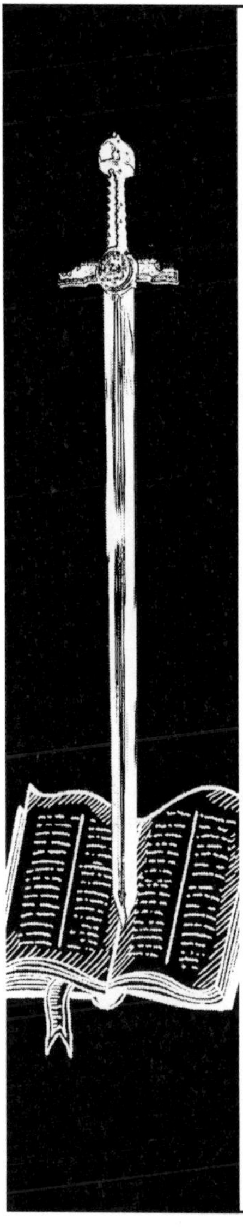

brought to Gideon as evidenced in 7:25.

In Judges 8:20–21, Gideon orders his first-born son to kill the kings Zebah and Zalmunna. Scripture relates, however, that the boy was afraid and did not draw his sword. So Gideon proceeds to finish them off.

Backtracking a little, Scripture reveals in 8:4–9 that while in pursuit of two of the Midianite kings, Gideon requested food for his army from the people in two towns along the way, Succoth and Penuel. The officials in Succoth refuse, as do those in Penuel.

After Gideon returns from battle, verses 14–17 recount Gideon's reprisal against those who refused to support his army:

• • •

[Gideon] caught a young man, one of the people of Succoth, and questioned him; and he listed for him the officials and elders of Succoth, seventy-seven people. . . . So [Gideon] took the elders of the city and he took thorns of the wilderness and briers and with them he trampled the people of Succoth. He also broke down the tower of Penuel, and killed the men of the city.

◆ ◆ ◆

If Gideon was a mighty warrior, he was also a fertile male. Judges 8:30–31 mentions that Gideon has seventy sons and many wives.

His concubine also bears him a son named Abimelech. In the next chapter of Judges, Abimelech murders sixty-nine[10] of his half-brothers in an attempt to

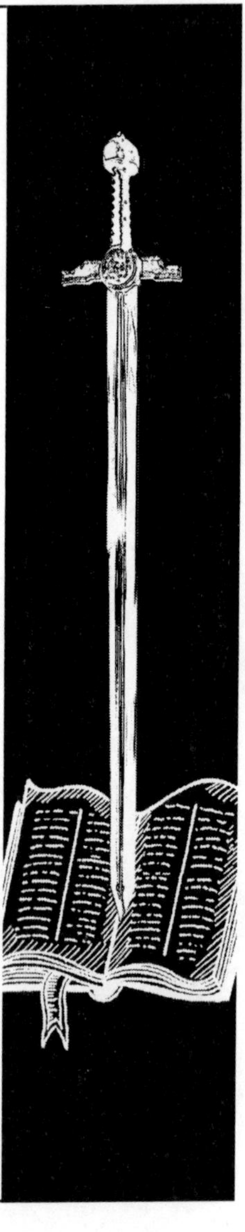

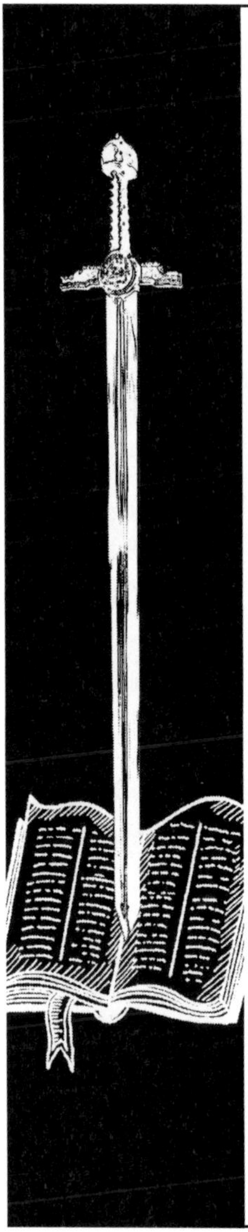

seize the leadership of his city. Only the youngest brother, hiding himself, manages to survive.

Abimelech himself comes to a disastrous end at 9:50–57. In one of his military campaigns, Abimelech approaches a city's tower in order to burn it, along with the men and women inside. A woman in the tower throws a millstone upon Abimelech's head, crushing his skull. However, Abimelech doesn't immediately die.

Not wanting to be remembered as being killed by a woman, Abimelech orders one of his young men to finish the deed with his sword.[11]

Jephthah, although not as well-known as either Gideon or Samson, was also a mighty Israelite warrior. But Jephthah suffers an almost unspeakable tragedy in Judges 11:29–39 during his military campaign against a native people called the Ammonites:

◆ ◆ ◆

And Jephthah made a vow to the Lord, and said, "If you will give the Ammonites into my hand, then whoever comes out of the doors of my house to meet me, when I return victorious from the Ammonites, shall be the Lord's, to be offered up by me as a burnt offering." So Jephthah crossed over the Ammonites to fight against them; and the Lord gave them into his hand. He inflicted a massive defeat on them...

Then Jephthah came to his home at Mizpah; and there was his daughter coming out to meet him with timbrels and with dancing. She was his only child; he had no son or daughter except her.

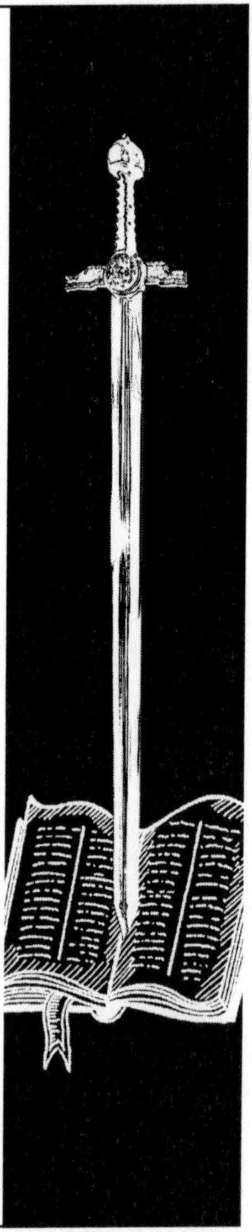

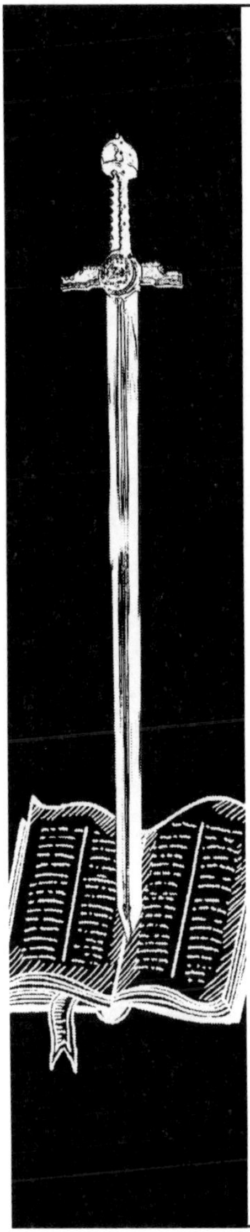

When he saw her, he tore his clothes, and said, "Alas, my daughter! You have brought me very low; you have become the cause of great trouble to me. For I have opened my mouth to the Lord, and I cannot take back my vow."

She said to him, "My father, if you have opened your mouth to the Lord, do to me according to what has gone out of your mouth, now that the Lord has given you vengeance against your enemies, the Ammonites."

And she said to her father, "Let this thing be done for me: Grant me two months on the mountains, so that I may go and wander on the mountains, and bewail my virginity, my companions and I."

"Go," he said and sent her away for two months. So she

departed, she and her companions, and bewailed her virginity on the mountains. At the end of two months, she returned to her father, who did with her according to the vow he had made.

◆ ◆ ◆

A human sacrifice of one's own daughter? And a burnt offering at that? One's first question might be, "Just who did Jephthah think would be the first out of his house?"

The *Oxford Bible*'s annotation attempts an explanation: given the arrangement of homes with courtyards that housed domesticated animals, it is likely that Jephthah assumed that one of these animals would be encountered first. The annotation adds that because a Hebrew woman could suffer no greater disgrace than to

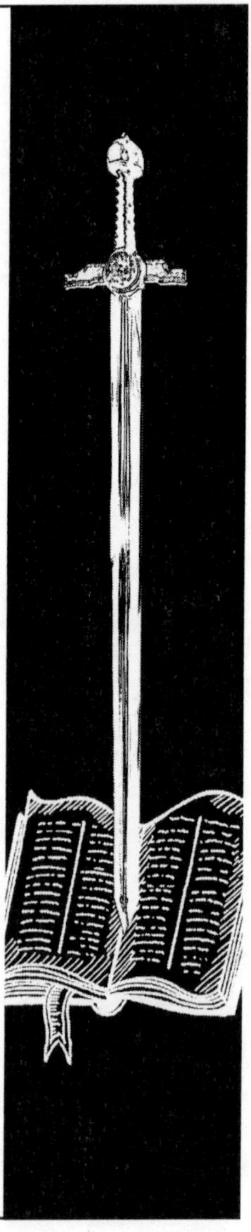

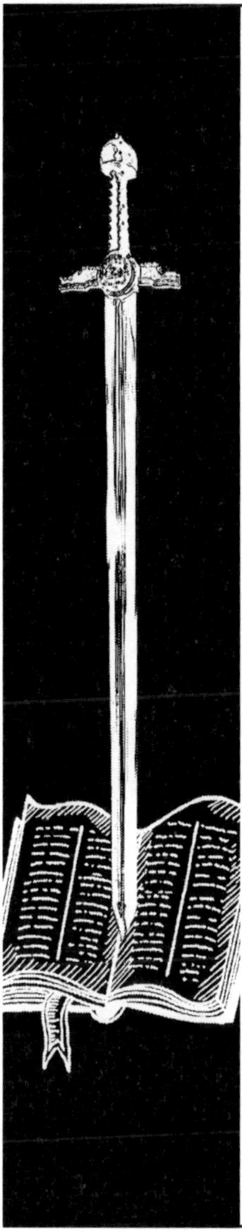

die childless, the daughter wanted to bewail her virginity.[12]

Jephthah's woes do not end. Immediately thereafter in Judges 12:1–6, Jephthah is criticized by Israelites from the tribe of Ephraim. Angry that Jephthah did not enlist their help in his war against the Ammonites, they threaten to burn down his house. The two sides fight, and Jephthah and his men end up killing 42,000 of their fellow Israelites. What's wrong with this picture: the Israelites fight against Jephthah because the Israelites were not called to fight *with* Jephthah.

The final mighty warrior is Samson — as in Samson and Delilah. Actually, Delilah was not Samson's first wife. In Judges 14:1–19, Samson marries a non-Israelite woman from the Philistine people in the land.

When Samson's parents travel to meet the woman, there is a feast, and Samson proposes a riddle to the Philistines. If the Philistines can guess the riddle, Samson will provide thirty pieces of clothing. And vice versa.

Samson's wife proceeds to coax the riddle's answer out of her husband and tells her kinsfolk. So when the Philistines answer correctly, Samson owes them thirty pieces of clothing. Samson then travels to another town, kills thirty men there, and takes their garments in order to pay his debt to the Philistines.

The father of Samson's wife, thinking that Samson must be angry with his wife over the riddle incident, gives the wife to another man in Judges 15:2. Samson takes revenge in verses 4–5:

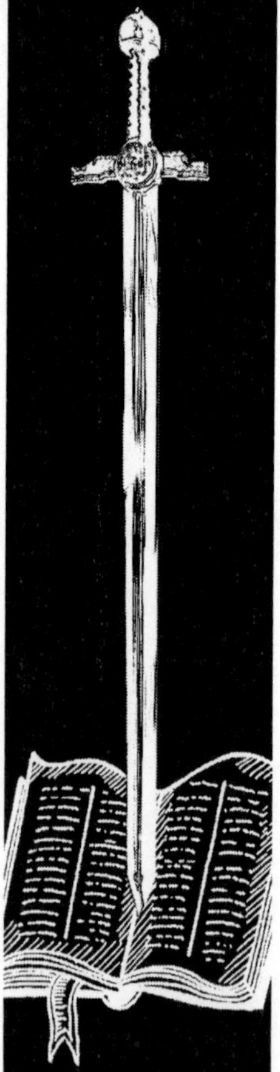

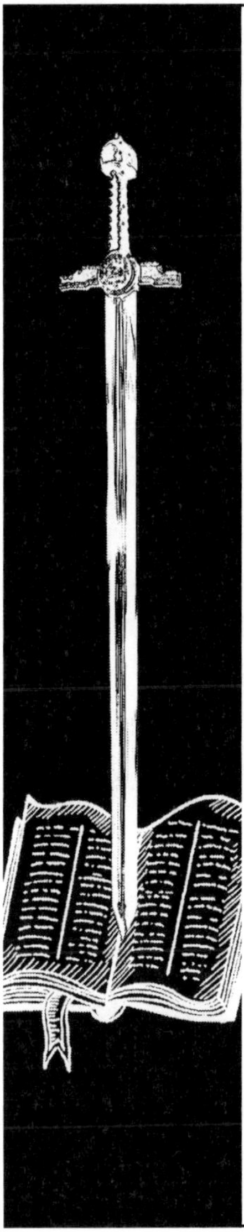

So Samson went and caught three hundred foxes, and took some torches; and he turned the foxes tail to tail, and put a torch between each pair of tails. When he had set fire to the torches, he let the foxes go into the standing grain of the Philistines, and burned up the shocks and the standing grain, as well as the vineyards and olive groves.

◆ ◆ ◆

Now the Philistines are angry and kill Samson's wife and her father. Samson avenges these deaths with a great slaughter of the Philistines, striking them down hip and thigh.

This back-and-forth narrative becomes even more dizzying: Samson tries to hide with a group of Israelites, but they refuse to provide him sanctuary from the Philistines. The Israelites bind Samson and give him back to the Philistines! But the Lord arrives to rescue Samson in verses 14–17:

◆ ◆ ◆

[A]nd the spirit of the Lord rushed on [Samson], and the ropes that were on his arms became like flax that has caught fire, and his bonds melted off his hands. Then he found a fresh jawbone of a donkey, reached down and took it, and with it he killed a thousand men. And Samson said, "With the jawbone of an donkey, heaps upon heaps, with the jawbone of an donkey, I have slain a thousand men."

When he had finished speaking, he threw away the jawbone.

◆ ◆ ◆

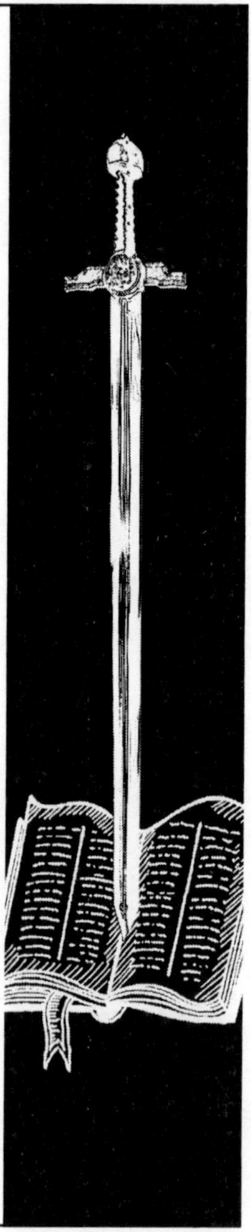

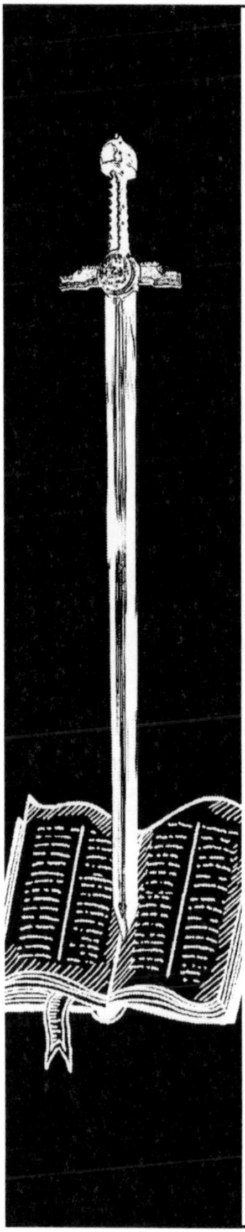

Delilah enters the stage in chapter 16, and Samson falls in love with her. Delilah, in a scene reminiscent of Samson's first wife, coaxes out of Samson the source of his strength: a razor has never touched his head. Delilah betrays Samson, has a man cut off his locks, and Samson is seized by the Philistines.

There they gouge out Samson's eyes and take him to one of their temples. Only the actual Scripture in verses 28–30 can adequately describe Samson's final revenge, which includes his suicide:

◆ ◆ ◆

Then Samson called to the Lord and said, "Lord God, remember me and strengthen me only this once, O God, so that with this one act of revenge I may pay back the Philistines for my two eyes."

And Samson grasped the two middle pillars on which the house rested, and he leaned his weight against them, his right hand on the one and his left hand on the other. Then Samson said, "Let me die with the Philistines." He strained with all his might; and the house fell on the lords and all the people who were in it. So those he killed at his death were more than those he had killed during his lifetime.

◆ ◆ ◆

Before we exit Judges, remember the (horrifying) tale from the Preface about the Baptist priest and the Methodists?

Refer to chapters 19 through 21 of Judges. The names, and their actual counterparts, are as follows:

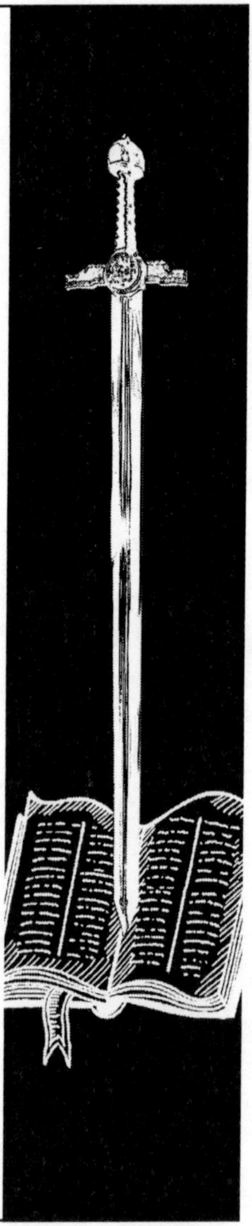

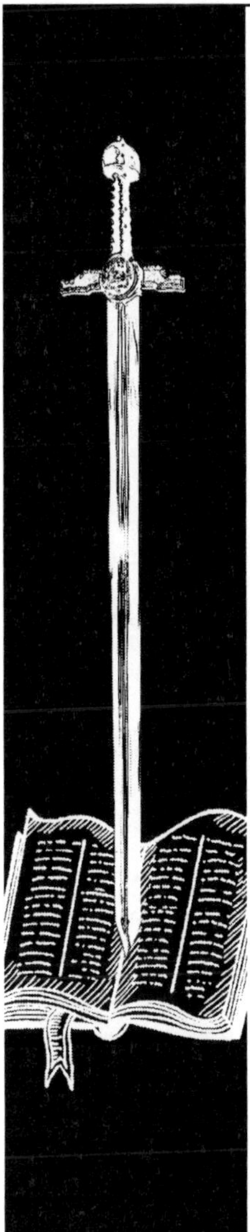

Twelve denominations of Christians (Preface) vs. twelve tribes of Israelites (Judges); Baptist preacher (Preface) vs. Israelite Levite priest (Judges); Baptist preacher's mistress (Preface) vs. Levite's concubine (Judges); Methodists (Preface) vs. Israelites from tribe of Benjamin (Judges); and City of Lutherans (Preface) vs. City of Israelites (Judges).

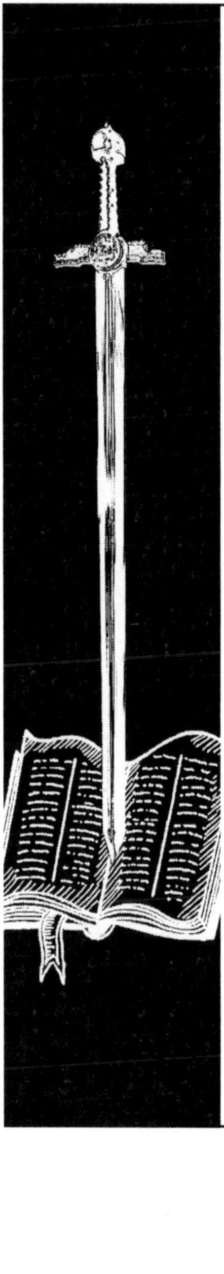

Chapter Five

The Murderous Reign of King David

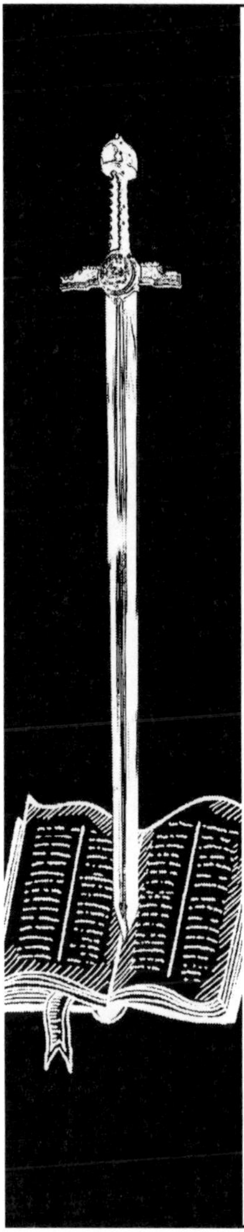

God's Chosen People are gradually conquering and settling the Promised Land. But there is no central government. The Israelites basically comprise a loose association of tribes led by judges or military heroes. To become a nation — to become a unified people in their own right — they want a king.

Following the book of Judges are the two books of Samuel. Samuel is the last Israelite judge, and he anoints Saul as the first king. Saul's military victories, along with other murders in 1 and 2 Samuel, are chronicled in Exhibit F. This chapter's focus, however, is the reign of King David — Israel's second and most renowned king.

The biblical reader first meets David as a boy in 1 Samuel 17:4–51, the famous story of Goliath. The ten-foot-tall Philistine giant[1] is taunting and challenging the Israelite armies when David asks, "Who is this uncircumcised Philistine that he should defy the armies of the living God?"

David fells Goliath with a sling and a stone, which sinks deep in the giant's forehead. David then kills Goliath with Goliath's own sword and cuts off his head, which is taken to Jerusalem.

The Israelites pursue the Philistines in 1 Samuel 17:52–53. Although these two verses do not mention killing or death, the assumption of murder proceeds from 1 Samuel 18:6–7:

◆ ◆ ◆

As [the Israelites] were returning home, when David re-

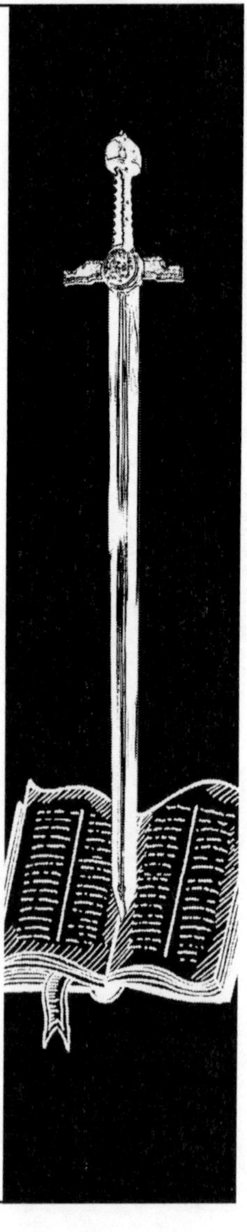

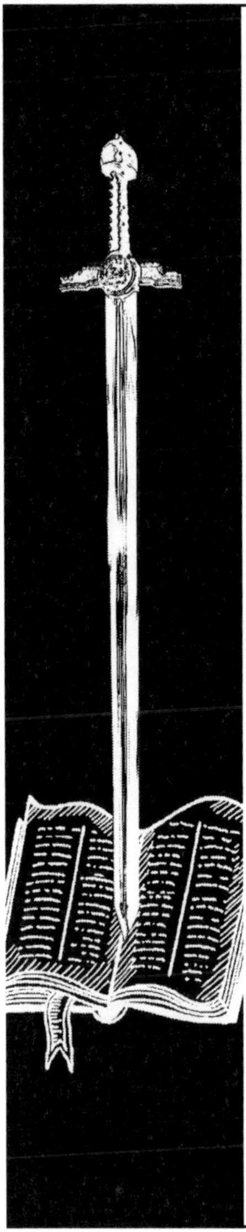

turned from killing the Philistine, the women came out of all the towns of Israel, singing and dancing, to songs of joy, and with musical instruments. And the women sang to one another as they made merry,

"Saul has killed his thousands, and David his ten thousands."

Verses 8–9 continue:

Saul was very angry, for this saying displeased him. He said, "they have ascribed to David ten thousands, and to me they have ascribed thousands; what more can he have but the kingdom?" So Saul eyed David from that day on.

The next day an evil spirit from God rushed upon Saul, and he raved within his house, while David was playing the lyre, as he did day by day. Saul had his spear in his hand; and Saul threw the spear, for he thought, "I will pin David to the wall." But David eluded him twice.

◆ ◆ ◆

An evil spirit from God in a case of attempted murder? Saul is both jealous of David's might and fearful that he is seeking the throne.

Throughout the next few chapters of 1 Samuel, Saul stalks David to try and kill him, but each time, David either flees or safely hides.

David, on the other hand, does not seem to share Saul's murderous intent. In two separate instances, David has the opportunity to murder Saul, but he does not. The first instance is noteworthy if for nothing else than its "personal" circumstances.

In 1 Samuel 24:1–7, David is hiding in a cave. While searching

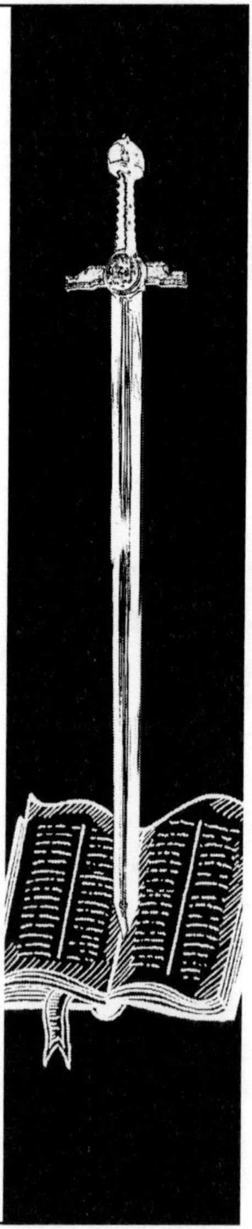

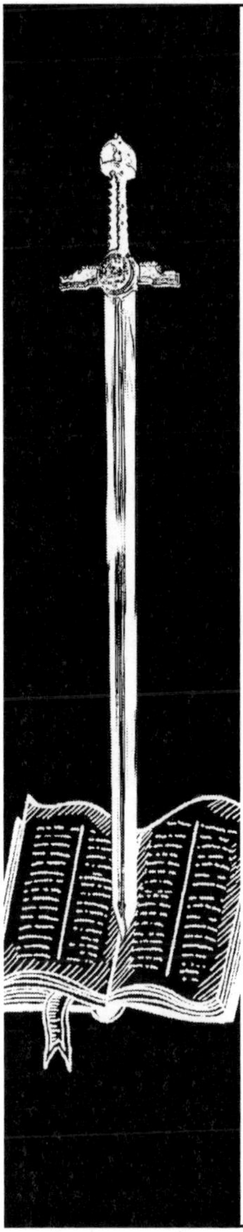

for David, Saul actually stops in the same cave to, as Scripture relates, "relieve himself."

David could kill his would-be assassin, but refuses to do so, telling his men:

◆ ◆ ◆

The Lord forbid that I should do this thing to my lord, the Lord's anointed, to raise my hand against him; for he is the Lord's anointed.

◆ ◆ ◆

Saul and David forge tenuous truces throughout their relationship, and David even seeks to marry Saul's daughter, Michal.

In 1 Samuel 18:20–27, the ever-conniving Saul again plots David's demise:

◆ ◆ ◆

Then Saul said, "Thus shall [my servants] say to David, 'The king desires no marriage pres-

ent except a hundred foreskins of the Philistines, that he may be avenged on the king's enemies.'" Now Saul planned to make David fall by the hand of the Philistines.

When his servants told David these words, David was well-pleased to be the king's son-in-law. Before the time had expired, David rose and went, along with his men, and killed one hundred of the Philistines; and David brought their foreskins, which were given in full number to the king, that he might become the king's son-in-law.

◆ ◆ ◆

So David gets the girl — at a price of 100 foreskins![2] How else was David to get 100 Philistine foreskins other than by killing 100 Philistines?

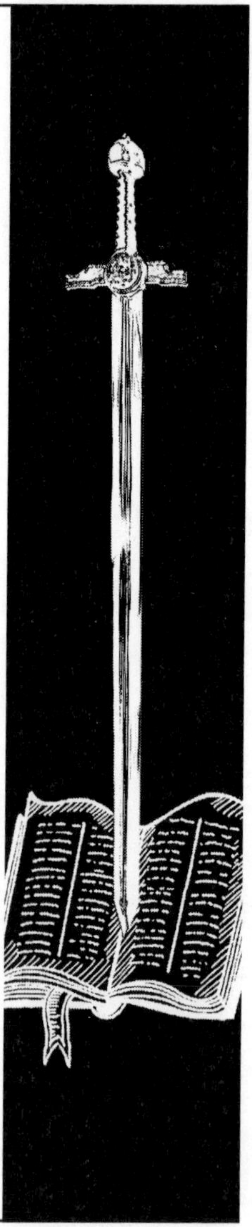

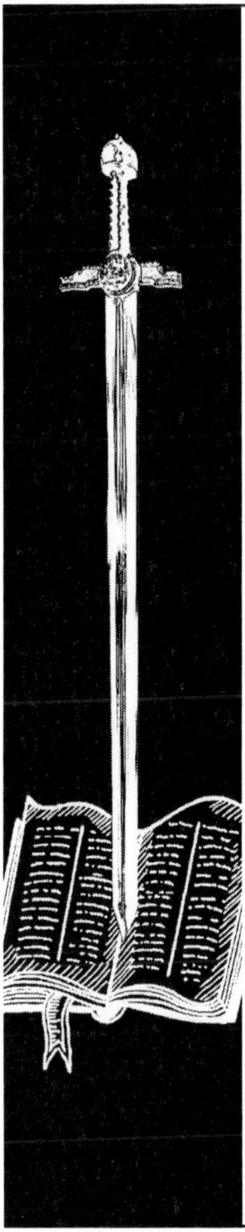

David marries another girl, too, but not before the Lord slays her husband on David's behalf. In 1 Samuel 25:2–35, David is in the wilderness of Paran and requests provisions for his men from a man named Nabal. Nabal refuses, and David readies to take revenge until Nabal's wife, Abigail, offers the provisions and begs for her husband's forgiveness.

David agrees, but then verses 38–39 announce:

◆ ◆ ◆

About ten days later the Lord struck Nabal, and he died. When David heard that Nabal was dead, he said, "Blessed be the Lord who has judged the case of Nabal's insult to me, and has kept back his servant from evil; the Lord has returned the evil-doing of Nabal upon his own head." Then Da-

vid sent and wooed Abigail, to make her his wife.

• • •

King Saul dies in a rather unusual way. The Israelites are again fighting the Philistines, and 1 Samuel 31:3–5 relates:

• • •

The battle pressed hard upon Saul; the archers found him, and he was badly wounded by them. Then Saul said to his armor-bearer, "Draw your sword and thrust me through with it, so that these uncircumcised may not come and thrust me through, and make sport of me." But his armor-bearer was unwilling; for he was terrified. So Saul took his own sword and fell upon it. When his armor-bearer saw that Saul was dead, he also fell upon his sword and died with him.

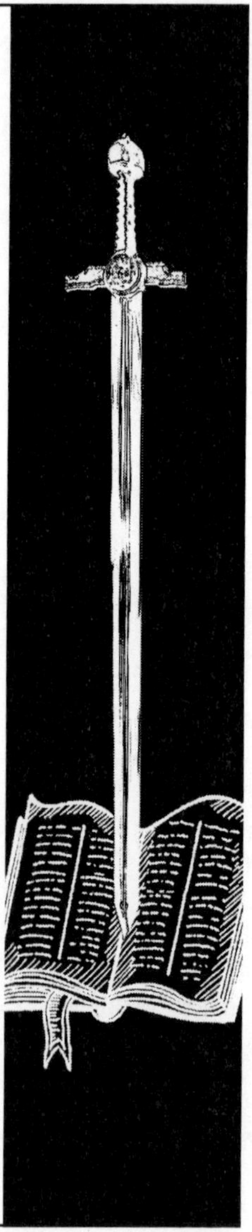

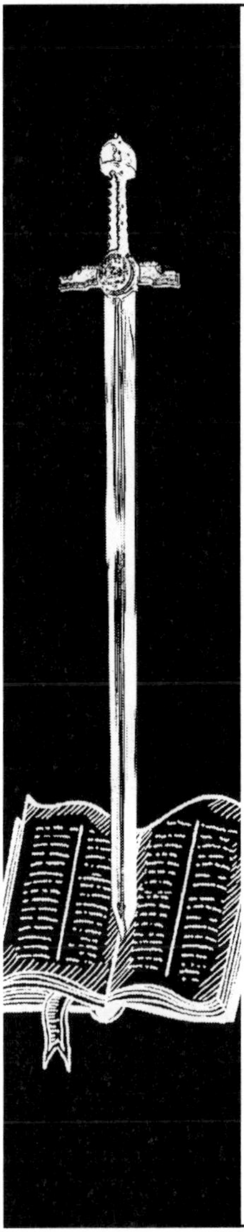

These two suicides will not be tallied in the murder count, but a following deception about Saul's death will affect the total.

Moving into the second book of Samuel, a non-Israelite apparently believes that David will be pleased with the death of Saul. The man lies to David, saying that he found Saul mortally wounded and killed him upon Saul's insistence. The man has brought Saul's crown to David, probably not expecting the outcome in 1:13–15:

David said to the young man who had reported to him, "Where do you come from?" He answered, "I am the son of a resident alien, an Amalekite." David said to him, "Were you not afraid to lift your hand to destroy the Lord's anointed?"

Then David called one of the young men and said, "Come here and strike him down." So he struck him down and he died.

◆ ◆ ◆

A yet third and conflicting account of Saul's death is found in 1 Chronicles 10:13–14: Saul died because of his unfaithfulness and for consulting a medium for guidance. Therefore, the Lord put Saul to death.

Seeking to curry David's favor also fails for two men in 2 Samuel 4:1–8. Ishbaal, one of the sons of Saul, is a potential rival king to David.

Two of Ishbaal's captains, Baanah and Rechab, murder Ishbaal and bring his head to David. In a scene reminiscent of David ordering the death of the Amalekite, David directs one of his young

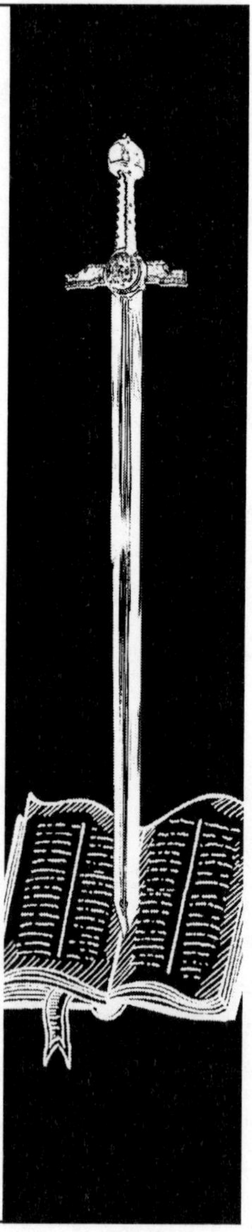

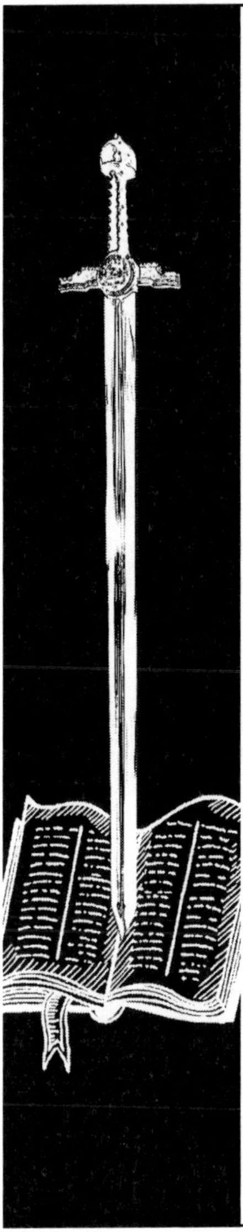

men to kill Baanah and Rechab. David goes further with the two captains, however. Their hands and feet are cut off, and their bodies are hung beside a pool of water.

Here is a peculiar aside about the last three murders: In each instance, David orders one of his young men to slay the offender. Does David not want the bloodshed on his hands? Is David training his young men to murder?

Most certainly, King David does murder his fair share, defeating tens of thousands of his adversaries. As stated, most of his "routine" military victories are charted in Exhibit F and not addressed in this narrative.

However, 2 Samuel 8:2 records an unusual method utilized by David to determine who would die and who would live:

◆ ◆ ◆

[David] also defeated the Moabites and, making them lie down on the ground, measured them off with a cord; he measured two lengths of cord for those who were to be put to death, and one length for those who were to be spared.

◆ ◆ ◆

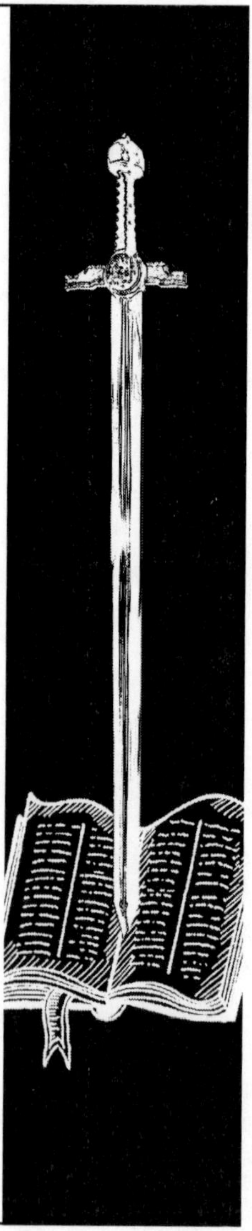

If King David was indiscriminate with who he murdered, he was also indiscriminate in his sexual relations. David's adultery with the married Bathsheba results in a pregnant Bathsheba.

In 2 Samuel 11:14–12:19, David orchestrates the death of Bathsheba's husband, Uriah, by arranging for Uriah to be sent to the front lines of a battle in which the Israelites are engaged. Uriah is killed in battle,[3] David marries Bathsheba, and their son is born.

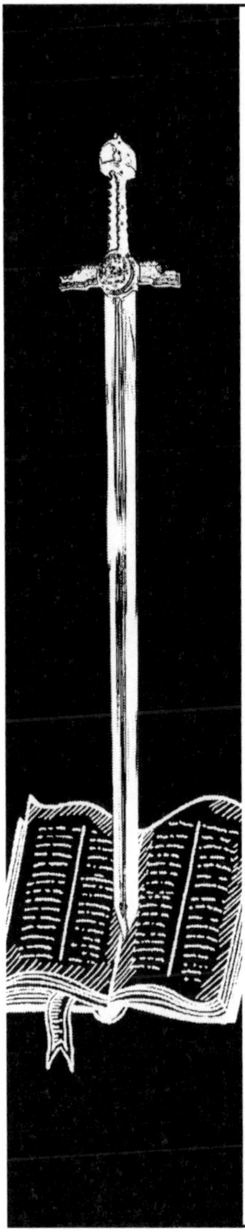

The Lord, however, angered over David's adultery and murder of Uriah, strikes the child dead after seven days.

David does have other children, and a family struggle and murder occur in 2 Samuel 13:1–30. By one wife, David has a son and daughter, Absalom and Tamar. By another wife, David has a son named Amnon. Therefore, Amnon is half-brother to both Absalom and Tamar.

Scripture describes Tamar as a beautiful virgin, and Amnon rapes her. Two years later, Absalom (Tamar's full brother) exacts revenge by having Amnon murdered.[4]

And many years later, Absalom revolts against his father, King David, in an effort to seize the throne. When the armies of the two men meet in 2 Samuel 18:1–17, David instructs his men to "deal gently for my sake with the young man Absalom."

The *Oxford Annotated Bible* provides that despite Absalom's rebellion, David still loves his son and wishes that his life might be saved.[5] But Joab, David's commander-in-chief, either doesn't hear or doesn't listen, as indicated in verses 9 and 14–15:

◆ ◆ ◆

Absalom was riding on his mule, and the mule went under the thick branches of a great oak. His head caught fast in the oak, and he was left hanging between heaven and earth, while the mule that was under him went on....[Joab] took three spears in his hand, and thrust them into the heart of Absalom, while he was still alive in the oak. And ten young

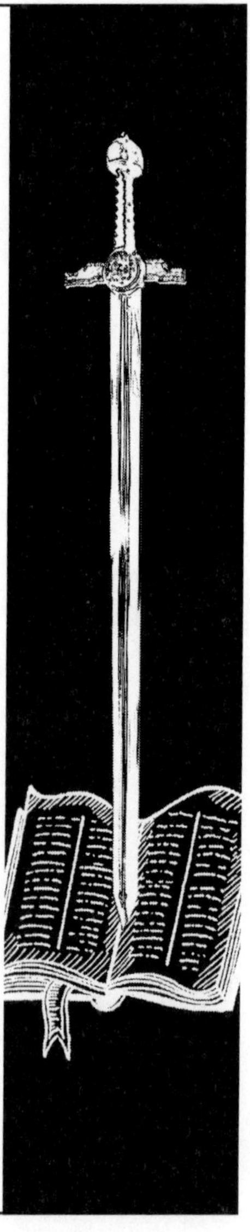

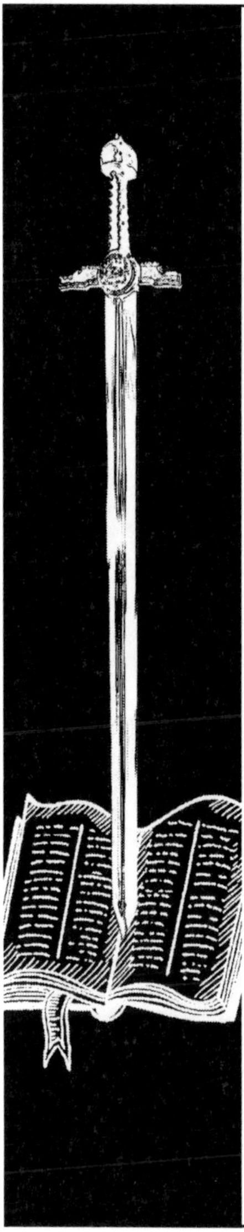

men, Joab's armor-bearers, surrounded Absalom and struck him, and killed him.

◆ ◆ ◆

David, resentful over Joab's murder of Absalom, replaces Joab with a man named Amasa. At his first opportunity, in 2 Samuel 20:7–12, Joab murders Amasa in order to regain his position as army commander. Joab strikes Amasa in the belly with a sword "so that his entrails poured out on the ground" and Amasa "lay wallowing in his blood."

Graphic descriptions of death in the Old Testament are commonplace, and another surfaces at 2 Samuel 21:1–9. The Lord informs David that a three-year famine on the land results from the bloodguilt of the former King Saul when he put the Gibeonites to death.[6]

David asks the Gibeonites, who are a non-Israelite people, how he might atone for the deaths in order to stop the famine. The Gibeonites demand seven sons of Saul. David hands over two sons and five grandsons of Saul, and the seven are impaled on a mountain before the Lord.

Although these deaths are technically by the hands of non-Israelites, it is David who negotiates the bargain and offers up Saul's descendants; therefore, these murders are included in the tally.

The conclusion to this story appears to violate the dictates of Deuteronomy 21:22–23:[7]

◆ ◆ ◆

When someone is convicted of a crime punishable by death and is executed, and you hang him on a tree, his corpse must not remain all night upon the

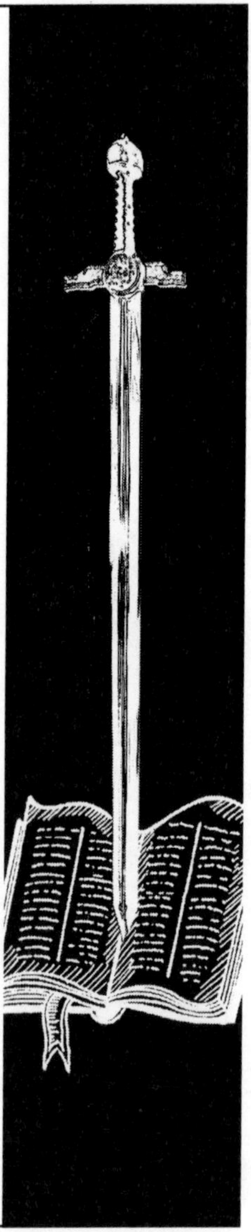

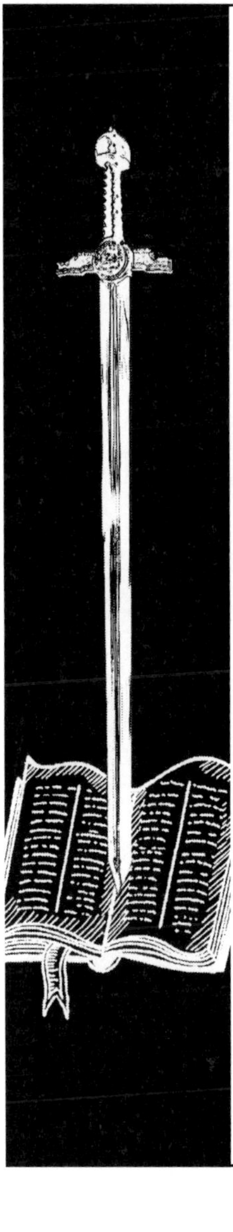

tree; you shall bury him that same day, for anyone hung on a tree is under God's curse. You must not defile the land that the Lord your God is giving you for possession.

◆ ◆ ◆

Verses 9–10 of the Samuel account disclose that Saul's seven descendants were impaled in the first days of the harvest (late April or May) and left exposed all summer until the rains came in late autumn.[8]

One of Saul's concubines, a woman named Rizpah, guards the seven decaying corpses and does not allow the birds to come feed by day or the wild animals by night (2 Samuel 21:10).

A final episode involving King David is perplexing if not downright troubling. In 2 Samuel 24:1, the text reads:

◆ ◆ ◆

Again the anger of the Lord was kindled against Israel, and he incited David against them, saying "Go, count the people of Judah and Israel."

◆ ◆ ◆

The reader is not apprised as to what has kindled God's anger, and a literal reading of the text indicates that God has instructed David to take a census. David obeys, directing his army officers to amass the figures.

But in 24:10–25, David is grieved because he has numbered the people, and David repents of this sin. For punishment, the Lord gives David three options: three years of famine, fleeing from his foes for three months, or three days of pestilence. David lets the Lord choose; there are three days of pestilence, and 70,000 Israelites die.

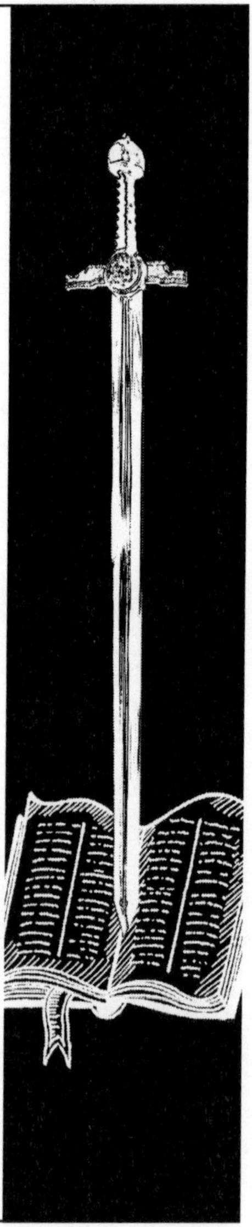

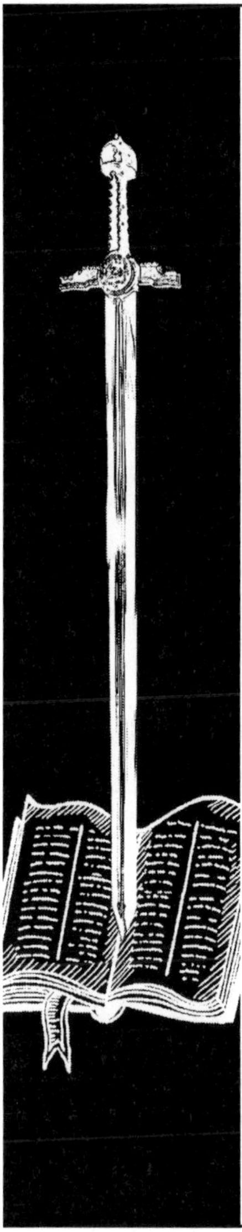

Scripture reveals that the Lord's angel is also stretching out his hand to destroy Jerusalem, but the Lord relents and stays the angel's hand. David averts further plague on the land by making offerings to the Lord.

But back to the beginning: Wasn't David told by God to count the people in the first place? The *Oxford Annotated Bible* offers this interpretation: taking a census was deemed an infringement upon the prerogatives of God, the sole arbiter of the destinies of the nation and its people.[9] The *Jewish Study Bible* submits that "inciting" does not mean commanding, but only putting the idea in David's mind; therefore, it remained David's decision whether or not to carry out the census.[10]

Neither explanation seems satisfactory. The later author of 1

Chronicles 21:1 attempts to solve this problem — of God apparently inciting David to sin — by substituting Satan for God.

Before leaving this chapter, three instances of murder are noteworthy as they relate to the Ark of the Covenant.

The Ark of the Covenant (which is also known as the Ark of the Lord or the Ark of God) was the sacred portable chest containing the stone tablets of the Ten Commandments.

The Israelites transported the ark with them, both in the wilderness and in the Promised Land, as it symbolized the presence and power of the Lord.

In 1 Samuel 5:1–12, the Philistines capture the ark and carry it to several of their cities. The Lord punishes the Philistines by striking some dead. Verse 12:

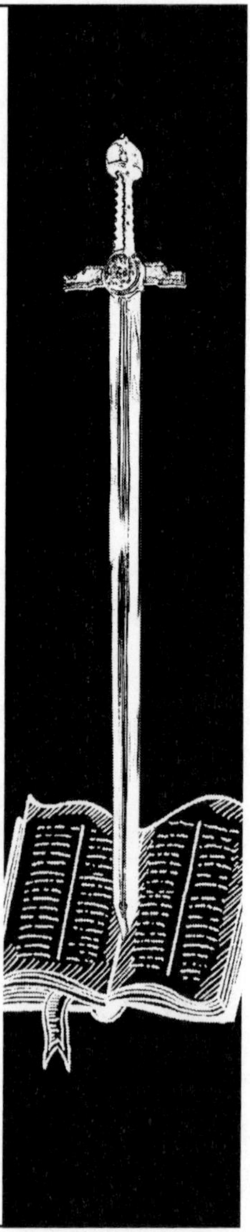

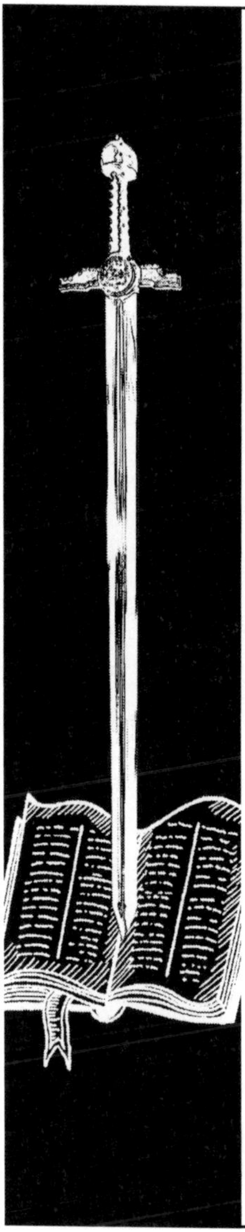

◆ ◆ ◆

. . . Those who did not die were stricken with tumors.

◆ ◆ ◆

The Philistines return the ark to reverse their bad fortune, and most of the Israelites rejoice at its homecoming.

However, 1 Samuel 6:19 relates that one group of Israelites do not rejoice when they greet the ark of the Lord; therefore, the Lord kills seventy of them. In contrast, verse 19 of the *Jewish Study Bible* states that the Israelites "looked into the Ark of the Lord," so the Lord killed "seventy men among the people [and] fifty thousand men."[11] For purposes of this study, only seventy deaths are recorded as the additional 50,000 is questionable.[12]

The third event occurs in 2 Samuel 6:1–8 while the Israelites are transporting the ark from one city to another on a cart driven by oxen. When the oxen shake the cart, a man named Uzzah reaches out his hand, presumably to prevent the ark from toppling.

Verse 7:

◆ ◆ ◆

The anger of the Lord was kindled against Uzzah; and God struck him there because he reached out his hand to the ark; and he died there beside the ark of God.

◆ ◆ ◆

The *Oxford Annotated Bible* suggests that Uzzah should not have touched the ark as only Levite priests were allowed to come in contact with holy things.[13] The *Jewish Study Bible* explains that touching a sacred object, loaded with awesome divine power, was fraught with danger.[14]

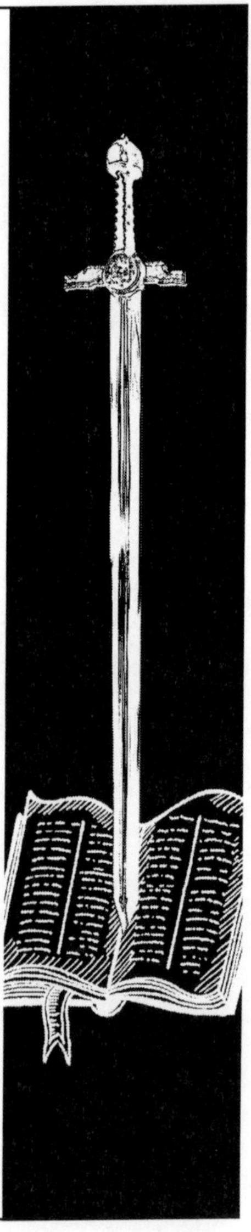

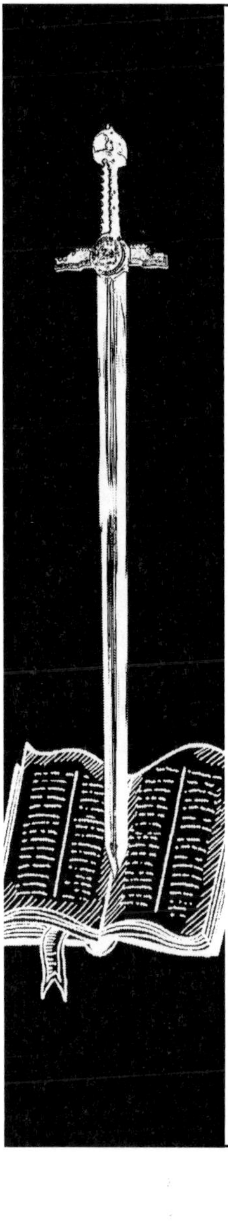

Chapter Six

Assassinations, Child Sacrifice, and Listening to Prophets

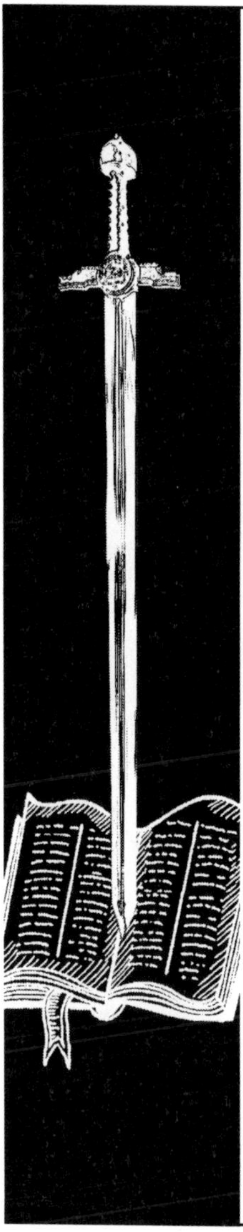

Apologies in advance as the two books of Kings can read like a cheap dime-store novel. King Joash is assassinated by two servants. His son, Amaziah, then murders the two servants. Then Amaziah is assassinated.

King Zechariah is assassinated by Shallum. Shallum is assassinated by Menahem. The son of Menahem, King Pekahiah, is assassinated by Pekah. Hoshea assassinates Pekah. When King Amon is assassinated by his servants, the people murder the servants.

After the unified reigns of King David and his son, Solomon, Israel splits into southern and northern kingdoms. The northern nation retains the name Israel, while the southern territory becomes Judah. The next four centuries are turbulent times as a total of nineteen different kings rule in Israel and twenty different kings in Judah.

Moreover, the narratives are complex and difficult to follow. The historical author switches back and forth between the nations and their kings, and the see-saw effect can be confusing to even the most careful biblical reader. For these reasons, the majority of killings and murders in the two books of Kings are summarized in Exhibit G.[1] The particularly murderous reign of King Jehu, however, merits special attention.

In 2 Kings 9:1–26, the prophet Elisha anoints Jehu to be the king of Israel. Jehu then proceeds to murder both the present king

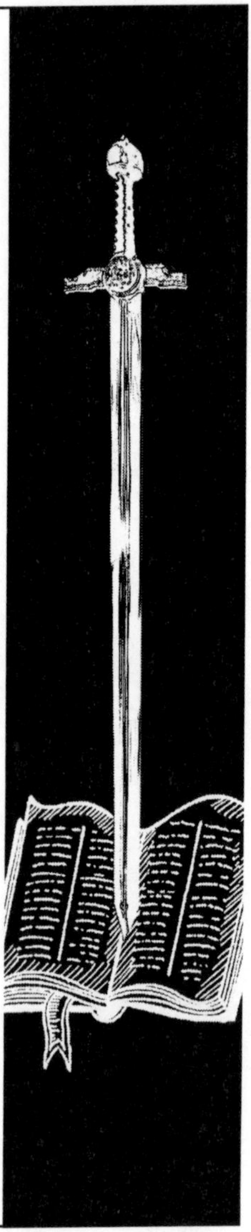

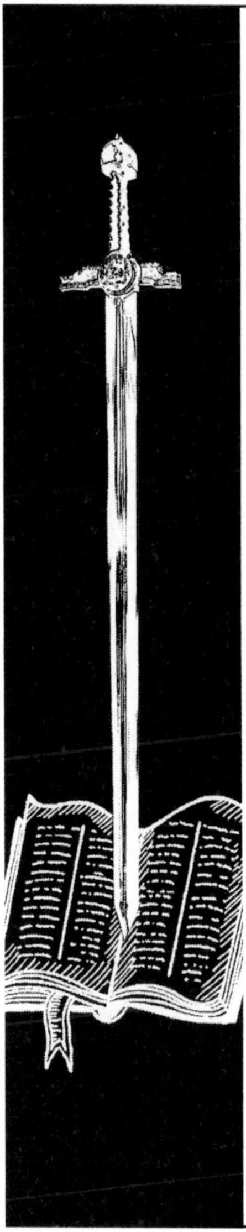

of Israel, King Joram, and King Ahaziah of Judah. With Joram, Jehu draws his bow with all his strength and shoots Joram between the shoulders so that the arrow pierces into his heart. Jehu then murders a former queen whose name is Jezebel by ordering eunuchs to throw her out a window. Verses 33–35:

◆ ◆ ◆

[Jehu] said, "Throw [Jezebel] down." So they threw her down; some of her blood spattered on the wall and on the horses, which trampled her. Then [Jehu] went in and ate and drank; he said, "See to that cursed woman and bury her; for she is a king's daughter." But when they went to bury her, they found no more of her than the skull and the feet and the palms of her hands.

◆ ◆ ◆

Jehu seeks to solidify his rule in the northern kingdom by demanding the heads of the sons of a former ruler, King Ahab. In 2 Kings 10:1–8, the leaders in Israel's capital city of Samaria kill the seventy sons, put their heads in a basket, and send the basket to Jehu. Jehu directs that the heads be laid in two heaps at the entrance to a gate until the morning.

Jehu continues his rampage in 2 Kings 10:11 by murdering all the remaining leaders, close friends, and priests of Ahab, until no survivor is left. Traveling to Samaria, Jehu meets forty-two relatives of the assassinated King Ahaziah in 10:12–14. Jehu slaughters all forty-two at a pit.

Jehu then arrives in Samaria, in verses 15–17, and murders every other person with connections to

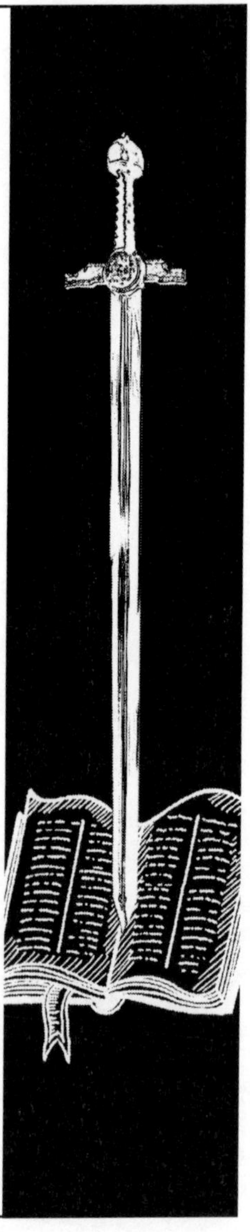

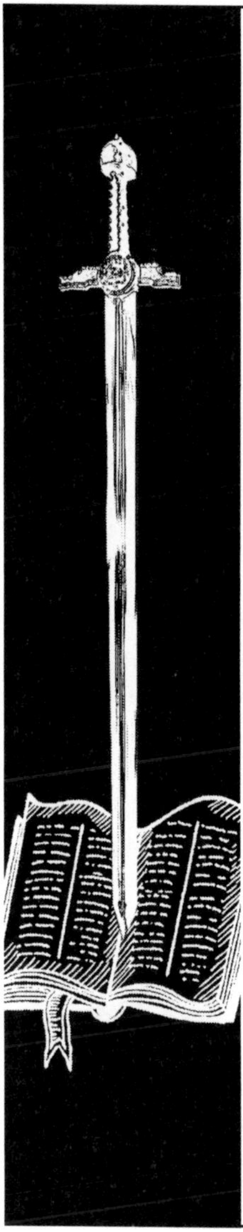

Ahab. In verse 16, Jehu indicates that these killings are representative of his "zeal for the Lord."

Jehu's uses deception in his last murderous act involving Baal, a god of the native people. In 2 Kings 10:18–28, Jehu pretends that he will sacrifice to Baal, so all the prophets, priests, and worshippers of Baal gather until the temple is "filled from wall to wall." Jehu then orders his guards to put all the people to the sword. The temple is destroyed and made into a latrine.

Molech was the national deity of the native Ammonites, whose worship included child sacrifice.[2] Leviticus 18:21 decries the practice:

* * *

You shall not give any of your offspring to sacrifice them to Molech, and so profane the name of your God.

◆ ◆ ◆

And participants in the practice are condemned in Psalm 106:37–38:

◆ ◆ ◆

They sacrificed their sons and daughters to demons . . . and the land was polluted with blood.

◆ ◆ ◆

The sacrifice of children was not unknown to the Israelites in the Old Testament[3] (remember Abraham's near sacrifice of his son, Isaac, in Genesis). In 2 Kings 16:3 and 21:6, two kings of Judah, Ahaz and Manasseh, make their sons pass through fire. An Israelite named Hiel, in 1 Kings 16:34, lays a foundation for Jericho

◆ ◆ ◆

. . . at the cost of Abiram his firstborn, and set up its gates

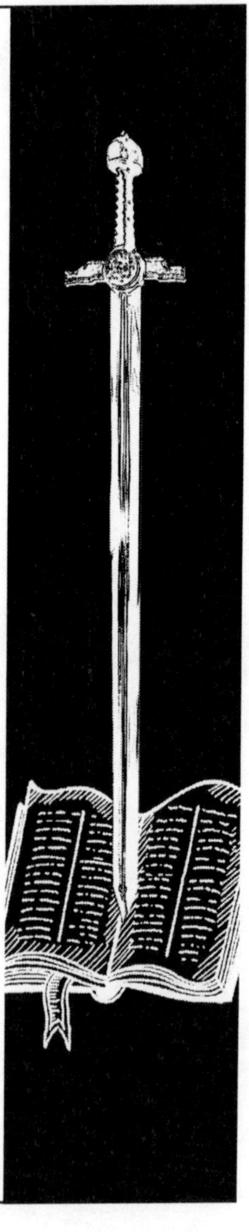

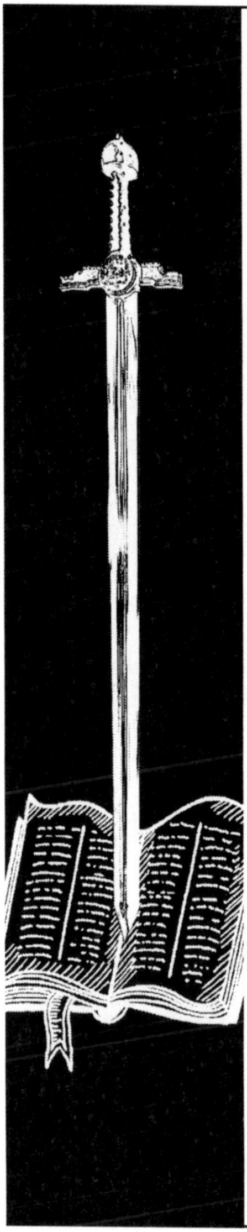

at the cost of his youngest son Segub.

◆ ◆ ◆

The *Oxford Annotated Bible* states that the bodies of children were often buried under foundations to bring good luck to the building project.[4]

One instance of cannibalism crops up in 2 Kings 6:25–29. There is a famine in Samaria, the capital of Israel, due to a siege by a foreign army. As the king of Israel is walking in the city, a woman cries out to him. When the king inquires of her complaint,

◆ ◆ ◆

She answered, "This woman said to me, 'Give up your son; we will eat him today, and we will eat my son tomorrow.' So we cooked my son and ate him. The next day I said to her, 'Give up your son and we will

eat him.' But she has hidden her son."

◆ ◆ ◆

The king is distressed to hear her complaint, but 2 Kings does not elaborate further.

The book of Lamentations, which recalls the siege of Judah, echoes the abomination in 4:10:

◆ ◆ ◆

The hands of compassionate women have boiled their own children; they became their food in the destruction of my people.

◆ ◆ ◆

Whether to listen to prophets becomes a puzzle in the two books of Kings. In 1 Kings 13:11–25, a "man of God" has been instructed by the Lord not to eat or drink anything. Another man, an "old prophet," lies to the man of God (no explanation is given why):

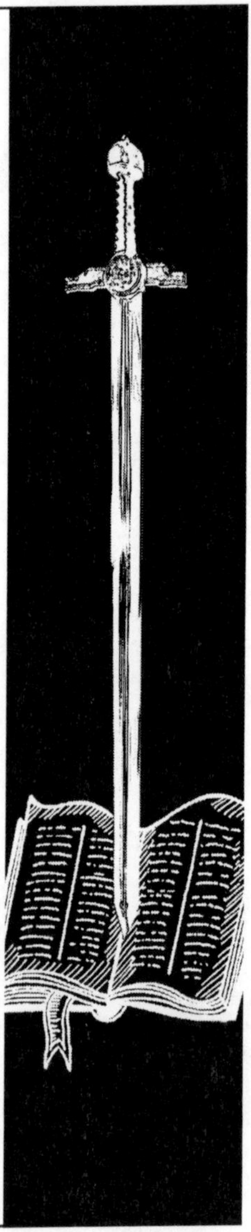

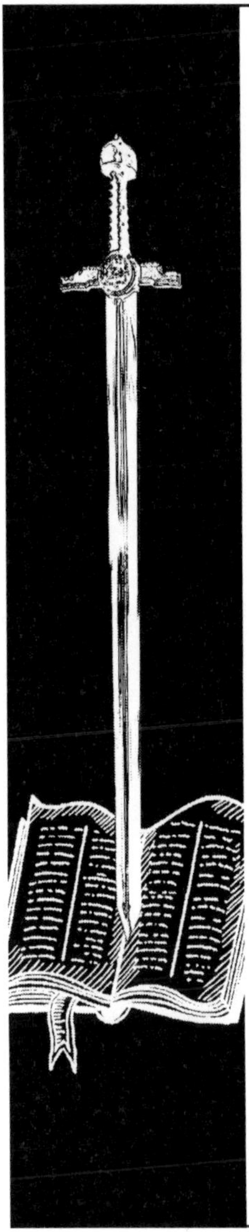

◆ ◆ ◆

Then the [prophet] said to [the man of God], "I also am a prophet as you are, and an angel spoke to me by the word of the Lord: Bring him back with you into your house so that he may eat food and drink water." But he was deceiving him. Then the man of God went back with him, and ate food and drank water in his house.

◆ ◆ ◆

As they are sitting at the old prophet's table, the prophet proclaims to the man of God:

◆ ◆ ◆

Thus says the Lord: "Because you have disobeyed the word of the Lord, and have not kept the commandment that the Lord your God commanded you, but have eaten food and drunk water in the place of which he said to you, 'Eat no food, and drink no water, your body shall not come to your ancestral home.'"

◆ ◆ ◆

Verses 23–25 conclude:

◆ ◆ ◆

After the man of God had eaten and had drunk, they saddled for him a donkey belonging to the prophet who had brought him back.

Then as he went away, a lion met him on the road and killed him. His body was thrown in the road, and the donkey stood beside it; the lion also stood beside the donkey. People passed by and saw the body thrown in the road, with the lion standing by the body.

◆ ◆ ◆

Contrast this story with 1 Kings 20:35–36:

◆ ◆ ◆

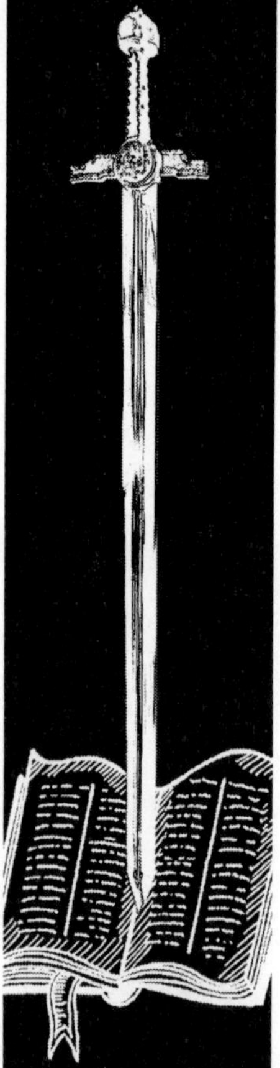

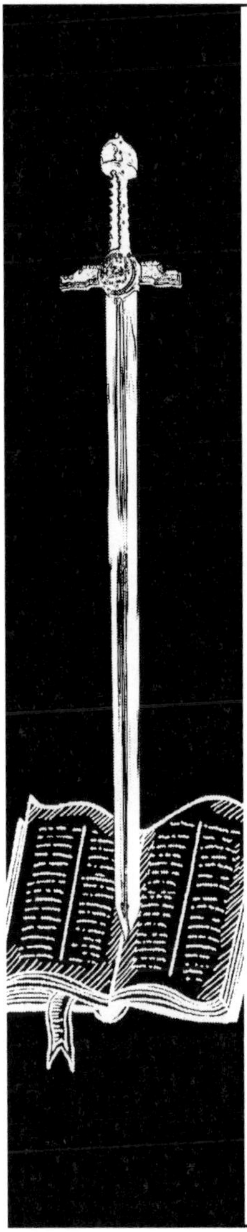

At the command of the Lord a certain member of a company of prophets said to another, "Strike me!" But the man refused to strike him.

Then he said to him, "Because you have not obeyed the voice of the Lord, as soon as you have left me, a lion will kill you." And when he had left him, a lion met him and killed him.

◆ ◆ ◆

Therefore, in the first story, listening to the prophet and acting seemingly reasonable (eating and drinking), results in death by a lion. In the second story, not listening to the prophet and acting seemingly reasonable (not striking someone else) results in death by a lion.

Skepticism of a prophet can also prove disastrous. In 2 Kings 7:1–2 and 17–20, the prophet Elisha predicts to the king of Israel that the current famine on the land will end the next day. An Israelite army captain expresses his doubt, and Elisha predicts his doom. The next day, the captain is trampled to death by people at a gate.

Although not included in the murder count, another interesting story concerning Elisha occurs in 2 Kings 2:23–24. While Elisha is journeying to the city of Bethel, some small boys jeer and taunt Elisha for his bald-headedness. Elisha curses them in the name of the Lord, and two bears emerge from the nearby woods and maul forty-two of the boys (the *Jewish Study Bible* uses the verb "mangle").

The account, although fascinating, is not entered into the murder charts as Scripture does not indi-

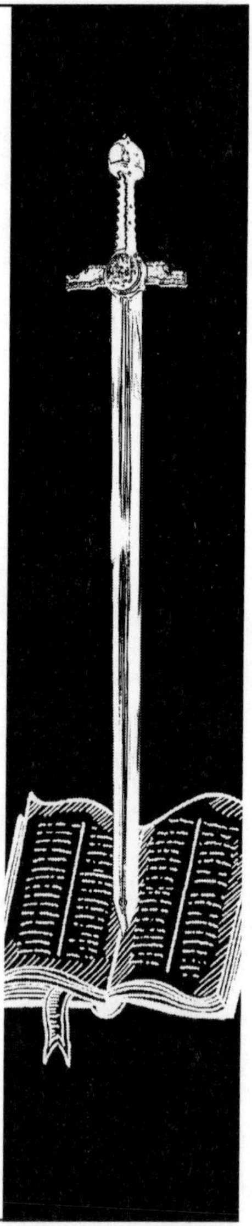

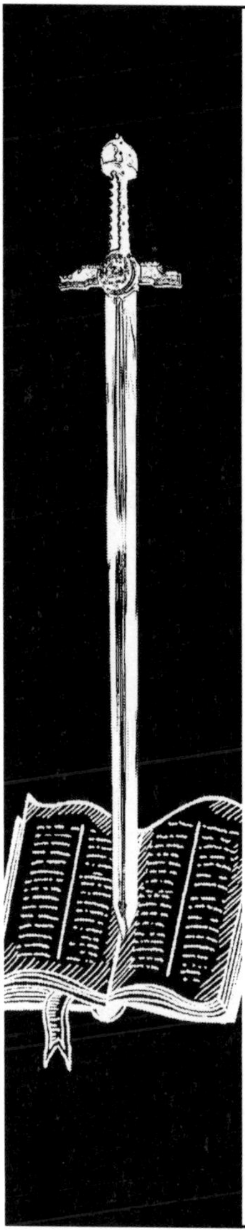

cate the forty-two boys died as a result of their encounter.

Heeding the advice of a prophet causes a murderous rampage in 2 Kings 14:7 and its companion story in 2 Chronicles 25:7–13. King Amaziah, preparing for war against a native people called the Edomites, assembles armies in both the northern kingdom (Israel) and southern kingdom (Judah).

But a prophet tells Amaziah to go into battle with only the southern army because "the Lord is not with Israel." Amaziah discharges the northern army, which returns home in fierce anger. Verse 13 reveals that the discharged army exacts revenge on its southern neighbor:

◆ ◆ ◆

But the men of the [northern] army whom Amaziah sent back, not letting them go with him to battle, fell on the cities of Judah from Samaria to Bethlehem; they killed three thousand people in them, and took much booty.

◆ ◆ ◆

A renowned prophet of the Old Testament, Elijah, concludes this chapter with two noteworthy occurrences. In 1 Kings 18:17–40, Elijah challenges 850 prophets of two false gods, Baal and Asherab, to see whose God can put fire to an animal offering. Only the Lord God consumes the offering with fire, and Elijah orders the Israelites to kill every one of the false prophets.

Finally, in 2 Kings 1:2–12, a king of Israel falls and lies injured. To learn whether he will recover, the king sends an envoy to make inquiries to Elijah. An angel of the

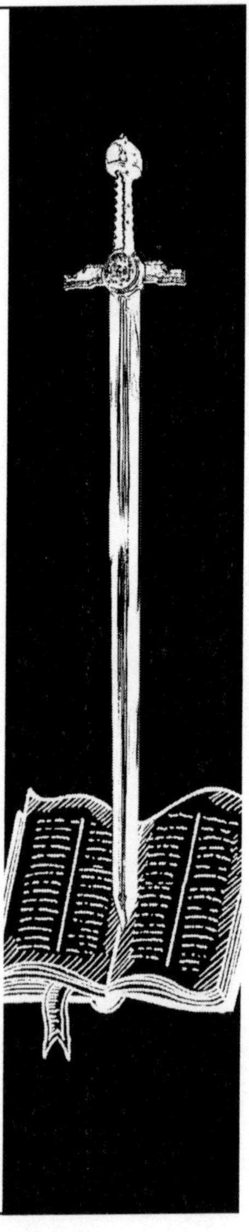

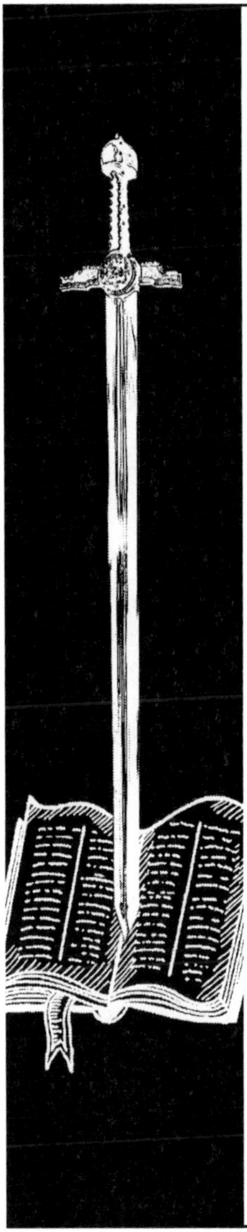

Lord instructs Elijah to meet the envoy, which consists of one captain and fifty men.

Elijah greets them, saying,

◆ ◆ ◆

If I am a man of God, let fire come down from heaven and consume you and your fifty men."

◆ ◆ ◆

Then fire comes down from heaven and consumes him and his fifty.

The king sends a second envoy of a captain and fifty men. And the scene repeats: fire comes down from heaven and consumes him and his fifty. The third envoy pleads for their lives, and Elijah spares them. Elijah also finally answers the king: the king will not leave his bed but will surely die.

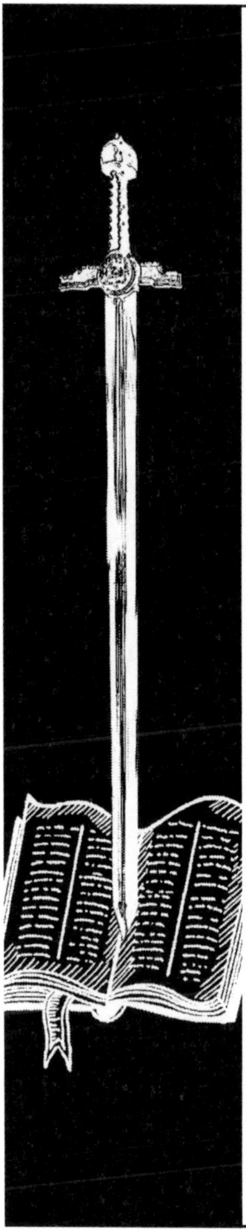

Interlude II

Can God Commit Murder?

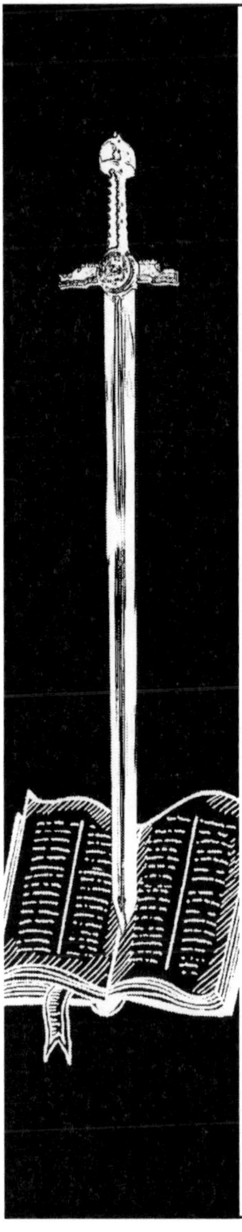

The final tally includes killings by both the Israelites and the Lord.[1] But the question arises: Can God commit murder? Should the deaths caused or orchestrated by God be included? And if not, what about the murders by Israelites in the name of God? Or the murders commanded by God?

The killings by the Lord are counted for the following reasons. First, the Lord God states that man was created in His image. Therefore, should not man act and behave like God? If God is allowed to murder, then man can also. If man is prohibited from committing murder, should the model of God be any different?

Second, the Fifth Commandment demands, "Honor Your Mother and Father." The Lord God is the father of the Israelites. To honor the Lord God, one must follow in his footsteps. If God murders, then man can murder. If man should not murder, then God, as the father, must set the example.

Finally, the killings by the Lord are included for a very practical reason. In many instances, it is difficult to ascertain whether a particular murder is solely at the hands of man or at the direction of God.

An Israelite battle with no mention of God follows one that states that the Lord handed over the Israelites' enemies. The line is often blurred between battles of the people and battles of the Lord. Attempting to separate them can

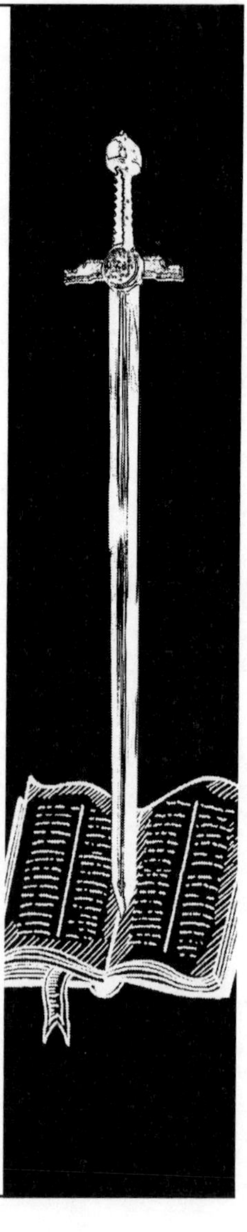

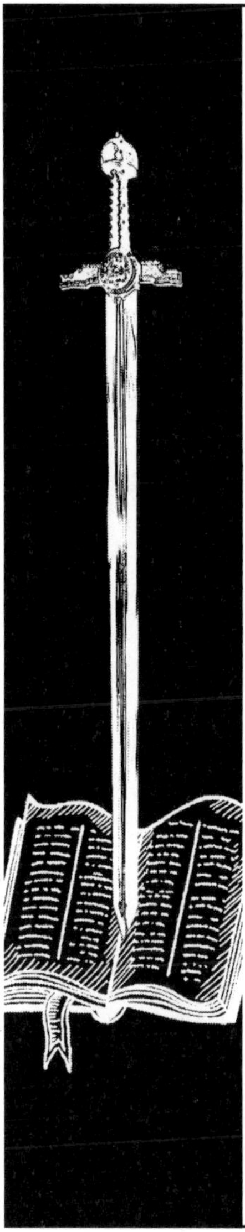

lead to more confusion than distinction.

For purposes of this study, then, deaths by the hand of God are tallied the same as murders by the Israelites. This is admittedly problematic due to the very divine and holy nature of the Lord — He who can do no wrong. But the premise has been stated, and it is acknowledged that there are those who will disagree.

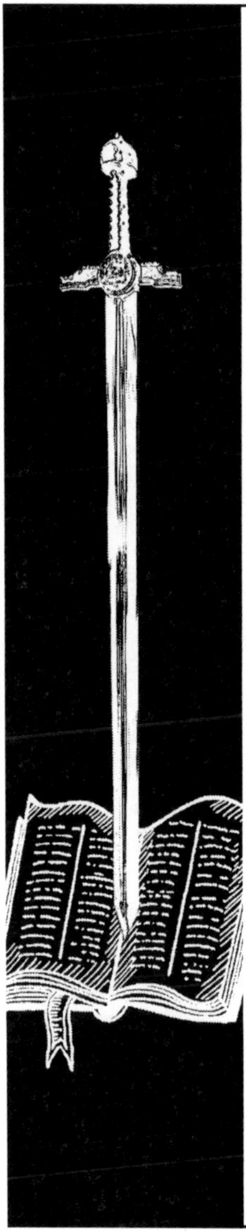

Chapter Seven

Chronicles (Killing Kin), Esther, and Job

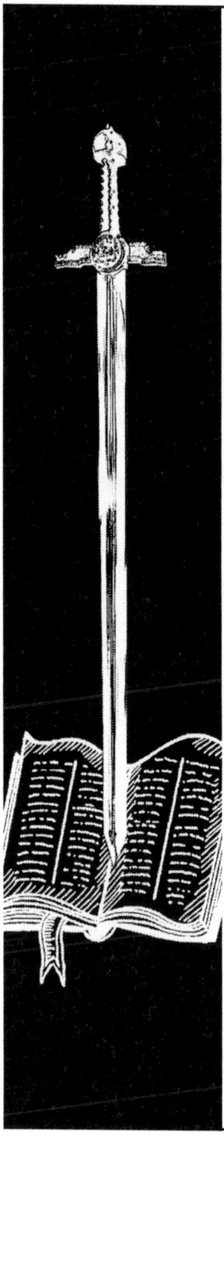

Following the books of Kings, the two books of Chronicles are really one long book chronicling the whole story of God's Chosen People from earliest times to their return from exile. Moreover, the Chronicles restate a large mass of material from earlier biblical books, particularly Samuel and Kings. The Chronicles are noteworthy, however, for their portrayal of Israelites murdering fellow Israelites. The second book also delivers the largest figure for our murder tally: one million.

The killings and murders in both books are charted in Exhibit H. The majority of entries describe heretofore unmentioned battles between the Israelites and native peoples. Two additional entries from the book of Esther are included in the exhibit, and this chapter concludes with a brief discussion of Job.

The two nations of the divided monarchy, Israel and Judah, have been at odds before. But in 2 Chronicles 13:1-20, the murder rate soars.

King Jeroboam of Israel goes to war with King Abijah of Judah, and Abijah and his army defeat Israel with a great slaughter — 500,000 picked men of Israel fall slain. Verse 20 wastes no words with regard to the king of Israel: "The Lord struck him down, and he died."

The two kingdoms war again at 2 Chronicles 28:1–15. Because of the apostasy of King Ahaz of Judah, the Lord executes judgment:

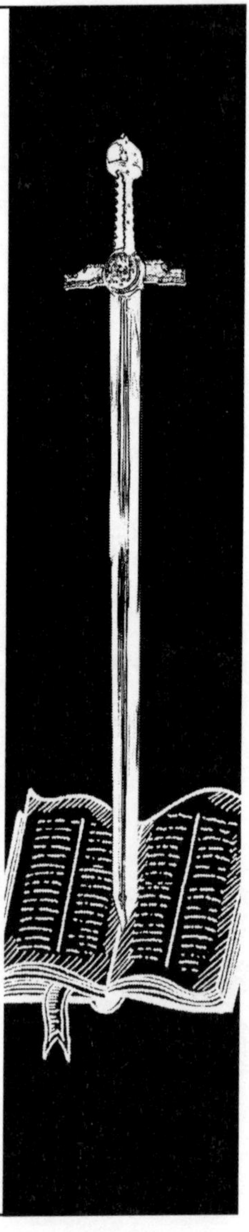

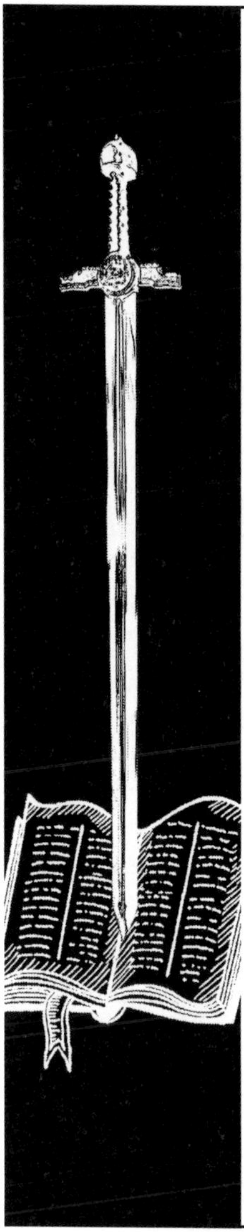

[Ahaz] was also given into the hands of the king of Israel, who defeated him with a great slaughter. Pekah son of Remaliah killed one hundred twenty thousand in Judah in one day, all of them valiant warriors, because they had abandoned the Lord, the God of their ancestors. And Zichri, a mighty warrior of Ephraim, killed the king's son Maaseiah, Azrikam the commander of the palace, and Elkanah the next in authority to the king.

◆ ◆ ◆

The people of Israel take an additional 200,000 captive, including women, sons, and daughters. However, a prophet warns of the Lord's fierce wrath at this attempt to subjugate fellow Israelites. As decreed in Deuteronomy 24:7, anyone kidnapping or enslaving a fellow Israelite will die. The chronicler concludes that the victorious Israelites promptly release their kin.

Throughout the Old Testament, any king's brothers are always potential rivals to the throne.

King Jehoram of Judah quickly solves any possible threat in 2 Chronicles 21:2–4. Upon ascending to the throne, Jehoram murders his six brothers and some Israelite officials with the sword.

An unpopular prophet meets his demise by the hands of fellow Israelites in 2 Chronicles 24:20–22. Zechariah, son of a priest, admonishes the people for forsaking the Lord and transgressing His commandments. The Israelites conspire against him, and by order of the king, Zechariah is stoned to death in the court of the house of the Lord.

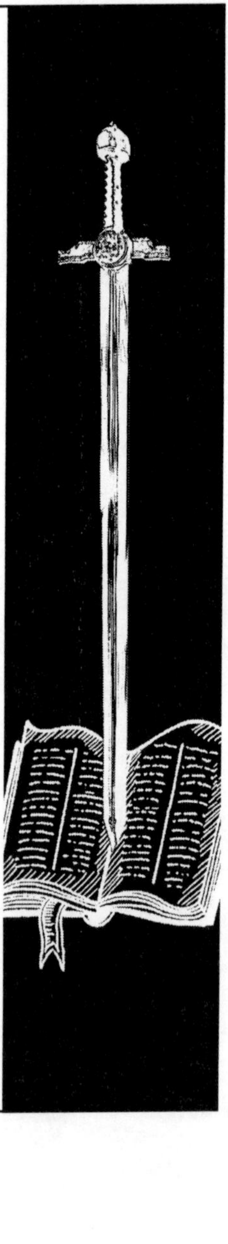

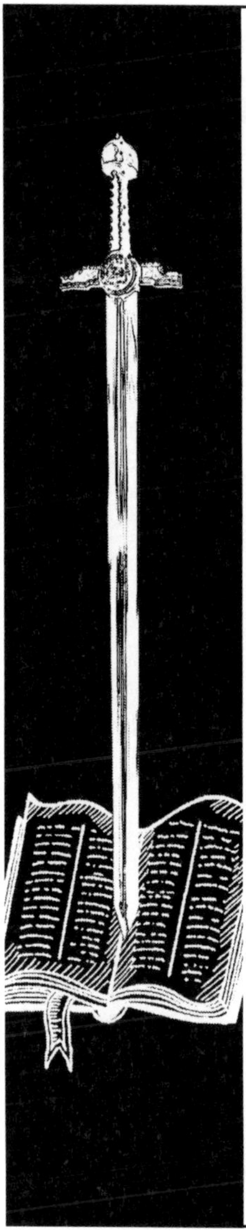

The murder tally takes a giant leap in 2 Chronicles 14:8–13. King Asa of Judah, with an army of 580,000 Israelites, draws battle lines against an Ethiopian army of 1,000,000 men and 300 chariots:

◆ ◆ ◆

Asa cried out to the Lord his God, "O Lord, there is no difference for you between helping the mighty and the weak. Help us, O Lord our God, for we rely on you, and in your name we have come against this multitude. O Lord, you are our God; let no mortal prevail against you." So the Lord defeated the Ethiopians before Asa and before Judah, and the Ethiopians fled. Asa and the army with him pursued them as far as Gerar, and the Ethiopians fell until no one remained alive;

for they were broken before the Lord and his army.

◆ ◆ ◆

The book of Esther weaves a fascinating tale of colorful characters, intrigue, and extraordinary circumstances. The story is brief but packed with action, excitement, suspense, and deceit. Moreover, the female heroine Esther combines beauty, courage, and shrewd intelligence.

The narrative has also, however, attracted much criticism. The Persian king, for instance, is mentioned 190 times whereas the word "Lord" or "God" does not appear once.[1] Further, the account portrays God's Chosen People as vengeful and bloodthirsty. The contrast between the murderous rampage of the Israelites and the uplifting tone of deliverance is both captivating and

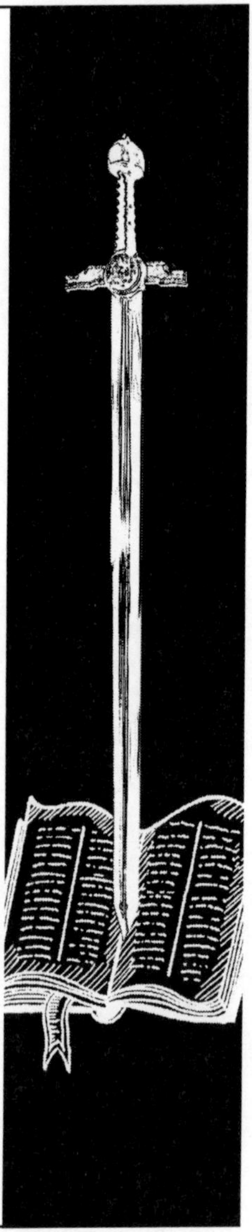

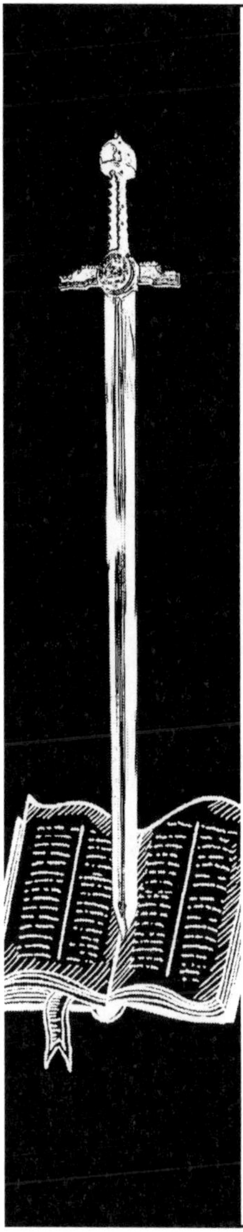

shocking.

The reader is encouraged to review the biblical text for a true appreciation of the story. In brief, Esther is a Jewish queen in Persia married to the non-Jewish king (who doesn't know she is a Jew).

A man named Haman finagles the Persian king into issuing an edict to annihilate the Jews in the region. By boldness and cunning, Esther procures a mandate from the king allowing the Jews to defend themselves against the attack.

When their enemies attack the city of Susa, the Jews slaughter and destroy 500 people as well as the ten sons of Haman.

Verses 12–16 of chapter nine say:

◆ ◆ ◆

The king said to Queen Esther, "In the citadel of Susa the

Jews have killed five hundred people and also the ten sons of Haman. . . .

Now what is your petition? It shall be granted you. And what further is your request? It shall be fulfilled."

Esther said, "If it pleases the king, let the Jews who are in Susa be allowed tomorrow also to do according to this day's edict, and let the ten sons of Haman be hanged on the gallows. So the king commanded this to be done; a decree was issued in Susa, and the ten sons of Haman were hanged.

The Jews . . . killed three hundred persons in Susa; but they did not touch the plunder.

Now the other Jews who were in the king's provinces also gathered to defend their lives, and gained relief from their en-

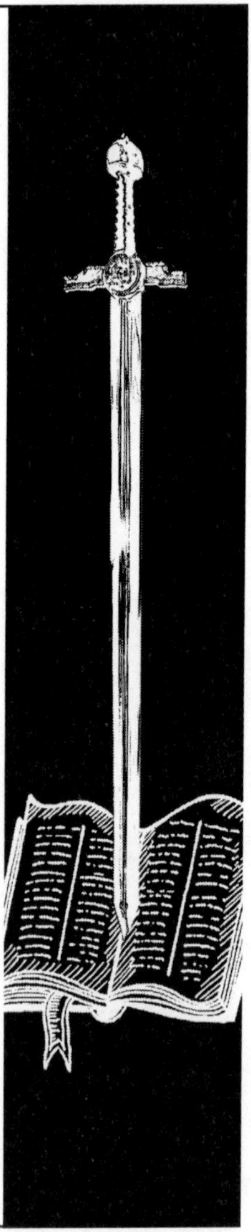

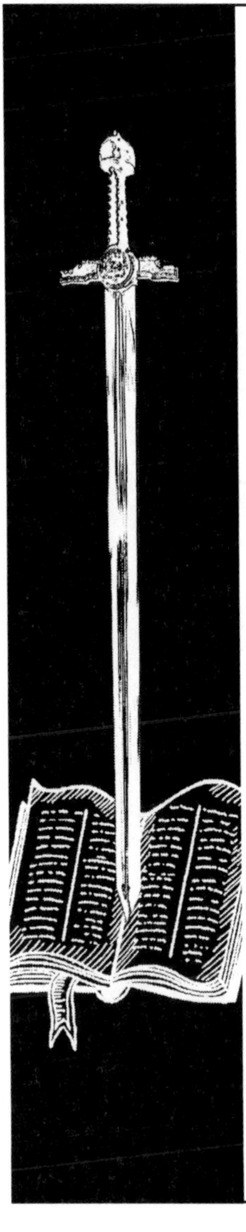

emies, and killed seventy-five thousand of those who hated them.

◆ ◆ ◆

Finally, the book of Job poses the age-old question: Why do good people suffer? Job's faith and devotion to God are tested when God allows Satan to inflict terrible sufferings on the righteous man.

In particular, Job's sons, daughters, and servants are killed by either foreigners or natural disasters. At Job 1:16, a messenger tells Job that the fire of God fell from heaven and burned up the sheep and the servants. This seems to indicate that a direct act of God killed the servants.

Verse 19 relates that a great wind strikes the house in which Job's children are eating and drinking. The house falls on the young people, and they all die.

Verse 16 aside, the argument is made that because God allowed Satan to cause the deaths of Job's children, then God is ultimately responsible. For purposes of this study, however, the death of Job's children (and servants) is laid on Satan's doorstep; therefore, the killings are not included in the tally.

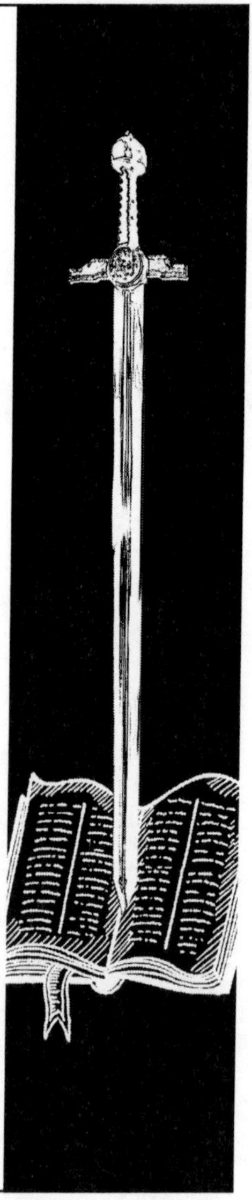

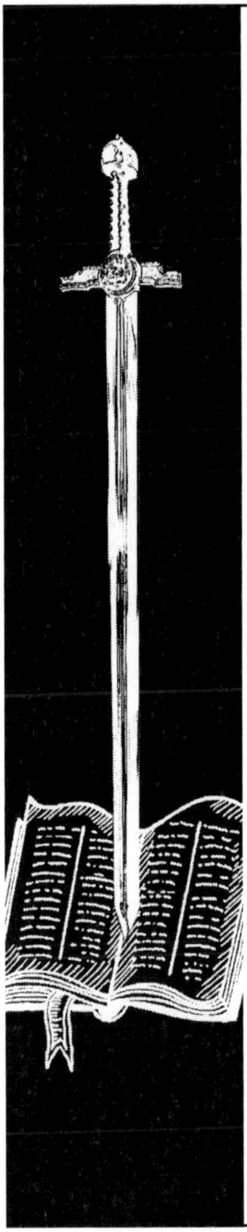

Chapter Eight

Prophetic Murder

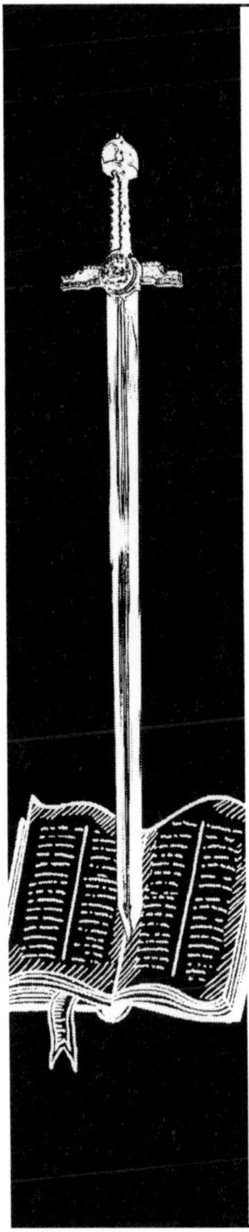

The remainder of the killings and murders in the Old Testament are found in the prophetic books of Isaiah, Jeremiah, and Ezekiel. A prophet was someone who spoke for God, one who courageously communicated God's message to a people who might not listen.

Isaiah, Jeremiah, and Ezekiel were prophets to the southern kingdom of Judah as the people became increasingly unfaithful to the Lord. The Israelites' apostasy ranged from false swearing and adultery to murder and child sacrifice.

Ezekiel 23:20 chastises the people for lusting after paramours in Egypt

• • •

. . . whose members were like those of donkeys, and whose emission was like that of stallions.

◆ ◆ ◆

In chapter 16, Ezekiel compares Judah's sins to the deeds of a brazen whore, and at 36:17, the prophet's comparison is to the uncleanness of a woman in her menstrual period.

All three prophets denounce the people of Judah for committing murder. A sampling from Scripture of their transgressions includes:

Isaiah 59:7 — the shedding of innocent blood;

Jeremiah 2:34 — the shedding of the lifeblood of the innocent poor;

Jeremiah 7:31 — burning their sons and daughters in the fire

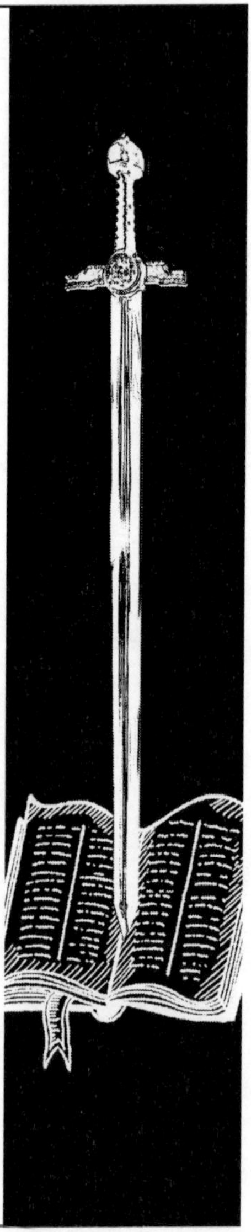

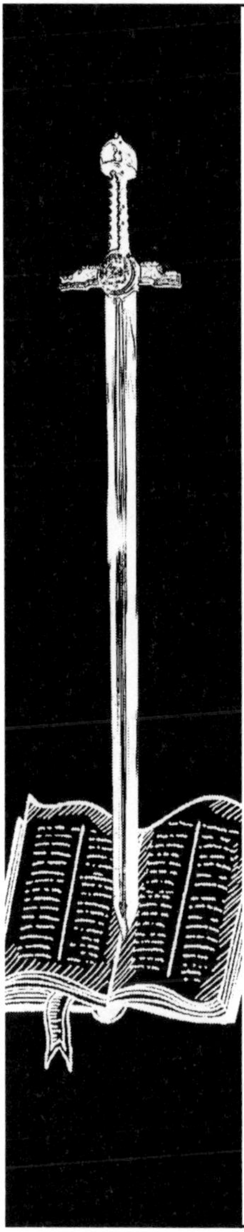

Ezekiel 11:6 — killing and filling the streets with the slain

Ezekiel 16:20 — sacrificing their sons and daughters

Ezekiel 23:37 — offering up their children as food for idols

The northern kingdom of Israel had also been accused of murder by the prophets Hosea, Amos, and Micah in earlier Old Testament books. Hosea further condemned Israel for sexual orgies, illegitimate children, excessive litigation, and people kissing calves. Amos added the sin of a father and son having sex with the same girl.

In Ezekiel 9:1–7, the Lord calls for six executioners to enforce God's judgment on the sinful Israelites in Jerusalem. Each executioner holds a weapon for slaughter, and one of them is clothed in linen with a writing case at his side. The Lord instructs the six men to mark those Israelites who grieve of the wickedness. The prophet Ezekiel explains:

◆ ◆ ◆

The Lord called to the man clothed in linen, who had the writing case at his side, and said to him, "Go through the city, through Jerusalem, and put a mark on the foreheads of those who sigh and groan over all the abominations that are committed in it."

To the others he said in my hearing, "Pass through the city after him, and kill; your eye shall not spare, and you shall show no pity. Cut down old men, young men and young women, little children and women, but touch no one who has the mark. And begin at my sanc-

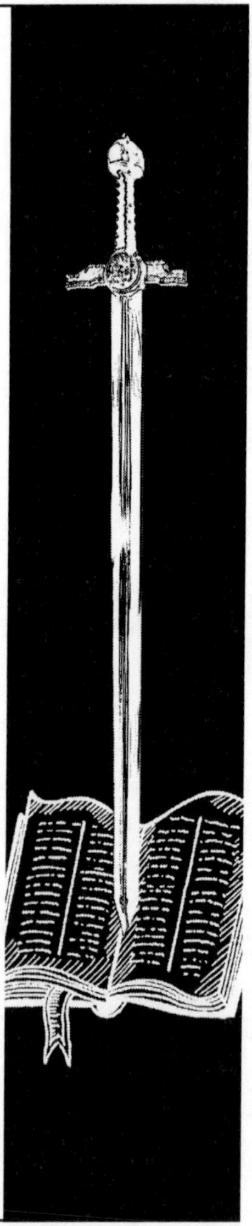

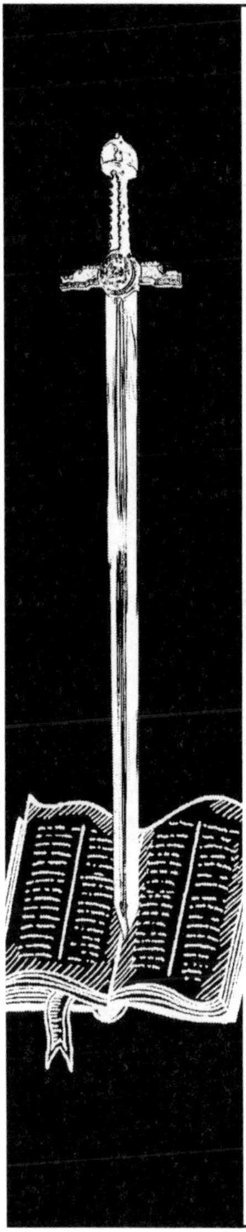

tuary." So they began with the elders who were in front of the house. Then he said to them, "Defile the house, and fill the courts with the slain. Go!" So they went out and killed in the city.

◆ ◆ ◆

Because the prophets criticized the people, their lives were often in danger. As stated in Chapter 7, the prophet Zechariah was stoned to death by Israelites for preaching a message they did not want to hear.

A prophet named Uriah prophesies about the Israelites' apostasy and God's punishment in Jeremiah 26:20–23. King Jehoiakim of Judah seeks to murder Uriah, but the prophet flees to Egypt. However, Uriah is found and brought back to the king, who strikes Uriah down with the sword.

Jeremiah also received death threats, and in Jeremiah 11:19, he feels like a gentle lamb being led to the slaughter. In verses 22–23, the Lord announces his punishment for those who seek Jeremiah's life:

◆ ◆ ◆

Thus says the Lord of hosts: I am going to punish them; the young men shall die by the sword; their sons and daughters shall die by famine; and not even a remnant will be left of them.

For I will bring disaster upon the people.

◆ ◆ ◆

Scripture, however, does not disclose an instance where the Lord actually metes out His death threat.

God also issues a threat of death to a man named Shebna in

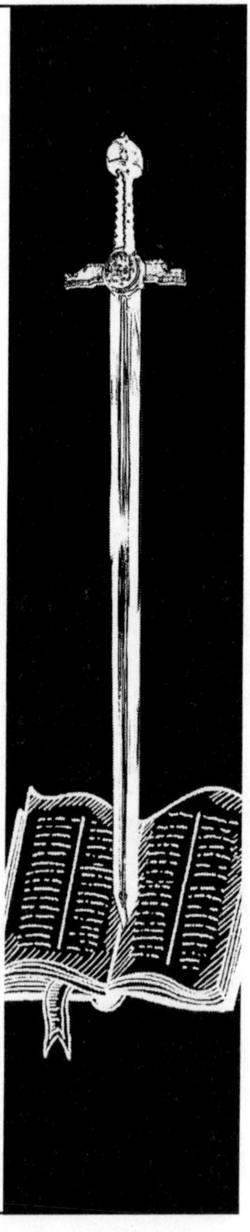

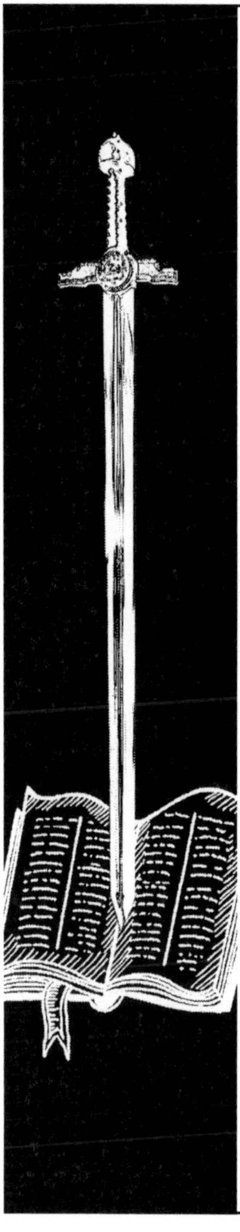

Isaiah 22:15–18. The text is unclear as to Shebna's exact sin, although the *Oxford Annotated Bible* states that Shebna apparently arrogated improper status to himself.[1]

Whatever his actual transgression, the Lord's retribution as it was relayed by Isaiah is unequivocal:

◆ ◆ ◆

The Lord is about to hurl you away violently, my fellow. He will seize firm hold on you, whirl you round and round, and throw you like a ball into a wide land; there you shall die, and there your splendid chariots shall lie, O you disgrace to your master's house!

◆ ◆ ◆

False prophets were not uncommon in biblical times. In Jeremiah 28:1–17, Jeremiah accuses Hananiah of falsely proclaiming a call to prophecy by the Lord. Jeremiah himself prophesies that the Lord will send Hananiah off the face of the earth within the year, and Hananiah dies in the seventh month.

Ahab and Zedekiah are accused of false prophecy in Jeremiah 29:21–23, and Jeremiah predicts that the king of Babylon will kill them. The Babylonian king roasts Ahab and Zedekiah in the fire. (Note: these two deaths are included in the murder tally for two reasons. First, the Israelite prophet predicts their deaths, and secondly, the Lord is the one who delivers the false prophets into the hands of the Babylonian king.)

The final entry from the prophetic books comes from the "suffering servant" songs in the book of Isaiah (42:1–4; 49:1–7; 50:4–9; 52:13–53:12).

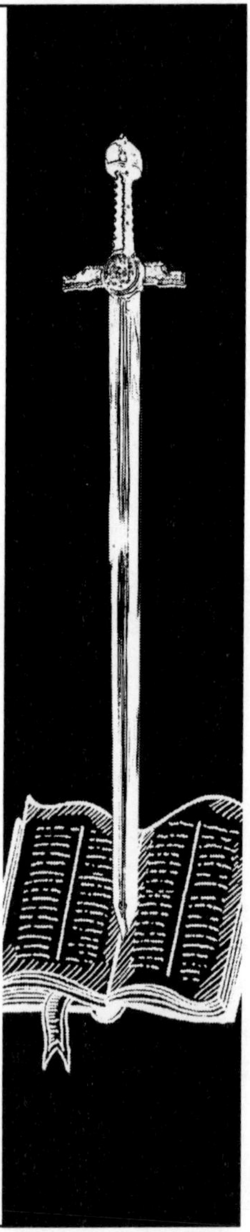

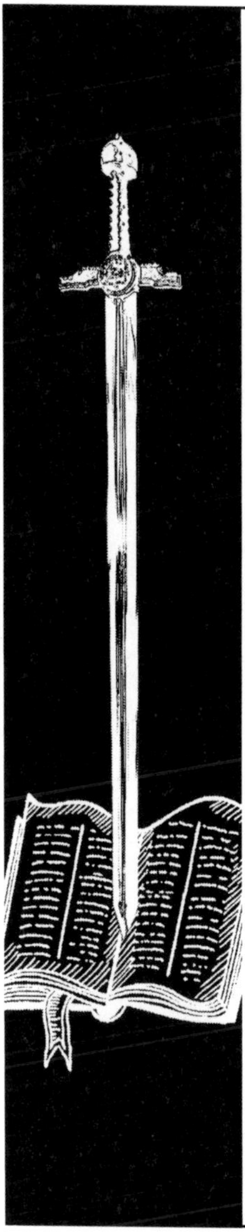

There are four different poems in Isaiah, each describing a servant enduring undeserved pain and death. In Isaiah 53:4, the servant is "struck down by God." And in verse 10, "it is the will of the Lord to crush him with pain," and the servant's life is made an offering for sin.

Although the passages indicate that God kills the suffering servant, the servant is not identified. Some think he is the prophet Isaiah, while others believe the servant is representative of the nation of Israel.[2]

Christians have often identified this suffering individual as the son of God, Jesus Christ. But *that* is a whole other story.

The killings and murders in the prophetic books of Isaiah, Jeremiah, and Ezekiel are outlined in Exhibit I.

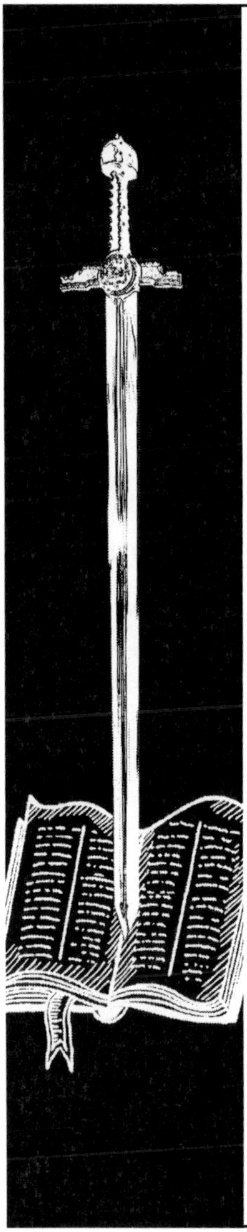

Chapter Nine

Judgment Against the Nations

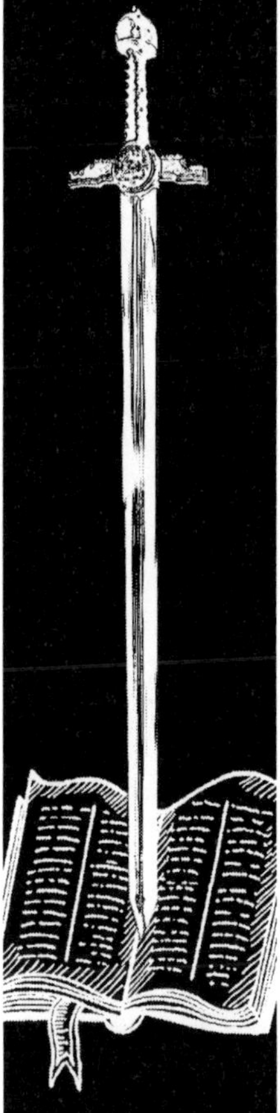

The Israelites' murders and apostasy prompt the Lord to banish them from the Promised Land. The nation of Israel is invaded by the Assyrians, and Judah falls to Babylon. The Israelites in both nations are exiled to these foreign lands, with only a remnant remaining behind. But exile appears the least of the Israelites' worries as the Lord pronounces his wrathful judgment throughout the books of the prophets.

The Old Testament, although replete with references to the invading Assyrians[1] and Babylonians, reveals few actual numbers. The reader is not told exactly how many Israelites are exiled, nor how many die by the hands of the foreign nations.[2] But sample passages from the prophets resonate with the murderous revenge of the Lord. The judgment against the northern nation includes:

Hosea 9:13 — The children will be led out to slaughter.

Hosea 9:16 — The Lord will kill the cherished offspring of the womb.

Hosea 11:6 — The sword will rage in the cities and consume the priests.

Hosea 13:16 — The Israelites will fall by the sword, their little ones shall be dashed to pieces, and their pregnant women ripped open.

Zechariah — 14:2 The women will be raped.

Malachi — 2:3 The Lord will spread dung on the faces of the priests.

The list of punishments seems endless. Besides widespread death

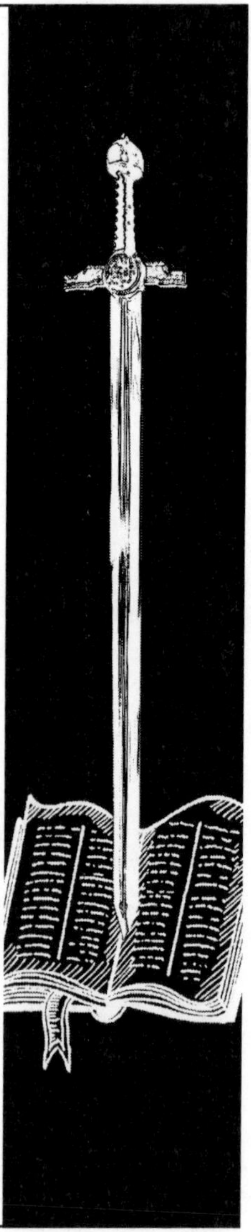

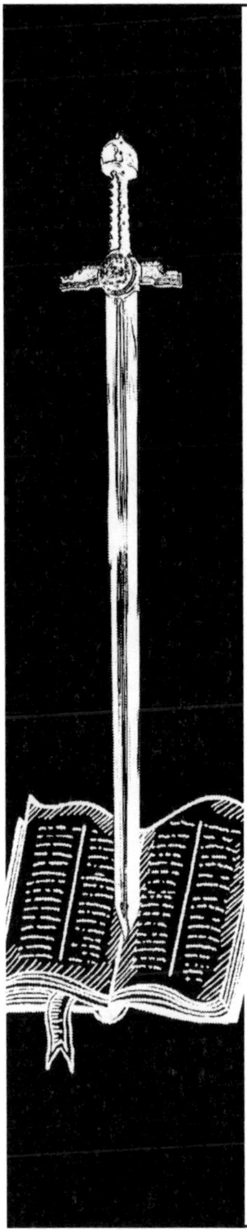

and destruction, the afflictions include pestilence, plagues, locusts, and showers of fire. Moreover, imagery abounds, such as when the Lord declares in Hosea 13:8:

◆ ◆ ◆

I will fall upon them like a bear robbed of her cubs, and will tear open the covering of their heart; There I will devour them like a lion, as a wild animal would mangle them.

◆ ◆ ◆

The Lord's judgment against the southern nation of Judah and its capital city Jerusalem is no less frightening or descriptive.

In Isaiah 51:17, the people will drink the cup of the Lord's wrath, down to the dregs from the bowl of staggering. Jeremiah 7:20 announces that the Lord's wrath shall burn and not be quenched. Other examples include:

Isaiah 3:17 — Daughters will be afflicted with scabs, and the Lord will lay bare their secret parts.

Isaiah 5:25 — Human corpses will be like refuse in the streets.

Jeremiah 5:17 — Enemies will eat their sons and daughters.

Jeremiah 7:32 — In a valley of slaughter, the Israelite corpses will be food for the birds and animals.

Jeremiah 13:14 — Parents and children will be dashed against one another.

Jeremiah 16:4 — Sons and daughters will die of diseases, sword, and famine.

Zephaniah 1:17 — The Israelites' blood will be poured out like dust and their flesh like dung.

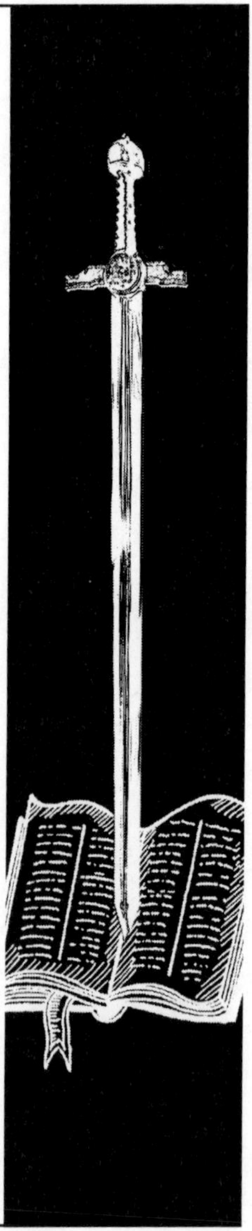

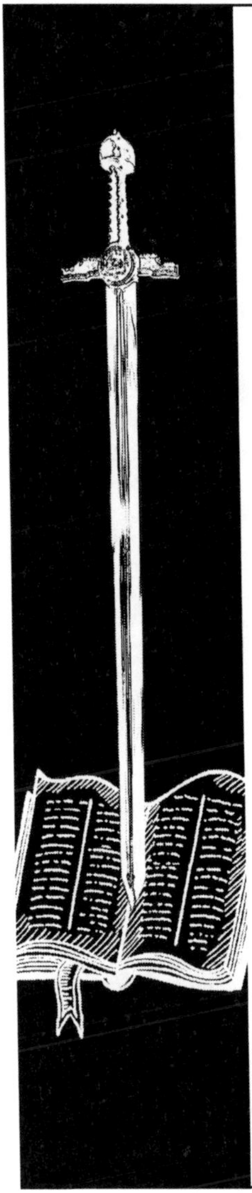

Against Judah, the Lord adds more instruments of death: poisoned water, biting adders, devouring animals, wormwood, arrows, and stoning.

The day of the Lord's vengeance will be like that in Zephaniah 1:15: a day of wrath, anguish, ruin, devastation, darkness, gloom, and clouds. Jeremiah 23:19–20 declares:

◆ ◆ ◆

[The Lord's] wrath has gone forth, a whirling tempest; It will burst upon the head of the wicked. The anger of the Lord will not turn back until he has executed and accomplished the intents in his mind.

◆ ◆ ◆

In short, as the Lord states in Ezekiel 5:9:

I will do to [Judah] what I have never yet done, and the like of which I will never do again.

◆ ◆ ◆

The scenes the prophets paint are almost beyond horrifying. Verse after verse cries out with killing, corpses, blood, violence, and cruelty. The mind reels with repeated images of slaughtered children, raped women, and murdered young men. The fury of the Lord and His terrifying retribution explode on the page.

But the Lord does not stop there. In fact, the Lord doubles back. Assyria and Babylon, once the instruments of the Lord's wrath against the Israelites, now become the objects of His wrath.

Moreover, the Lord hands down a verdict of destruction against the peoples in Moab, Philistia, Egypt, Ammon, Edom, Tyre, and Sidon.

The Lord's will is implemented by either invading armies or na-

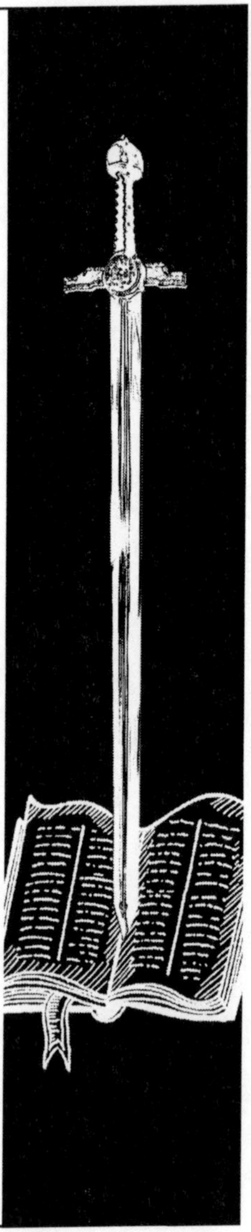

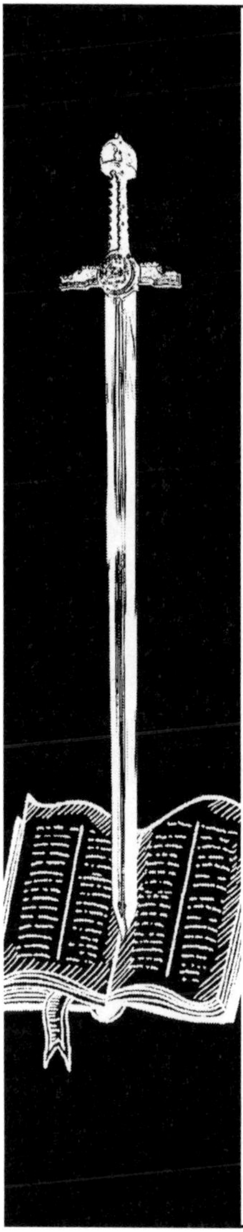

tions battling among themselves. Scripture presents a picture in which the Lord oversees the devastation and orchestrates the eventual outcome. To spare the reader from an overload of doom and gloom, the oracles against foreign nations have been ruthlessly edited. But to afford some concept of the Lord's pronouncements, a sampling is provided.

Judgment Against Assyria

Isaiah 30:33—

The burning place for the Assyrian will be prepared and made ready for the king. Its pyre is deep and wide, with fire and wood in abundance. The breath of the Lord, like a stream of sulfur, kindles it.

◆ ◆ ◆

Ezekiel 32:22—

Assyria is full of graves; all will . . . fall by the sword.

◆ ◆ ◆

Nahum 3:3—

The charging horsemen, with flashing sword and glittering spear, will stumble over the piles of dead, heaps of corpses, and dead bodies without end.

◆ ◆ ◆

Nahum 3:10—

Infants will be dashed to pieces at the head of every street.

◆ ◆ ◆

Zephaniah 2:14–15—

Assyria will become a lair of wild animals: the desert and screech owls shall lodge on its capital; the owl shall hoot at the window; the raven croak on the threshold. Everyone who passes by shall hiss and shake the fist.

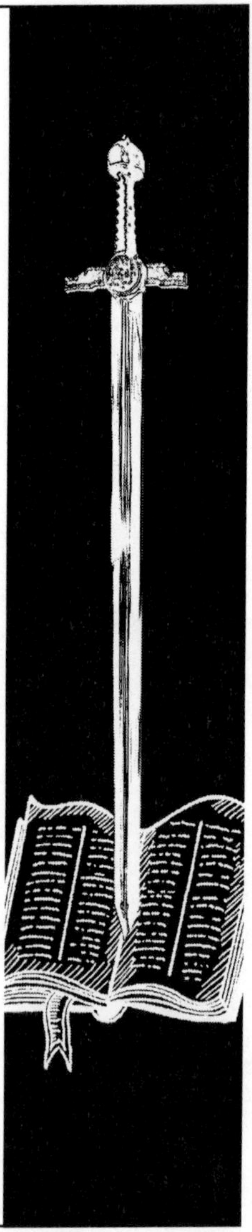

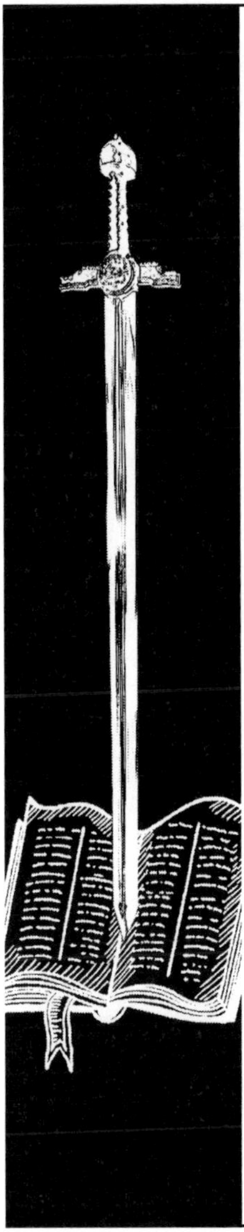

Judgment Against Babylon

Isaiah 13:15–16—

[They] will be thrust through, and whoever is caught will fall by the sword. Their infants shall be dashed to pieces before their eyes; their houses will be plundered and their wives ravished.

◆ ◆ ◆

Isaiah 14:9—

Sheol beneath stirs up to meet Babylon; it raises its shades to greet them.

◆ ◆ ◆

Isaiah 14:11—

Maggots are the bed beneath the Babylonians, and worms are their covering.

◆ ◆ ◆

Isaiah 14:19—

The Babylonians will be cast away from their grave like loathsome carrion.

Isaiah 14:23—

The Lord will sweep Babylon with the broom of destruction.

⬥ ⬥ ⬥

Isaiah 47:3—

The Lord will execute vengeance and spare no one.

⬥ ⬥ ⬥

Isaiah 47:9—

The loss of children and widowhood will come in full measure.

Jeremiah 50:25—

The Lord will open his armory and bring out his weapons of wrath.

⬥ ⬥ ⬥

Jeremiah 51:13—

The thread of life will be cut.

⬥ ⬥ ⬥

Jeremiah 51:40—

The Lord will bring down the Babylonians like lambs to the slaughter.

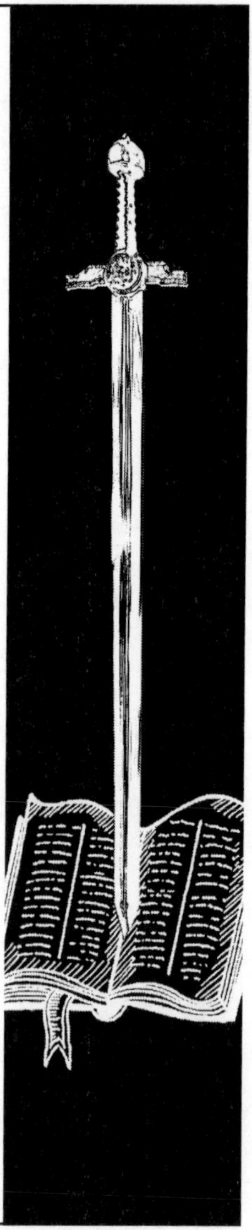

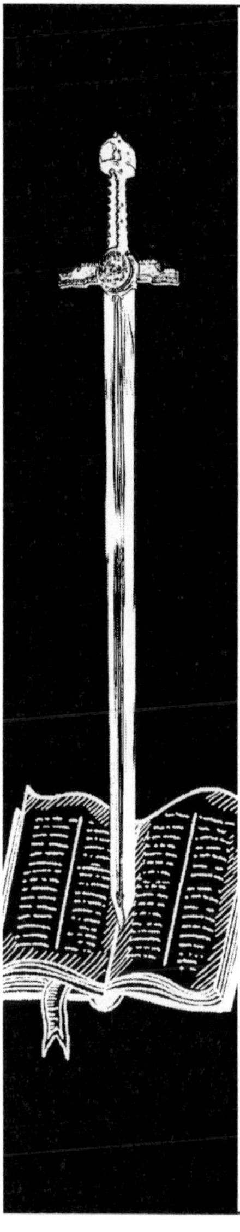

Jeremiah 51:57—

The Babylonians will sleep a perpetual sleep and never wake.

Judgment Against Moab

Isaiah 25:10—

The Moabites shall be trodden as straw is trodden down in a dung-pit.

• • •

Jeremiah 48:15—

The choicest of the young men will go down to slaughter.

• • •

Jeremiah 48:26—

Moab will wallow in its vomit.

• • •

Jeremiah 48:38—

The Lord will break Moab like a vessel no one wants.

• • •

Jeremiah 48:41—

The hearts of the Moab warriors shall be like the heart of a woman in labor.

◆ ◆ ◆

Amos 2:2—

Moab shall die amid uproar, shouting, and the sound of the trumpet.

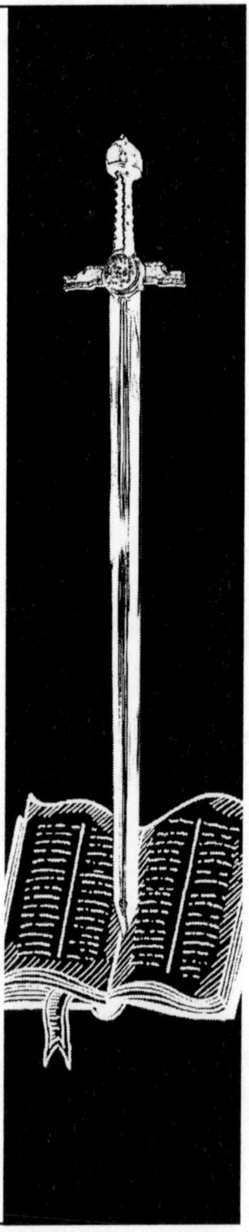

Judgment Against Philistia

Ezekiel 25:17—

The Lord will execute great vengeance and wrathful punishments on the Philistines.

◆ ◆ ◆

Zephaniah 2:5—

The Lord will destroy until no one is left.

◆ ◆ ◆

Zechariah 9:7—

The Lord will take away the Philistines' blood from its mouth

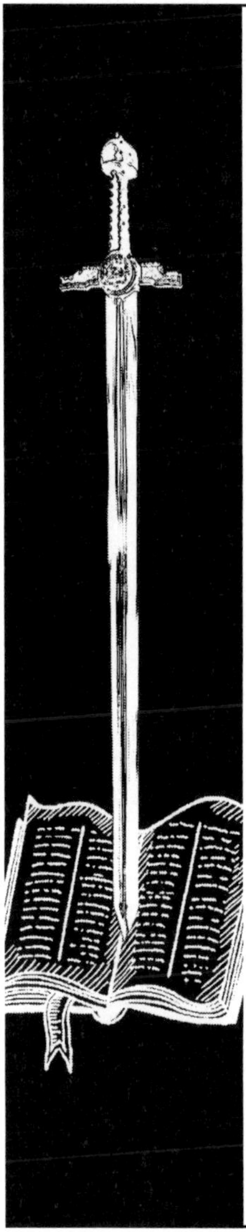

and its abominations from between its teeth.

Judgment Against Egypt

Isaiah 19:14—

Egypt will be made to stagger as a drunkard staggers around in vomit.

◆ ◆ ◆

Ezekiel 30:11—

The land will be filled with the slain.

◆ ◆ ◆

Ezekiel 32:4–6—

The wild animals of the whole earth will gorge themselves on the Pharaoh. The Lord will strew Pharaoh's flesh on the mountains, fill the valleys with his carcass, and drench the land with his blood up to the mountains.

Judgment Against Ammon

Ezekiel 21:31–32—

The Lord will pour out his indignation and the fire of his wrath. Ammon shall be fuel for the fire, and its blood shall enter the earth.

Zephaniah 2:9—

The Ammonites shall become like Gomorrah, a land possessed by nettles and salt pits, and a waste forever.

◆ ◆ ◆

Judgment Against Sidon

Ezekiel 28:23—

The Lord will send pestilence and bloodshed into the streets; the sword is against it on every side.

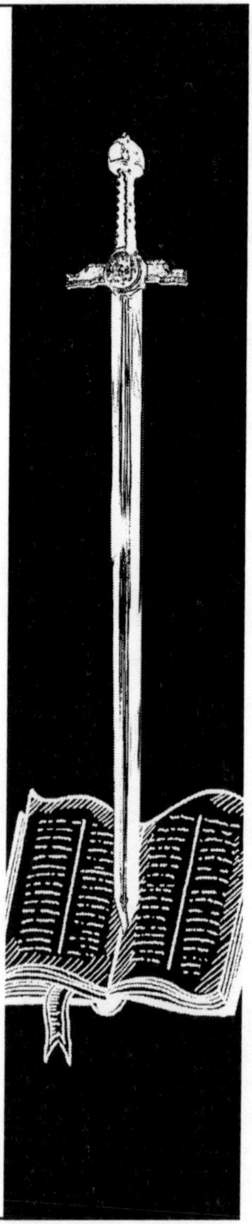

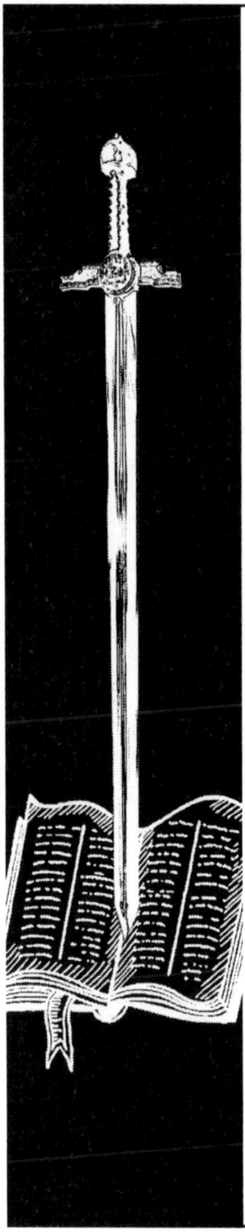

JUDGMENT AGAINST EDOM

Isaiah 63:3—

The Lord will tread upon the people in His anger and trample them in His wrath; their juice will spatter on His robes and stain all His robes.

Jeremiah 49:17—

Everyone who passes by Edom will be horrified and will hiss because of all its disasters.

◆ ◆ ◆

Ezekiel 32:29—

The kings and princes of Edom will lie in Sheol with all those killed by the sword; they will lie with the uncircumcised, with those who go down to the Pit.

◆ ◆ ◆

Ezekiel 35:6–8—

Bloodshed shall pursue Edom, and the Lord will fill its mountains with the slain; those killed with the sword will fall in the hills, valleys, and watercourses.

◆ ◆ ◆

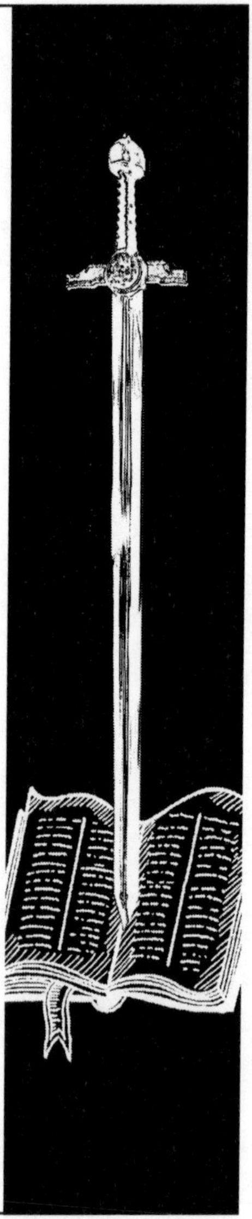

Judgment Against Tyre

Isaiah 23:15,17—

Tyre will be forgotten for seventy years, the lifetime of one king. At the end of seventy years, Tyre will prostitute herself with all the kingdoms of the world.

◆ ◆ ◆

Ezekiel 28:8—

Tyre shall die a violent death in the heart of the seas.

◆ ◆ ◆

Ezekiel 28:19—

The king shall come to a dreadful end.

◆ ◆ ◆

Zechariah 9:4—

Tyre shall be devoured by fire.

The Lord's revenge on specific nations is accompanied by a

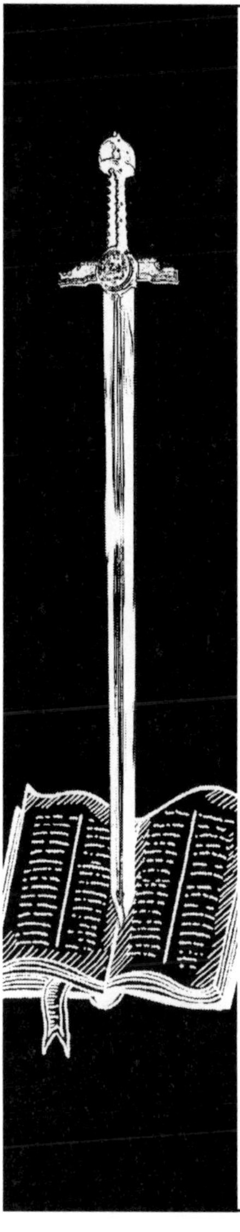

promise of universal judgment. God's fierce anger and cruel sword will reign throughout the world, as Jeremiah 25:33 vows:

◆ ◆ ◆

Those slain by the Lord on that day shall extend from one end of the earth to the other. They shall not be lamented, or gathered, or buried; they shall become dung on the surface of the ground.

◆ ◆ ◆

And the news persists:

Isaiah 26:21—

The earth will disclose blood and will no longer cover its slain.

◆ ◆ ◆

Isaiah 30:28—

The Lord will sift the nations with his sieve of destruction.

Isaiah 34:3—

The stench of the corpses shall

rise, and the mountains shall flow with blood.

◆ ◆ ◆

As evident, the wrath of the Lord manifests itself in many different ways and is visited upon an immense number of people.

As Psalm 18:7–8 clearly illustrates:

◆ ◆ ◆

Then the earth reeled and rocked; the foundations also of the mountains trembled and quaked, because [the Lord] was angry.

Smoke went up from his nostrils, and devouring fire from his mouth; glowing coals flamed forth from him.

◆ ◆ ◆

No wonder the psalmist queried in Psalm 76:7:

Who can stand before the Lord once his anger is roused?

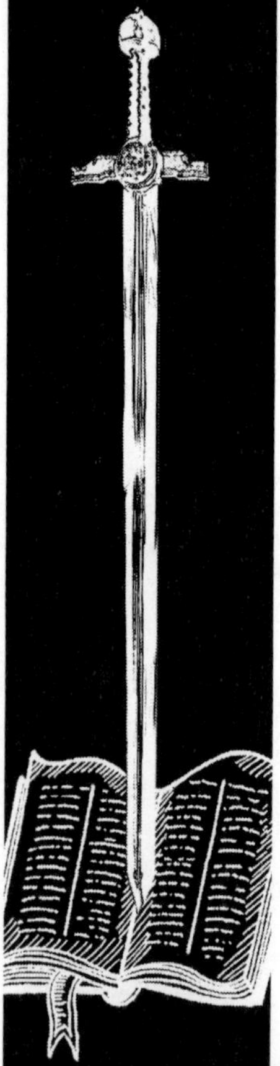

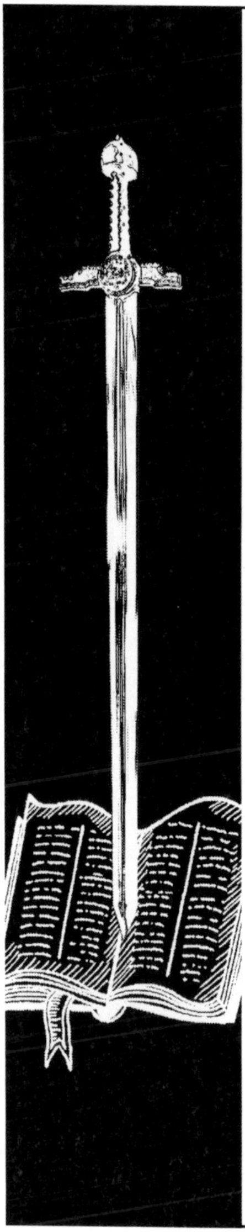

And the prophet in Nahum 1:6:

Who can stand before the Lord's indignation?

Who can endure the heat of his anger?

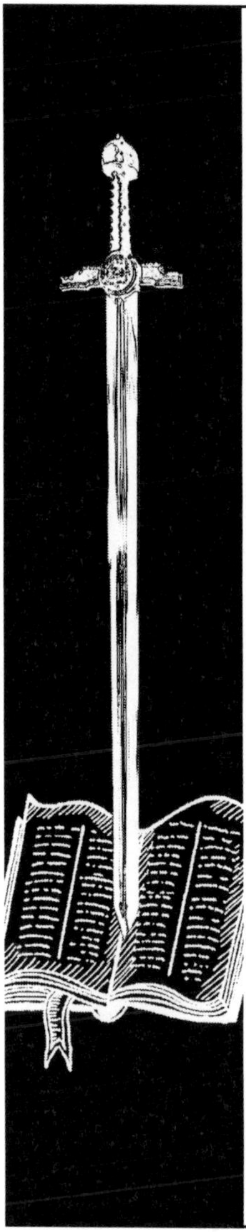

Interlude III

Bibles, Dates, & Numbers

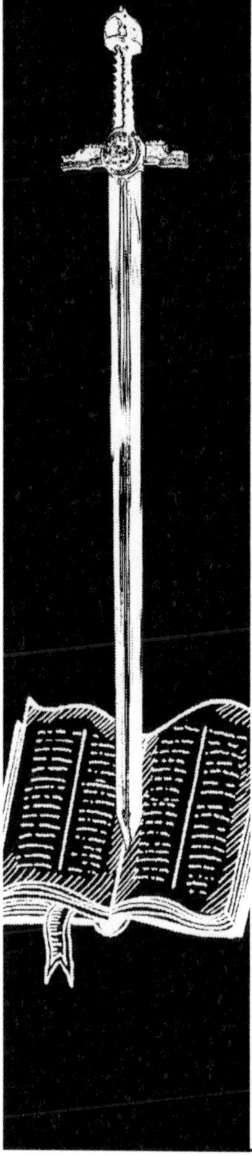

The Christian Old Testament and Hebrew Bible provide basically the same text with a different organization of the books. The first seven books are the same in each, but the order varies thereafter.

For example, the Christian Old Testament places the books of the prophets at the end of the testament; the prophetic books comprise the middle section of the Hebrew Bible. The last book of the Old Testament is Malachi, whereas the final book of the *Tanakh* is Second Chronicles. Again, Scripture is essentially the same, but the books are arranged differently.

The reader of this study will detect an absence of dates and events in the narratives and charts. The reason for this omission is two-fold. First, biblical dating often differs from scholar to scholar. Second, the question was whether to consistently offer Scripture references (that contain numbers) or provide dates. The inclusion of both Scripture references and dates would have resulted in pages filled as much with numbers as with narrative.

The preference for Scripture prevailed, so dates have been omitted in the narrative. The reader is referred to Bible references books for applicable time periods.

Numbers and figures in the Bible are very often disputed among scholars, and many believe they are outright exaggerations. In Genesis, for example, Noah fathers three children after he is 500 years old (Gen. 5:32), and

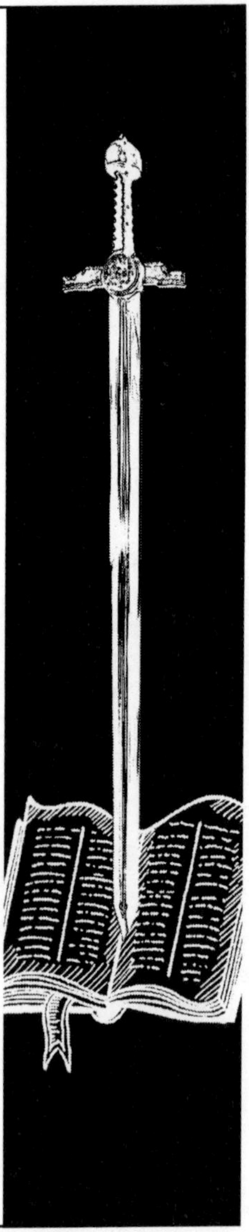

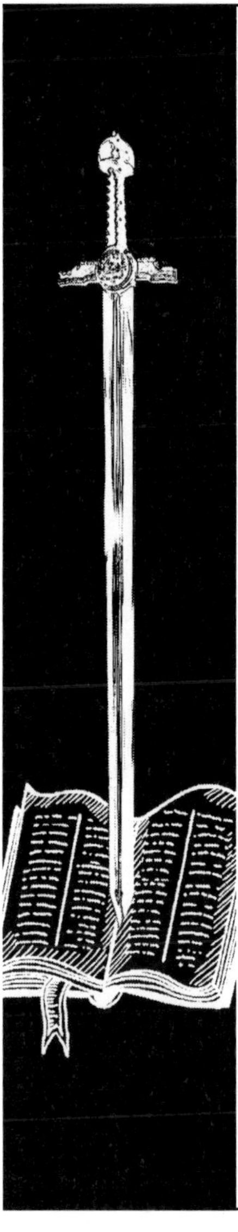

Noah lives to the ripe old age of 950 (Gen.9:29).

King David's army in 1 Chronicles 12:23–37 adds up to 340,822, and the king's military divisions total 288,000 in 27:1–24. In 2 Chronicles 17:14–19, King Jehoshaphat of Judah is represented as having an army of 1,160,000 men.

If ages and armies are exaggerated, the number of murders and killings might also be overestimated. The death of one million Ethiopians in 2 Chronicles 14:9–13 certainly seems unrealistic. However, as stated in the Preface, this study reviews the Bible through the lens of black-letter law: it says what it says. Whether the numbers are exaggerated is not the issue. The focus is what the Scripture states as the truth.

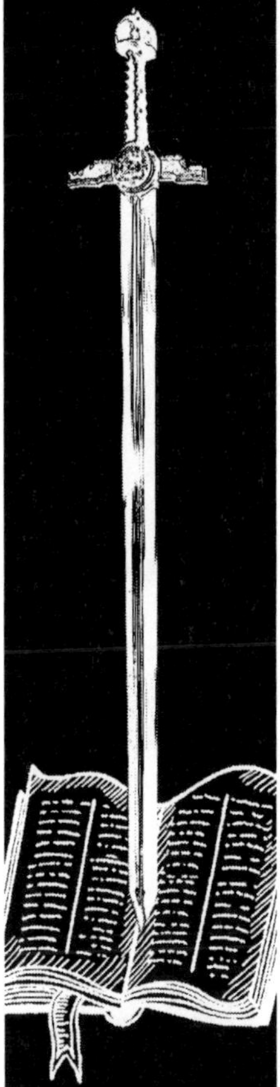

Chapter Ten

Suicides and Assassinations Revisited

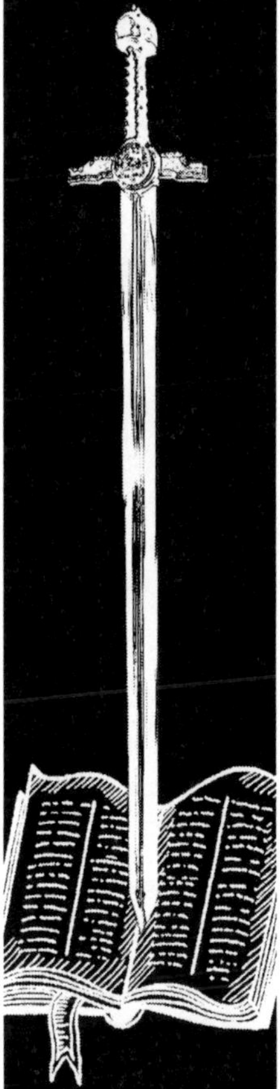

Ecclesiastes 7:17 declares, "Do not be too wicked, and do not be a fool; why should you die before your time?"

Suicide — or self-murder — occurs several times in the pages of the Old Testament. Recall the story of Samson in Judges 16:18–31. Samson's revenge on his Philistine captives — the destruction of the Philistine temple — leads to his own death when the temple walls collapse over him. Samson's last words in verse 30: "Let me die with the Philistines."

And recall the two cases involving requests for assisted suicide. In Judges 9:50–54, Abimelech is wounded when a woman in a tower throws a millstone on his head. Not wanting to be remembered as being killed by a woman, Abimelech orders one of his young men to finish him off.

In 1 Samuel 31:3–5, King Saul lies mortally wounded in a battle with the Philistines. Saul orders one of his armor-bearers to thrust him through with the sword. When the terrified armor-bearer refuses, Saul takes his own sword and falls upon it. The armor-bearer then commits suicide, too.

Finally, remember the instance where King David murders a man who claims to have abetted the suicide of King Saul. In 2 Samuel 1:1–16, a non-Israelite deceives David, alleging that he found Saul mortally wounded and killed him upon Saul's insistence. David, unaware of the deception, kills the non-Israelite for assisting in the suicide of one of the Lord's anointed.

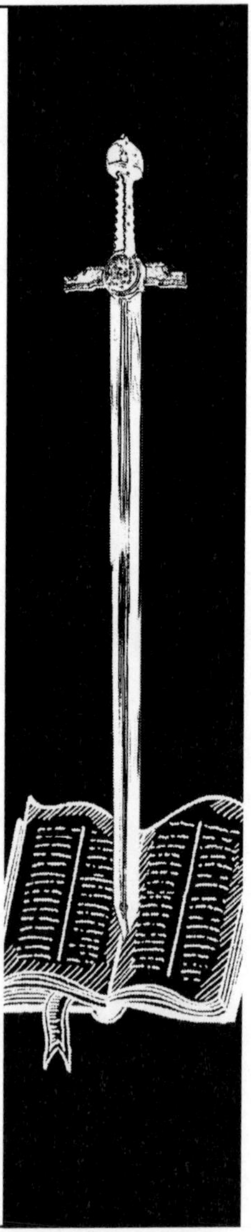

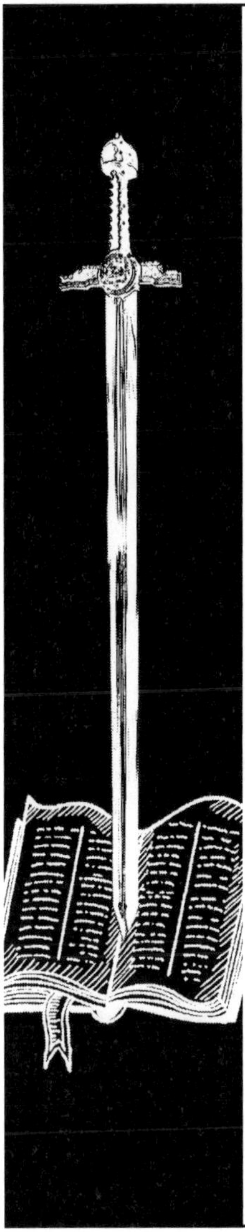

Rejection results in suicide in 2 Samuel 17:23. Absalom, the son of David, has two army counselors named Athithophel and Hushai. When Absalom takes the advice of Hushai over that of Athithophel, Athithophel saddles his donkey and returns home. After setting his house in order, Athithophel hangs himself.

One of the kings ruling the nation of Israel commits suicide with arson in 1 Kings 16:18. King Zimri has only been on the throne for seven days when the Israelites rebel against his rule. The people appoint Omri, the commander of the army, as king over Israel. When Omri and the army besiege the city in which Zimri is staying, Scripture informs:

◆ ◆ ◆

When Zimri saw that the city was taken, he went into the

citadel of the king's house; he burned down the king's house over himself with fire, and died.

◆ ◆ ◆

Finally, an example of offered suicide occurs in Jonah 1:1–12. Jonah has been summoned by the Lord to preach to the wicked city of Nineveh, but Jonah flees on a ship heading to Tarshish. The Lord hurls such a great wind upon the sea that the ship threatens to break apart. Jonah tells his shipmates:

◆ ◆ ◆

Pick me up and throw me into the sea; then the sea will quiet down for you; for I know it is because of me that this great storm has come upon you.

◆ ◆ ◆

The shipmates initially refuse Jonah's offer, but when the storm

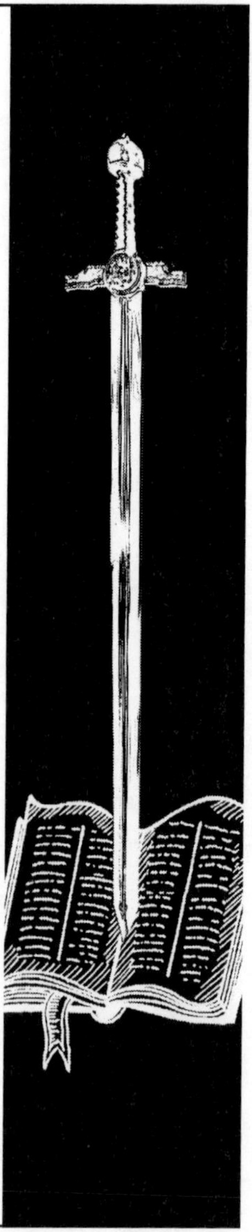

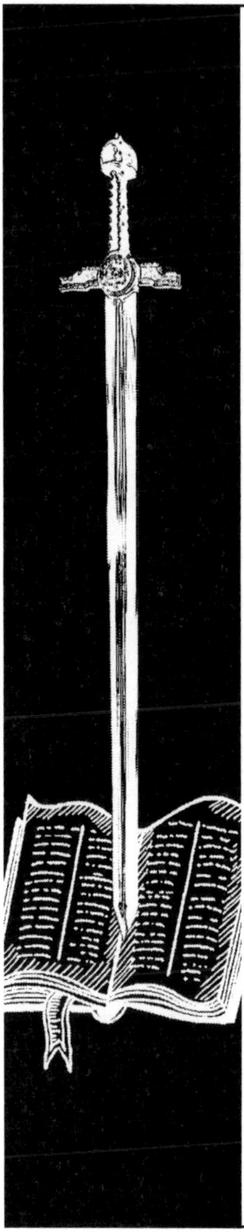

intensifies, Jonah is thrown overboard, and the seas cease raging. As even most children know, Jonah does not die but is swallowed by a big fish.

Although suicides are technically self-murders, they are not figured in the murder tally. Assassinations are. Because the twenty assassinations in the Old Testament span five different books and are therefore included in different exhibits, they are repeated here for ease of reference.

Below is a list of victims, their assassins, and the Scripture passage that relates the story:

Victim	Assassin	Scripture
Abner	Joab	2 Samuel 3:27
Absalom	Joab	2 Samuel 18:14
Ahaziah	Jehu	2 Kings 9:27
Amasa	Joab	2 Samuel 20:10
Amnon	Absalom	2 Samuel 13:28–29

Amon	servants	2 Kings 21:23
Athaliah	Jehoiada	2 Kings 11:16,20
Eglon	Ehud	Judges 3:21
Elah	Zimri	1 Kings 16:8–10
Gedaliah	Ishmael	2 Kings 25:25
Ishbaal	Baanah/Rechab	2 Samuel 4:5–8
Joram	Jehu	2 Kings 9:24
Jezebel	Jehu	2 Kings 9:30–37
Joash	servants	2 Kings 12:20–21
Pekah	Hoshea	2 Kings 15:30
Pekahiah	Pekah	2 Kings 15:25
Sisera	Jael	Judges 4:17–21
Shallum	Menahem	2 Kings 15:14
Zechariah	Shallum	2 Kings 15:10
Zechariah	Joash	2 Chronicles 24:21

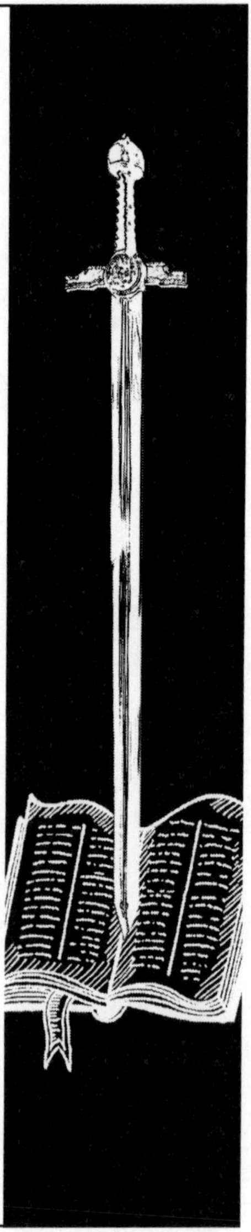

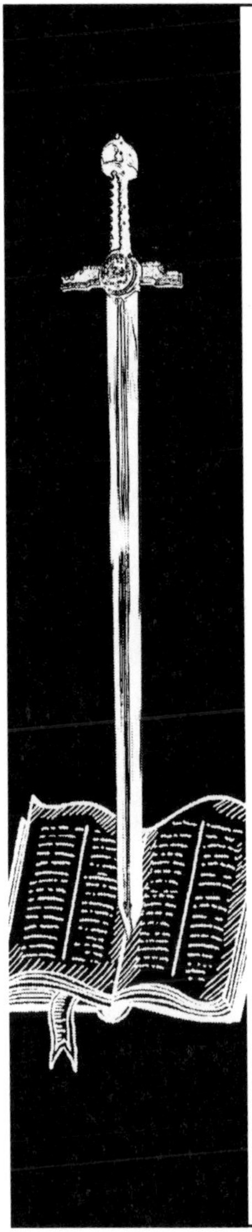

Chapter Eleven

Thy Will Be Dead

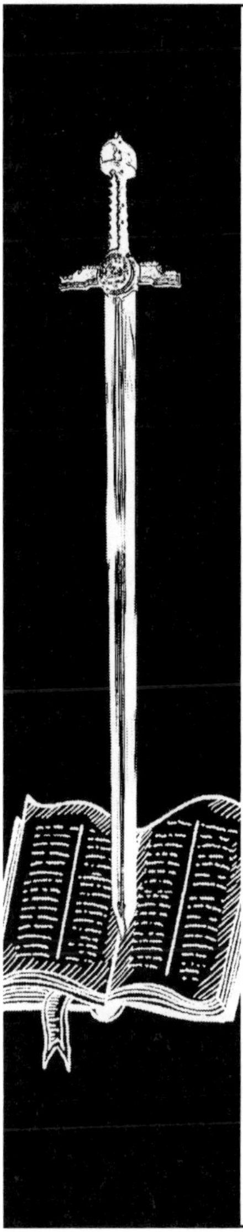

"The murderer shall be put to death." So declares Numbers 35:18 — a law of murder for murder. This law was an addendum to the Sixth Commandment of "Thou shalt not murder."

After Moses descended Mount Sinai for the final time, the Lord imposed some additional restrictions on the Israelite people, many of which are found in Numbers 35:9–33. This code of murder and revenge governed the Israelites throughout the Old Testament.

One innovative law, the establishment of "cities of refuge," was an attempt to restrain the ancient law of blood revenge before a person who had killed another might receive a trial.[1] A city of refuge was a place of asylum for one who committed an unpremeditated murder (today's manslaughter).

Verses 11–12:

◆ ◆ ◆

[A] slayer who kills a person without intent may flee there. The cities shall be for you a refuge from the avenger, so that the slayer may not die until there is a trial before the congregation.

◆ ◆ ◆

If the slayer claimed the murder was unpremeditated, the congregation of the people judged between the slayer and the avenger of blood, usually the next of kin.[2] If the murder was deemed unpremeditated, the slayer was sent back to the city of refuge with the conditions in verses 25–28:

◆ ◆ ◆

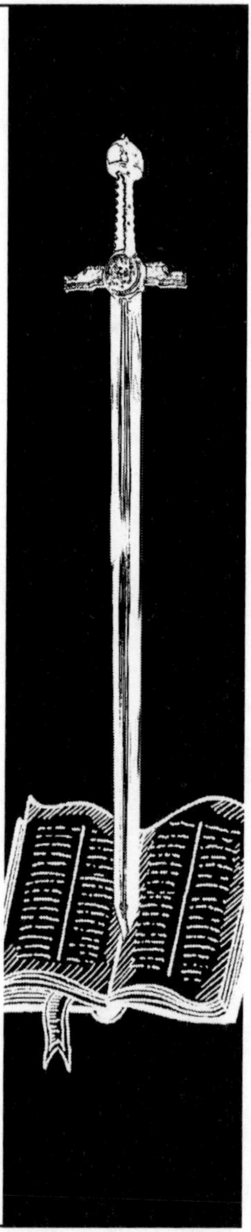

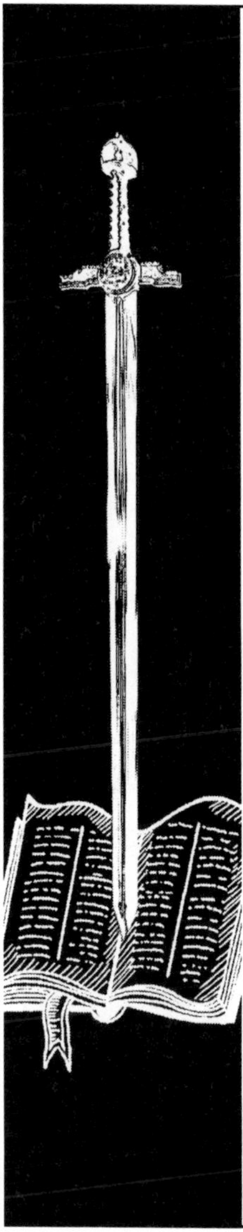

The slayer shall live in it until the death of the high priest who was anointed with holy oil. But if the slayer shall at any time go outside the bounds of the original city of refuge, and if found by the avenger of blood outside the bounds of the city of refuge, and is killed by the avenger, no bloodguilt shall be incurred. For the slayer must remain in the city of refuge until the death of the high priest; but after the death of the high priest, the slayer may return home.

◆ ◆ ◆

Distances to the cities of refuges was an important consideration, as evidenced in Deuteronomy 19:5–6:

◆ ◆ ◆

Suppose someone goes into the forest with another to cut wood, and when one of them swings the ax to cut down a tree, the head slips from the handle and strikes the other person who then dies; the killer may flee to one of these cities and live. But if the distance is too great, the avenger of blood in hot anger might pursue and overtake and put the killer to death, although a death sentence was not deserved, since the two had not been at enmity before.

◆ ◆ ◆

The additional rules also attempted to categorize murder. Striking another with an iron object, a stone, or a weapon of wood could be grounds for murder.[3] A verdict of murder could also result from pushing another in hatred, hurling something at another, lying in wait, or striking another with the hand.[4] If the

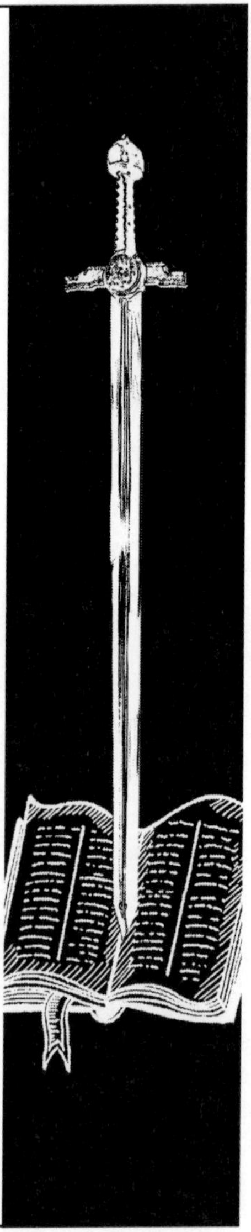

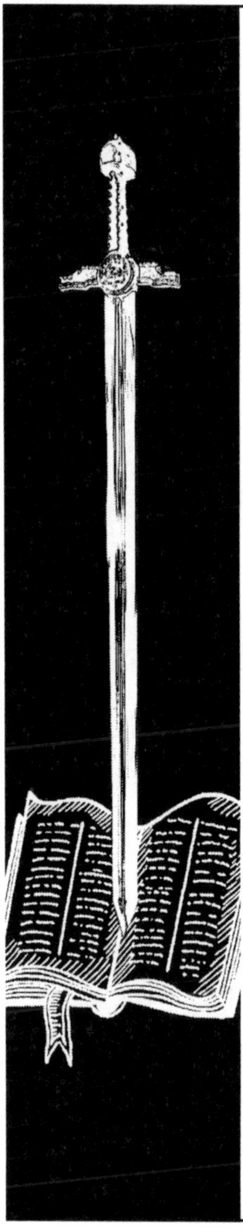

congregation of the people determined a slaying was premeditated, then the avenger of blood was allowed to carry out the sentence of death.[5]

Significantly, the law required the testimony of more than one witness for a murder conviction. In biblical times, witness testimony was generally the sole offering of evidence. The requirement of corroboration for proof of murder was a method to ensure justice before someone was put to death. Deuteronomy 19:15–20 states:

A single witness shall not suffice to convict a person of any crime or wrongdoing. . . . If a malicious witness comes forward to accuse someone of wrongdoing, then both parties to the dispute shall appear before the Lord, before the priests and the judges who are in offices in those days, and the judges shall make a thorough inquiry.

If the witness is a false witness, then you shall do to the false witness just as the false witness had meant to do to the other. So you shall purge the evil from your mist.

◆ ◆ ◆

Laws concerning sexual relations are outlined in Deuteronomy 22. In verse 21, a woman found not to be a virgin at marriage must be stoned to death. Sex with a betrothed woman could have two consequences, depending on where the act takes place, as revealed in verses 23–27:

◆ ◆ ◆

If there is a young woman, a virgin already engaged to be married, and a man meets her in the town and lies with her,

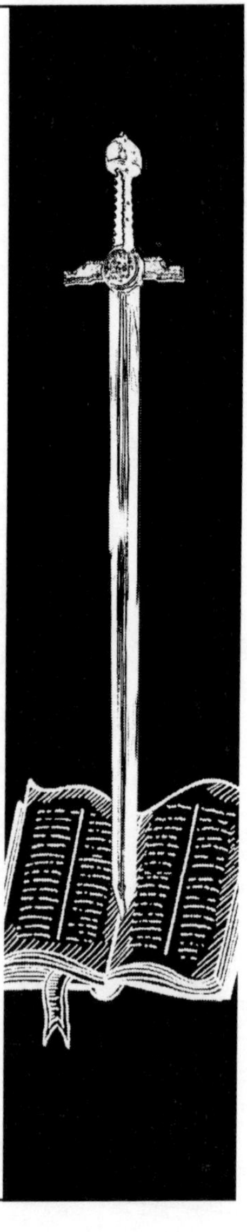

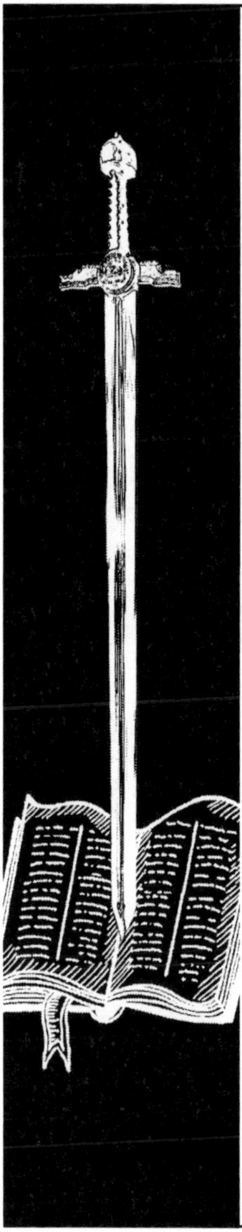

you shall…stone them to death, the young woman because she did not cry for help in the town and the man because he violated his neighbor's wife.

But if the man meets the engaged woman in the open country, and the man seizes her and lies with her, then only the man who lay with her shall die. You shall do nothing to the young woman; the young woman has not committed an offense punishable by death, because this case is like that of someone who attacks and murders a neighbor.

Since he found her in the open country, the engaged woman may have cried for help, but there was no one to rescue her.

◆ ◆ ◆

Other prohibited actions for which the penalty was death are:

Exodus 19:12 — touching Mount Sinai;

Exodus 21:16 — kidnapping;

Exodus 21:29 — not restraining a dangerous animal;

Exodus 22:19 — lying with an animal;

Numbers 1:51 — coming near the tabernacle of the Lord;

Numbers 4:15 — touching a holy thing;

Numbers 4:20 — looking at holy things;

Numbers 17:10 – complaining about the Lord;

Exodus 33:30 – seeing the Lord's face;

Leviticus 20:2 — sacrificing one's child to a pagan god;

Leviticus 20:11–12 — committing incest;

Leviticus 20:13 — lying with a person of the same sex;

Leviticus 20:14 — having sex

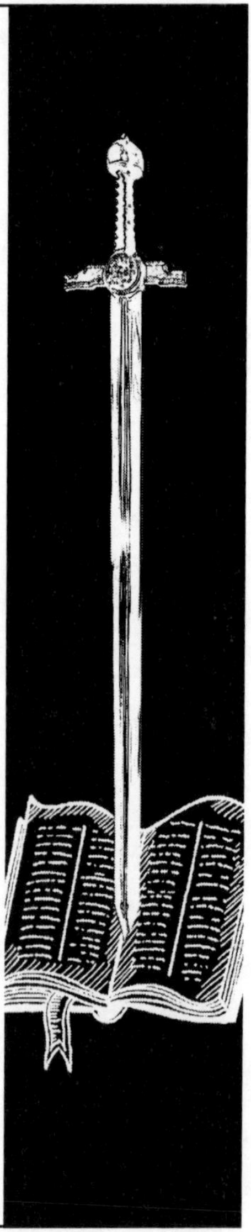

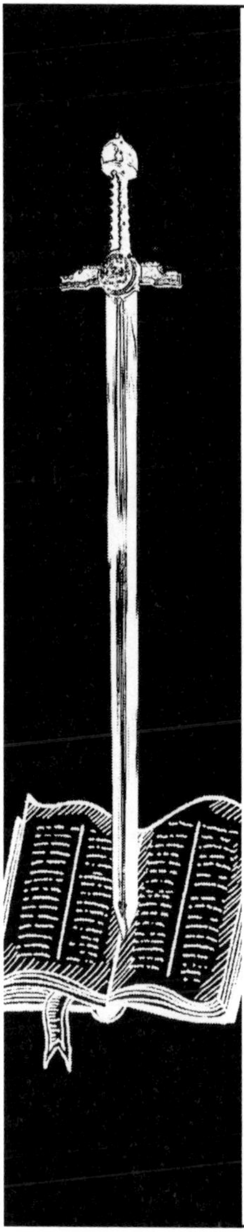

with both a mother and daughter;

Leviticus 20:18 — lying with a woman during her menstrual period;[6]

Leviticus 21:9 — playing the whore;

Leviticus 24:16 — blaspheming the name of the Lord;

Deuteronomy 17:12 — disobeying a priest appointed to minister;

Deuteronomy 19:19 — testifying falsely;

Deuteronomy 22:21 — engaging in sex before marriage; and

Deuteronomy 24:7 — kidnapping, enslaving, or selling another Israelite.

◆ ◆ ◆

Finally, the murder of a transgressor of the Ten Commandments (other than the previously-discussed Sixth) was considered appropriate punishment. The specific commandment and associated Scripture passages are as follows:

First Commandment

No Other Gods before Me

Exodus 22:18 — You shall not permit a female sorcerer to live.

Exodus 22:20 — Whoever sacrifices to any god, other than to the Lord alone, shall be devoted to destruction.

Leviticus 20:2 — Anyone sacrificing a child to Molech shall be stoned to death.

Leviticus 20:27 — Mediums and wizards shall be stoned to death.

Deuteronomy 6:14–15 — Do not follow other gods or

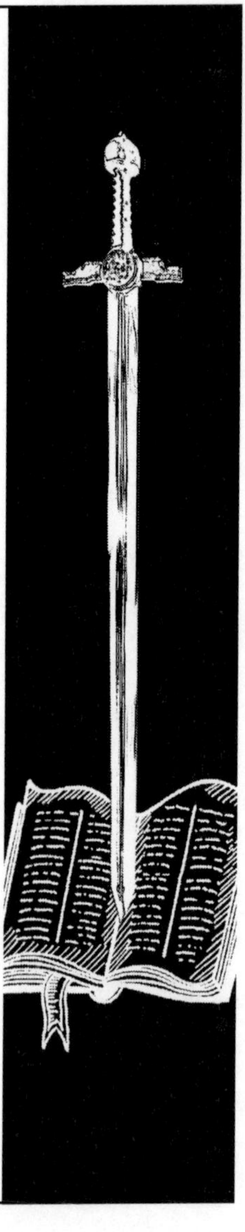

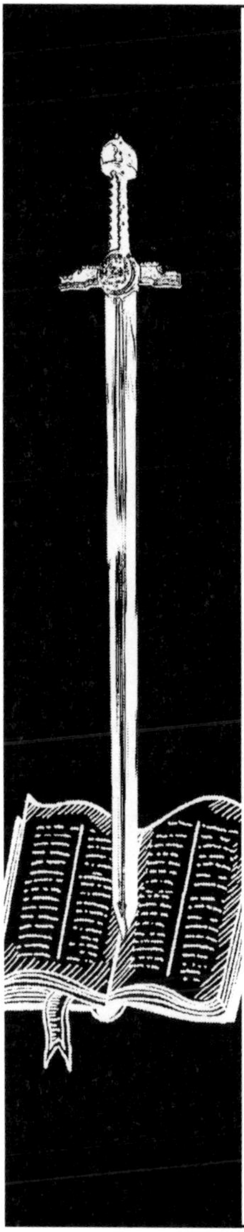

else the jealous Lord will destroy you.

Deuteronomy 13:5 — Prophets and diviners of dreams shall be put to death.

Deuteronomy 13:6–9 — Kill anyone, including one's own family member, who entices you to worship other gods.

Deuteronomy 17:2–5 — Worshippers of other gods must be stoned to death.

Joshua 23:16 — Allegiance to other gods will kindle God's anger and you will perish.

◆ ◆ ◆

Fourth Commandment

Remember the Sabbath and Keep It Holy

Exodus 31:15 — Anyone who does work on the Sabbath shall be put to death.

Fifth Commandment

Honor your Father and Mother

Exodus 21:15 — Whomever strikes his mother or father shall be put to death.

Leviticus 20:9 — Whoever curses his mother or father shall be put to death.

Deuteronomy 21:21 — A stubborn and rebellious son shall be stoned to death.

◆ ◆ ◆

Seventh Commandment

You Shall Not Commit Adultery

Deuteronomy 22:22 — If a man is caught lying with the wife of another man, both of them shall die.

Proverbs 2:18 — The way of the adulteress leads down to death.

◆ ◆ ◆

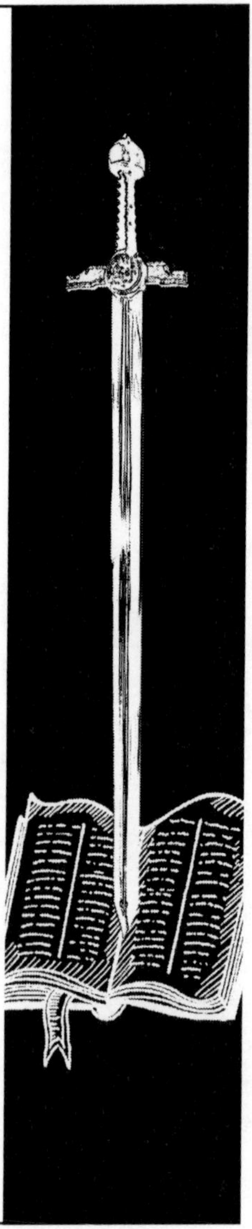

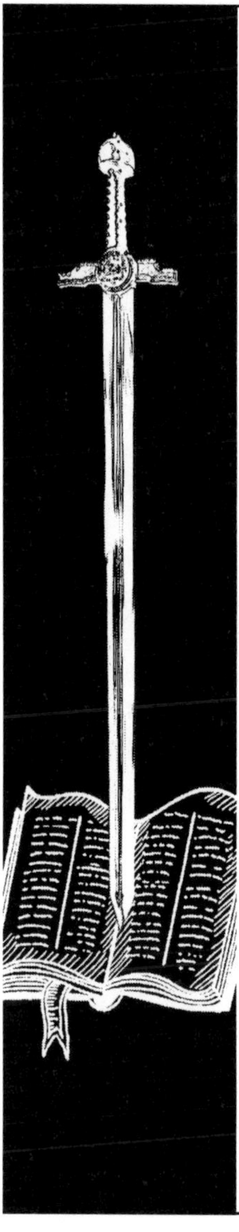

Ninth Commandment

You Shall Not Bear

False Witness

Psalms 5:6 — The Lord will destroy those who speak lies.

◆ ◆ ◆

A famous saying from the Old Testament is "an eye for any eye." In this study, "a murder for a murder and a whole lot more" seems appropriate.

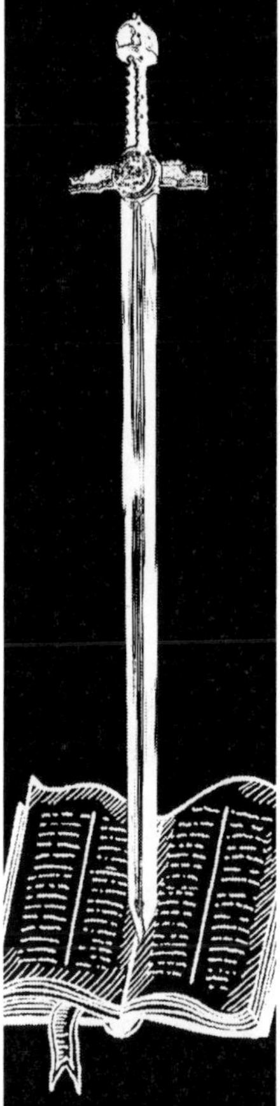

Chapter Twelve

Psalms of Death and Proverbs of Doom

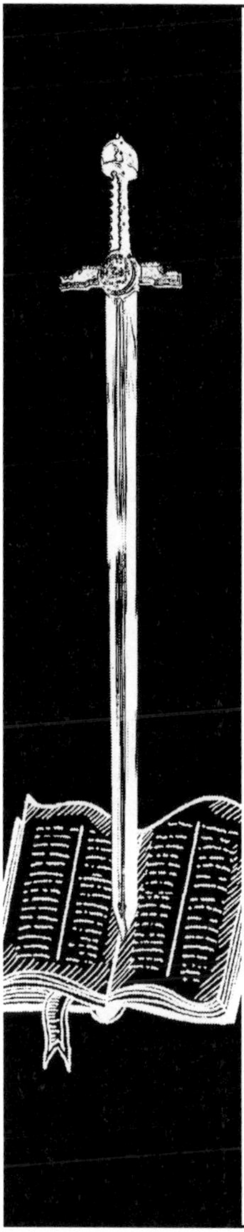

The book of Psalms is a diverse collection of hymns and prayers. Proceeding directly on the heels of the violent books of Chronicles and Job in the Christian Old Testament, the psalms are profuse in their praise of a God of faithfulness, mercy, justice, grace, and steadfast love. The reader cannot help but notice the stark contrast.

The Psalm writers cover a wide range of experiences: praise and exultation versus death and destruction. An exhaustive listing of all the Psalms dealing with murder would be impractical. For the purposes of this study, only selected passages are documented.

Variety and interest to the reader were the primary considerations upon condensing such a vast amount of material.

◆ ◆ ◆

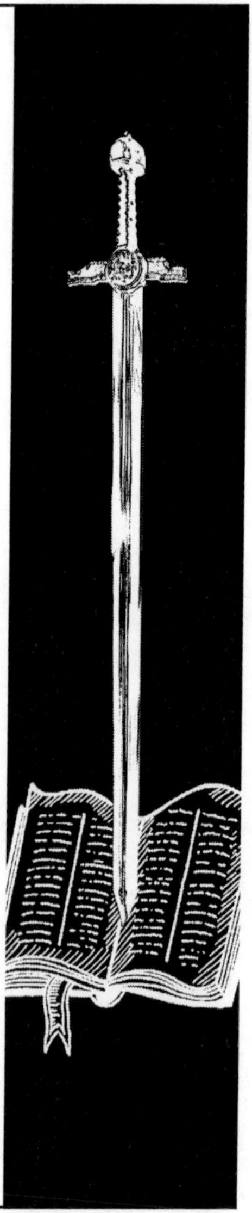

Psalms of the Victorious in Battle

18:37–38, 42—

I pursued my enemies and overtook them; and did not turn back until they were consumed. I struck them down, so that they were not able to rise; they fell under my feet. I beat them fine, like dust before the wind; I cast them out like the mire in the streets.

60:11–12—

O grant us help against the foe, for human help is worthless. With God we shall do valiantly; it is he who will tread down our foes.

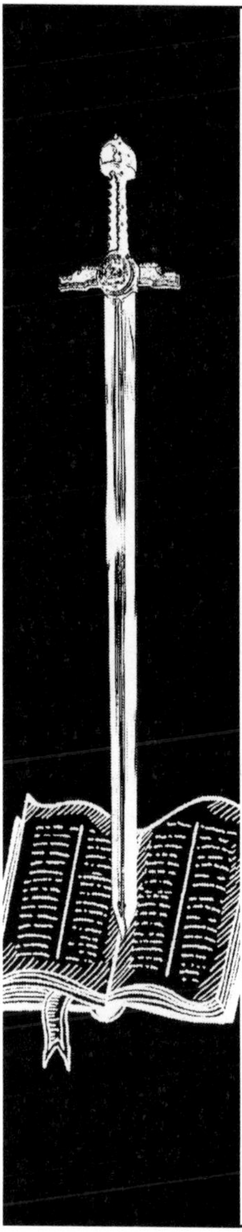

69:28—

Let my enemies be blotted out of the book of the living.

97:3—

Fire goes before the Lord and consumes his adversaries on every side.

◆ ◆ ◆

Psalms of the Lord's Judgment

2:11–12—

Serve the Lord with fear, with trembling kiss his feet, or he will be angry, and you will perish in the way; for his wrath is quickly kindled.

7:12–13—

If one does not repent, God will whet his sword; he has bent and strung his bow; he has prepared his deadly weapons, making his arrows fiery shafts.

21:9b—

The Lord will swallow up his enemies in his wrath, and fire will consume them.

37:15—

The sword of the wicked shall enter their own heart.

37:38—

Transgressors shall be altogether destroyed; the posterity of the wicked will be cut off.

53:5—

God will scatter the bones of the ungodly.

55:23—

The bloodthirsty and the treacherous shall not live out half their days.

68:2—

As wax melts before the fire, let the wicked perish before God.

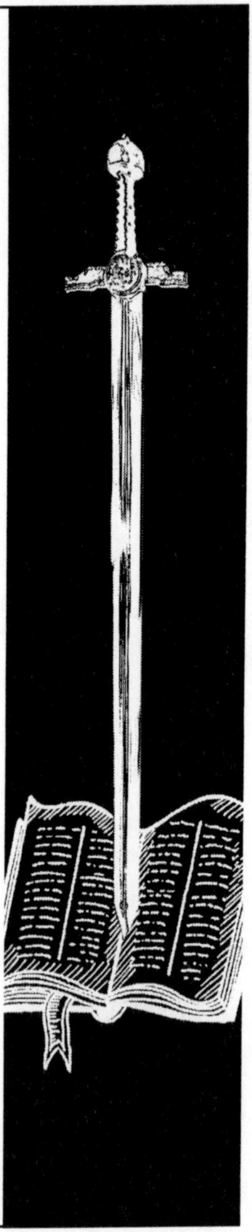

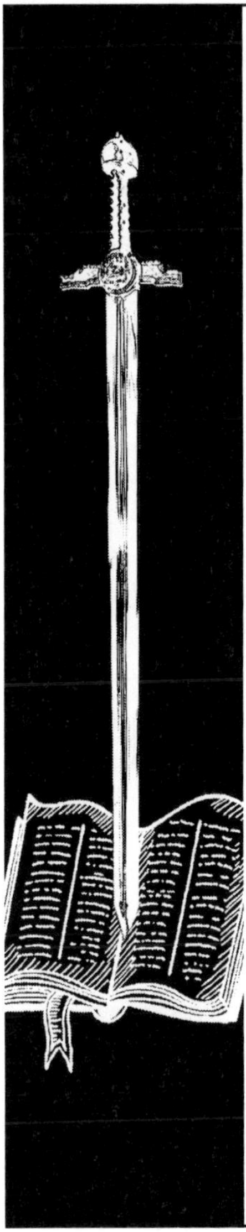

140:10–11—

Let burning coals fall on the wicked. Let them be flung into pits, no more to rise . . . let evil speedily hunt down the violent.

141:7—

Like a rock that one breaks apart and shatters on the land, so shall the bones of the wicked be strewn at the mouth of Sheol.

◆ ◆ ◆

And an imagery-laden rebuke to the wicked in Psalm 58:3–9:

The wicked go astray from the womb; they err from their birth, speaking lies.

They have venom like the venom of a serpent, like the deaf adder that stops its ear, so that it does not hear the voice of charmers or of the cunning enchanter.

O God, break the teeth in their mouths; tear out the fangs of the young lions, O Lord!

Let them vanish like water that runs away; like grass let them be trodden down and wither.

Let them be like the snail that dissolves into slime; like the untimely birth that never sees the sun.

Sooner than your pots can feel the heat of thorns, whether green or ablaze, may he sweep them away!

◆ ◆ ◆

The book of Proverbs, immediately following Psalms, offers the reader a varied collection of wise sayings.

[As an aside, the careful reader will note that numerous proverbs denounce the loose or contentious woman. There are no prov-

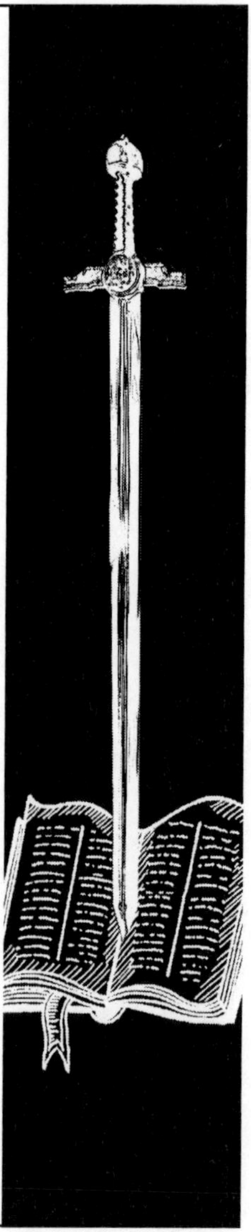

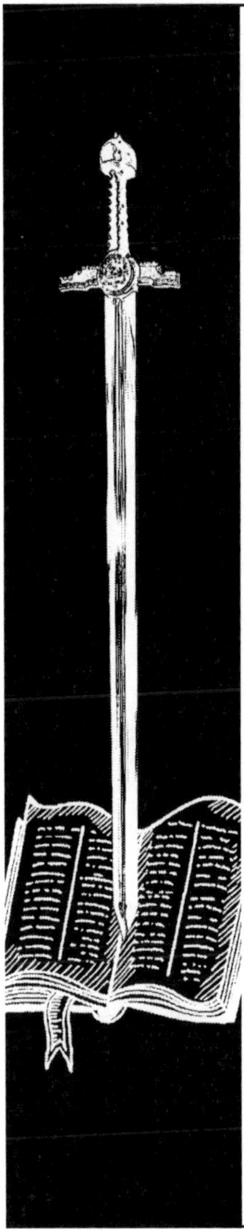

erbs, however, with comment regarding a loose or contentious male.]

Some proverbs relating to the Sixth Commandment are as follows:

◆ ◆ ◆

3:31—

Do not envy the violent and do not choose any of their ways; for the perverse are an abomination to the Lord.

6:16–17—

One of the six things that the Lord hates: hands that shed innocent blood.

21:27—

The sacrifice of the wicked is an abomination.

28:17—

If someone is burdened with the blood of another, let that killer be a fugitive until death; let no one offer assistance.

◆ ◆ ◆

Finally, Proverbs 16:4 states:

The Lord has made everything for its purpose, even the wicked for the day of trouble.

◆ ◆ ◆

The implication is disturbing — similar to the prophet's allusion that the Lord intentionally decreed laws that the Israelites could not follow. To which the psalmist might reply, as he does in 135:6:

Whatever the Lord pleases he does.

Or as the Lord might respond, as He does in Jeremiah 49:19:

For who is like me?

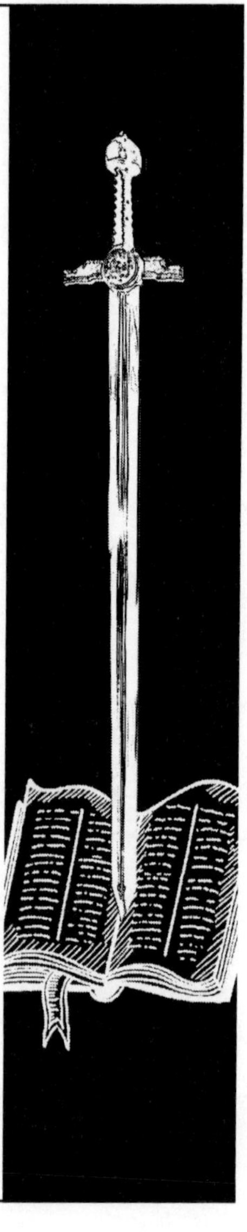

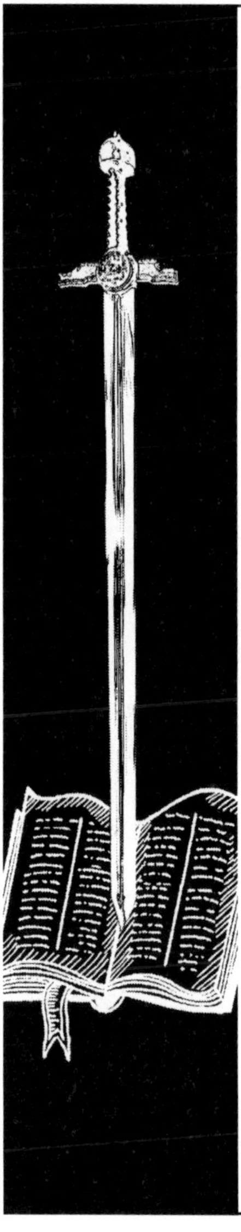

Epilogue

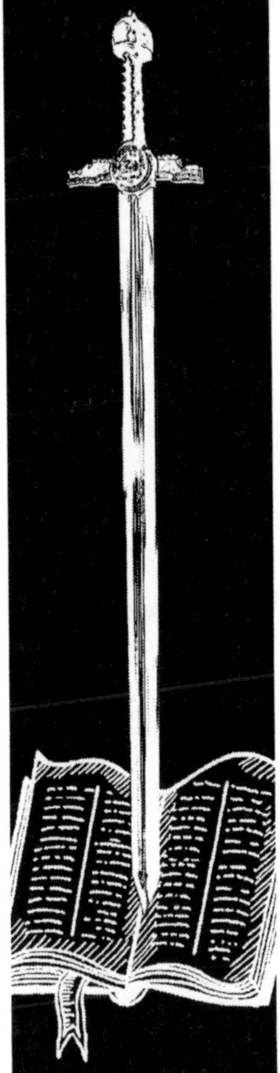

For the final murder toll, the easy and objective part is the addition — just get the calculator and total it up. The official tally for killings and murders in the Old Testament, either by the Lord or the Israelites, comes to 2,471,998 (see Exhibit J).

The harder and more subjective aspect is the instances of murder labeled as either massacres or possible massacres. In this area, I have taken some liberties, which understandably may be questioned. I tried to err on the side of caution, and an entry was only designated as a massacre when the text or context indicated large numbers of deaths.

For example, 1 Chronicles 4:39–41 states that the Israelites attacked the Menuim and in the process "exterminated" them. This was entered as a massacre. The next three verses state that 500 Israelites destroyed a remnant of the Amalekites. Because only 500 Israelites warriors were mentioned and they destroyed a "remnant, this was listed as a possible massacre.

In numerous instances, only "not known" is posted in the exhibits. This designation was utilized when an official count was not stated, but the text implied a limited number of deaths, such as within a family. This designation was also used when Scripture related that a portion or only "some" died.

I have explained in the "comment" section when assumptions were made and why. For example, 2 Kings 15:16 recounts when

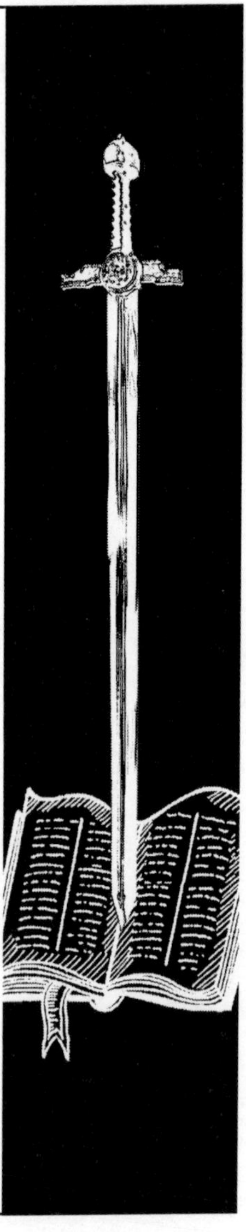

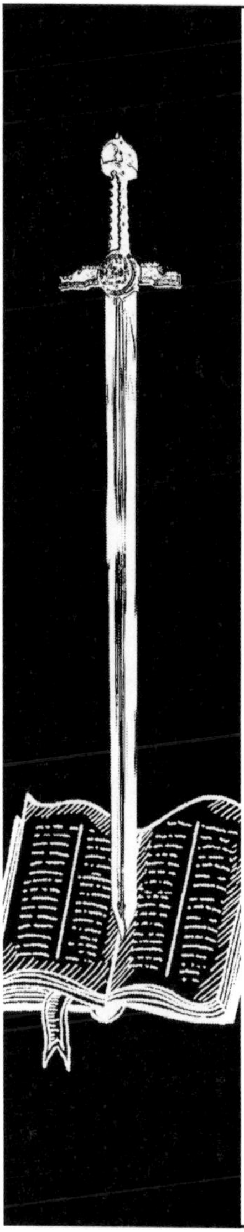

King Menahem sacked the city of Tipshah and "ripped open all the pregnant women in it."

I note in the comment section that I assumed that pregnant women and/or their fetuses died. A designation of "not known" was entered in the final column.

As with any subjective accounting, another person will total it differently. I make no claim that the tallies of massacres are accurate, not even (as the pollsters like to say) within several percentage points. But instances of mass slaughter most certainly did occur, especially when the Israelites were conquering the Promised Land. The specific number should not be the stumbling block to the reader's understanding.

Finally, as explained in the Preface, the text had to mention death, killing, burial, etc. in order to be included as an occurrence of murder.

In 2 Samuel 8:2, King David attacks and subdues the Philistines. There is no mention of death, so the passage was omitted.

But actual numbers are objective. Moreover, in many passages, Scripture implies that probably more were killed than the figure supplied. For these entries, the tally column notes "at least" that number died. The figure of 2,471,998 is therefore a minimum count.

As part of my research, I read the Old Testament word for word from beginning to end. I may have overlooked a murder or two. But as the total stands as a minimum, any missed murders are hopefully not consequential.

Finally, when in doubt, I consulted the Hebrew Bible and oth-

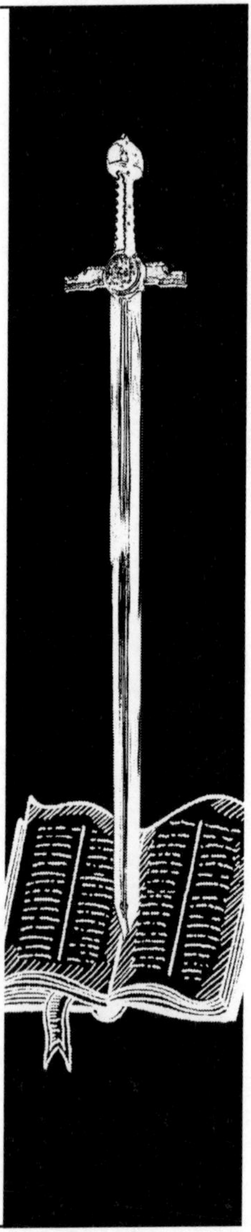

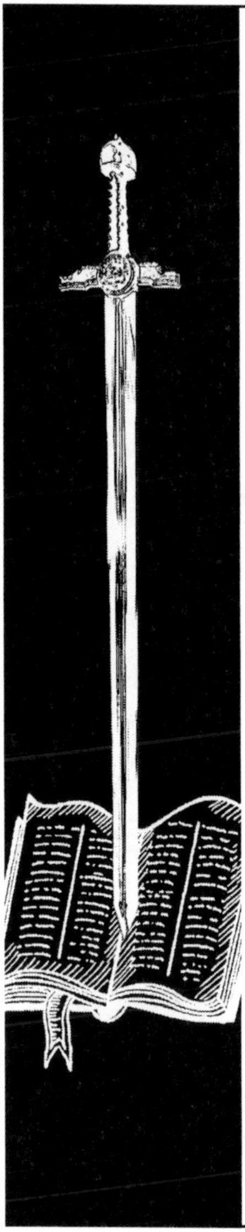

er source material as indicated in the annotations. Every attempt at accuracy and exactness has been made.

But remember, only God is perfect.

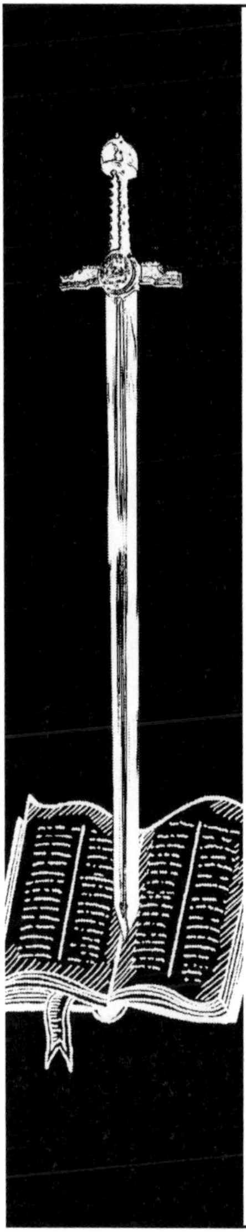

Exhibit A

Murders Prior to Mount Sinai

EXHIBIT A — Murders Prior to Mount Sinai

SCRIPTURE	OCCURRENCE	COMMENT	#Killed
Gen. 4:8	Cain kills Abel.	[see Chapter 2 discussion]	1
Gen. 4:23	Lamech, a descendant of Cain, tells his wives that he has killed a man.	Assumption is made that Lamech is telling the truth.	1
Gen. 7	God sends flood to destroy all mankind, which has become corrupt and violent.	[see Chapter 2 discussion] "all mankind"	not known Massacre
Gen. 19:24-26	Because of the wickedness of Sodom and Gomorrah, God rains down sulfur and fire on the two cities, the plain, and all the inhabitants.	As with the worldwide flood, God again saves a remnant of Lot and his family.	not known Massacre
Gen. 19:26	Lot's wife looks back on the cities of Sodom and Gomorrah and is turned into pillar of salt.[1]	In verse 17, the angels of God had told Lot's family not to look back.	1
Gen. 34:25-31	Two sons of Jacob kill Shechem and all the males of his city for allegedly raping their younger sister, Dinah.	[see Chapter 2 discussion]	not known Massacre

EXHIBIT A – Murders Prior to Mount Sinai – Continued

SCRIPTURE	OCCURRENCE	COMMENT	#Killed
Gen. 38:1-7	Judah, the son of Jacob and Leah, marries Canaanite woman named Shua. Their firstborn, Er, is married to Tamar. But Er does what is wicked in the sight of the Lord, and Lord puts Er to death.	[see Chapter 2 discussion]	1
Gen. 38:8-10	Judah order Er's younger brother, Onan, to bear a child with Er's widow, Tamar. Onan refuses to impregnate Tamar, and Lord puts Onan to death.	[see Chapter 2 discussion]	1
Ex. 2:11-12	Prior to Moses' call from the Lord, Moses sees an Egyptian beating a fellow Hebrew. Moses kills the Egyptian and hides him in the sand.	Remember that Moses was a Hebrew baby saved by the Pharaoh's daughter after being placed in a basket in the water.	1
Ex. 9:22-26	Lord sends the 7th plague of hail and thunder upon Pharaoh and Egypt. God states that every human not under shelter will die when hit by hail.	Verse 25: The hail struck down both human and animal.	not known

EXHIBIT A – Murders Prior to Mount Sinai – Continued

SCRIPTURE	OCCURRENCE	COMMENT	#Killed
Ex. 12:29-30	As part of the 10th plague on Pharaoh and the Egyptians, the Lord strikes down all the firstborn in the land, from the firstborn of Pharaoh to the firstborn of the prisoner in the dungeon.	Psalm 78:49-51 commemorates this plague, where God lets loose his "fierce anger, wrath, and indignation" by a company of destroying angels.	not known Massacre
Ex. 14:26-30	After Moses leads the Israelites out of Egypt and they cross the sea parted by God, Moses stretches out his hand, the water returns, and the Lord tosses the Egyptians into the sea.[2]	Verse 6 indicates that Pharaoh had at least 600 charioteers.[3] Psalm 106:11 "Not one of them was left."	total not known; at least 600.[4]
Ex. 17:8-13	Israelites go to war against Amalek and defeat them.	The text does not specifically say the Amalekites were killed, but verse 13 states they were defeated by the sword.	not known Massacre

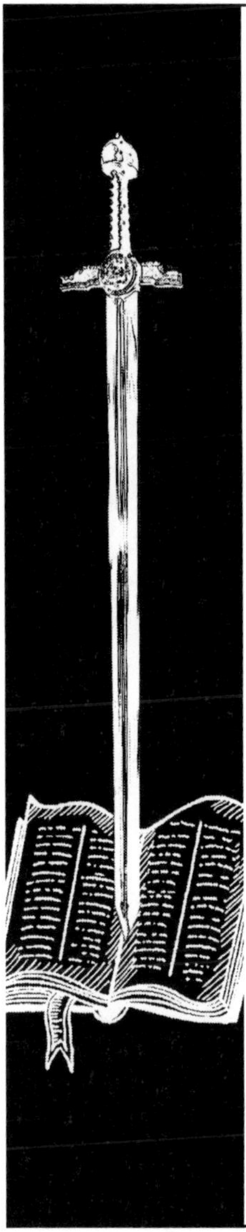

Exhibit B

Attempted or Plotted Murder

EXHIBIT B – Attempted or Plotted Murder

SCRIPTURE	OCCURRENCE	COMMENT
Gen. 22:1-13	God tells Abraham to sacrifice his son, Isaac. As Abraham prepares to comply, God stops Abraham and provides a ram for the offering instead.[5]	Story is usually interpreted as a test of Abraham's loyalty to God. Assumption is made that Abraham would have killed Isaac if God had not intervened.
Gen. 27: 41-45	Esau and Jacob are the two sons of Isaac and Rebekah. Jacob steals Esau's blessing from their father,[6] and Esau plans to murder Jacob. Rebekah foils the plot by telling Jacob to flee.	Esau, being the firstborn son, had the right to the father's blessing. Jacob "steals" the blessing by dressing up as Esau and deceiving the dim-eyed Isaac.
Gen. 37:21-24	Joseph is the youngest son of Jacob and Rachel. Joseph's brothers are jealous and conspire to kill him. The oldest brother intervenes and persuades the others to throw Joseph into a pit instead.	Joseph is subsequently retrieved from the pit by his brothers and sold to traders on their way to Egypt.
Ex. 2:11-15	After Moses kills the Egyptian (see Ex. A, 9th entry), the Egyptian Pharaoh hears of the incident and seeks to kill Moses.	Moses flees from the angered Pharaoh to the land of Midian, where he receives the call from God.
Ex. 4: 24-26	Lord tries to kill Moses on his way to Egypt.	[see Chapter 2 discussion]

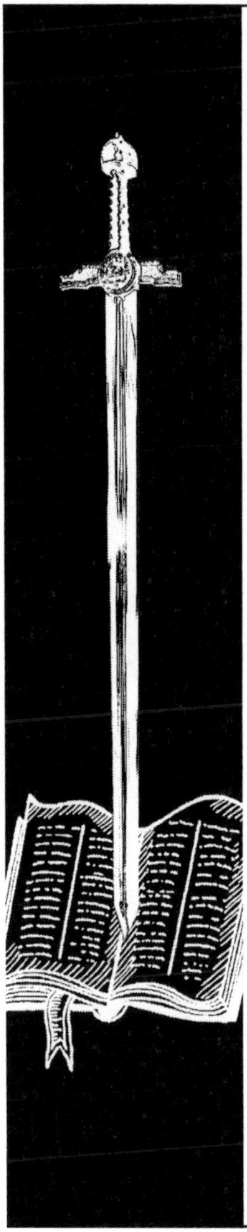

Exhibit C

In the Wilderness

EXHIBIT C – In the Wilderness

SCRIPTURE	OCCURRENCE	COMMENT	#Killed
Ex. 32:25-29	After the golden calf incident, Moses asks who is on Lord's side. Sons of Levi gather around him, and Moses orders them to kill "your brother, your friend, and your neighbor."	[see Chapter 3 discussion]	3,000
Lev. 10:1-2	Aaron's sons, Nadab and Abihu, offer unholy fire before the Lord. The Lord's fire comes and consumes them, and they die before the Lord.	[see Chapter 3 discussion]	2
Lev. 24:10-23	A man whose mother is Israelite and father Egyptian begins fighting with another Israelite, and the woman's son is blasphemed. Lord tells Moses to have whole congregation stone blasphemer.	[see Chapter 3 discussion]	1
Num. 11:31-34	Lord, angry over the Israelites' craving for meat, strikes them with a very great plague while they still have meat in their mouths.	[see Chapter 3 discussion] No mention of death, but verse 34 records burial of people.	not known

EXHIBIT C — In the Wilderness - Continued

SCRIPTURE	OCCURRENCE	COMMENT	#Killed
Num. 14:36-38	Ten scouts who bring back unfavorable report about the land of Canaan die under Lord's plague. Only Joshua and Caleb are spared because they trusted the Lord.	The unfavorable report was that formidable obstacles stood in the way of taking Canaan.[7] See Num. 13:1-16	10
Num. 15:32-36	A man found gathering sticks on the Sabbath[8] is stoned to death by the whole Israelite congregation.		1
Num. 16:1-35	Korah, Dathan, Abiram and On take 250 Israelite men and challenge Moses' authority. Lord causes earth to open up and swallow them along with their households.	[See Chapter 3 discussion] Ancient belief held that corporate guilt involved a person's whole family.[9]	at least 250 Israelite men
Num. 16:41-50	The following day, the whole congregation rebels against Moses. Lord sends plague and only stops when Moses tells Aaron to run into middle of assembly and make atonement for the people.	[See Chapter 3 discussion] What would have happened if Aaron had not made atonement?	14,700

EXHIBIT C – In the Wilderness - Continued

SCRIPTURE	OCCURRENCE	COMMENT	#Killed
Num. 21:1-3	Israelites go to war against King Arad and the Canaanites in the Negeb. The Israelites "utterly destroy" the Canaanites and their towns.		not known Massacre
Num. 21:4-9	Israelites become impatient and complain to Moses about the food and water. The Lord sends poisonous serpents and many Israelites die after being bitten until the people recant and Moses prays for them.	[see Chapter 3 discussion]	not known
Num. 21:21-31	Israelites send messengers to King Sihon of Amorites requesting passage through his land. King Sihon refuses, the two sides go to war, and Israel puts King Sihon to the sword.	Although Numbers scripture implies only king killed, Deut. 2:32-34 and Josh. 13:21-22 indicate everyone killed, including women and children.	not known Massacre
Num. 21:33-35	Israelites battle with King Og of Bashan and his people. Lord tells Moses to do as was done to King Sihon. Israelites kill King Og, his sons, and all his people.	Deut. 3:3-6 relates that not a single survivor was left. Men, women, and children were all killed.	not known Massacre

EXHIBIT C — In the Wilderness - Continued

SCRIPTURE	OCCURRENCE	COMMENT	#Killed
Num. 25:1-9	Lord sends plague on Israelites for having sex with Midianite women and worshipping their god.	[see Chapter 3 discussion]	24,000
Num. 25:6-8	Grandson of Aaron stops plague by taking spear and piercing through Israelite man having sex with Midianite woman.	[see Chapter 3 discussion]	2
Num. 31:1-18, 35	Lord tells Moses to take revenge on the Midianites, so 12,000 Israelites kill every Midianite male as well as their five kings and Balaam. The women and children are taken captive, but Moses instructs troops to kill every male and any non-virgin female.	[see Chapter 3 discussion] The Israelite troops were going to let male children and non-virgin women survive, but Moses orders them killed.	6 (five kings and Balaam) not known Massacre

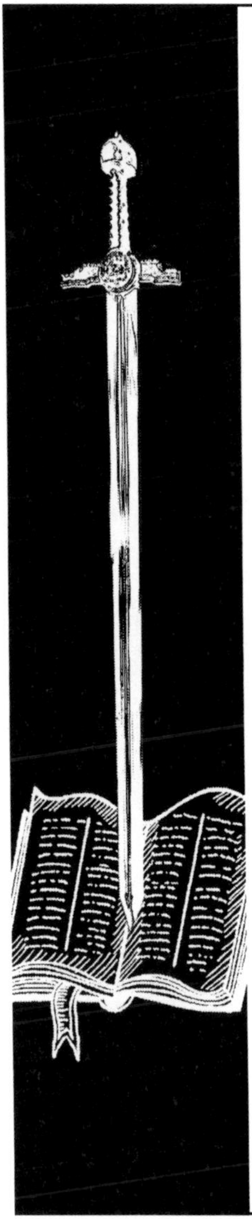

Exhibit D

Conquering the Promised Land

Exhibit D – Conquering the Promised Land

SCRIPTURE	OCCURRENCE	COMMENT	#Killed
Joshua 6:15-25	Israelites lay siege to Jericho[10] and kill all its inhabitants except Rahab and her family.	[see Chapter 4 discussion]	not known Massacre
Joshua 7:1-26	Joshua and Israelites stone Achan and his family for stealing some of the devoted things from city of Jericho.	[see Chapter 4 discussion]	at least 1 (Achan)
Joshua 8:18-29	30,000 Israelites ambush city of Ai[11] and slaughter all its inhabitants; all men and women fall by sword. The king is captured and hung on tree until sunset.		12,001 (12,000 plus king)
Joshua 10:1-14	Joshua and the Israelites help Gibeon defeat the Amorites and their five kings. Lord also sends down huge stones from heaven and makes sun stand still to lengthen the day so killing can continue.[12]	Verse 20: The Israelites inflict great slaughter on the Amorites until they are wiped out.	not known Massacre

Exhibit D – Conquering the Promised Land - Continued

SCRIPTURE	OCCURRENCE	COMMENT	#Killed
Joshua 10:22-27	Five Amorite kings, who had fled from above-mentioned battle, are captured. Israelite warriors put their feet on kings' necks, and Joshua kills them. Joshua hangs their dead bodies on trees until evening.	See Joshua 10:1-14	5
Joshua 10:28	Israelites take city of Mekkedah and strike down king and everyone with the sword. No one is left remaining.	Joshua does to king of Mekkedah what he had done to king of Jericho.	1 (the king) not known Massacre
Joshua 10:29-30	The Lord gives Libnah and its king into the hands of the Israelites. No one is left remaining.	Every person struck with edge of sword.	1 (the king) not known Massacre
Joshua 10:31-32	The Lord gives Lachish into the hands of the Israelites.	Every person struck with edge of sword.	not known Massacre
Joshua 10:33	King Horam of Gezer comes to help Lachish in above-mentioned battle. Joshua strikes him and his people.	No survivors are left.	1 (the king) not known Massacre

Exhibit D – Conquering the Promised Land - Continued

SCRIPTURE	OCCURRENCE	COMMENT	#Killed
Joshua 10:34-35	Israelites lay siege and assault Eglon. Everyone is struck with sword.	Israelites utterly destroy Eglon.	not known Massacre
Joshua 10:36-37	Israelites assault Hebron and kill the king and all the people. No one is left remaining.	Israelites utterly destroy Hebron.	1 (the king) not known Massacre
Joshua 10:38-39	Israelites assault and kill king and all the people of Debir. No one is left remaining.		1 (the king) not known Massacre
Joshua 10:40-41	Joshua defeats the whole land and all their kings. All that breathes is destroyed. The defeat is from Kadesh-barnea to Gaza and all the country of Goshen as far as Gibeon.		not known Massacre
Joshua 11:1-9	At least 11 kings join forces and wage war against the Israelites. Israelites strike everyone down until no one is left remaining.	Verse 4: The kings and their troops were a great army, in number like sand on the seashore.	11 (kings) not known Massacre

Exhibit D – Conquering the Promised Land - Continued

SCRIPTURE	OCCURRENCE	COMMENT	#Killed
Joshua 11:10-15	Israelites strike down city of Hazor, its king, and all the towns and kings over which Hazor was head.	There was no one left who breathed.	1 (the king) not known Massacre
Joshua 11:21-22	Israelites utterly destroy the Anakim and all their towns. None of the Anakim are left in the land of the Israelites.	Deut. 9:2 indicates that the Anakim are a strong and tall people.	not known Massacre
Joshua 19:47	When the tribe of Israelites known as Dan lose some territory, the Danites fight against Leshem, capture it, and put it to the sword.	see Judges 18:1, 27-28	not known Massacre

Note: Joshua 12:1-24 states that Joshua and the Israelites defeated 33 kings (two on the east side of Jordan and 31 on the west side). Because only the word "defeated" is used, no automatic assumption of 33 murders is made. However, some of these kings are specifically identified in earlier Scripture references as having been killed — these are included in the murder tally. In some instances (for example, Joshua 10:34-35), Scripture relates that everyone in the city is killed, but there is no specific mention of a king being killed. No individual death is thereby recorded.

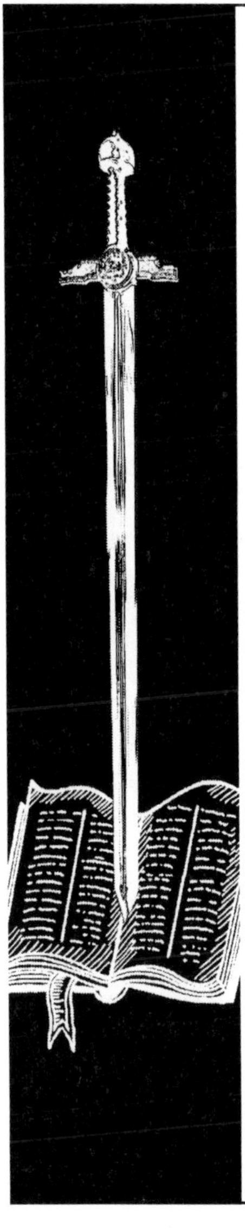

Exhibit E

Settling the Promised Land

EXHIBIT E – Settling the Promised Land

SCRIPTURE	OCCURRENCE	COMMENT	#Killed
Judges 1:8	Israelites from tribe of Judah fight against Jerusalem and take it. They put the city to sword and set on fire.	At the time, Jerusalem is not an Israelite city.	not known Massacre?
Judges 1:22-25	Israelites from the house of Joseph put city of Bethel to the sword.		not known Massacre?
Judges 3:15-30	An Israelite named Ehud murders King Eglon of Moab in order to free some Israelites held there in captivity. The Israelites then fight the Moabites.	Ehud thrusts sword into Eglon's fat belly. The hilt goes in after blade, and the fat closes over the blade.	10,001 (10,000 Moabites plus king)
Judges 3:31	An Israelite named Shamgar kills 600 Philistines with an oxgoad.	[See Chapter 4 discussion]	600
Judges 4:1-16	Deborah, a prophetess, tells Barak to take 10,000 Israelite warriors and fight Sisera, the general for King Jabin, who has oppressed the Israelites for 20 years. All of Sisera's army are killed.	[See Chapter 4 discussion]	Not known Massacre

EXHIBIT E – Settling the Promised Land - Continued

SCRIPTURE	OCCURRENCE	COMMENT	#Killed
Judges 4:17-22	Sisera flees on foot to tent of Jael. While Sisera is sleeping, Jael hammers a tent peg through his skull and he dies.	[See Chapter 4 discussion] Assumption made that Jael is the agent of Deborah.	1
Judges 4:23-24	Israelites bear harder and harder on King Jabin of Canaan until he is destroyed.	see Psalms 83:9-10	1
Judges 6:1-8:21	Gideon takes 300 Israelites and goes to war against Midianites, Amalekites, and all of the people of the east. The 300 Israelites kill 120,000. The remaining 15,000 are thrown into a panic.	[See Chapter 4 discussion]	120,000
Judges 7:25; 8:21	Gideon's army also kills the four Midianite kings. The heads of Oreb and Zeeb are brought to Gideon, and Gideon kills Zebah and Zalmunna.	[See Chapter 4 discussion]	4

EXHIBIT E – Settling the Promised Land - Continued

SCRIPTURE	OCCURRENCE	COMMENT	#Killed
Judges 8:4-7, 13-16	Gideon and his 300 warriors ask for food from people of Succoth, but officials of Succoth refuse. Gideon returns and tramples people of Succoth.	[See Chapter 4 discussion] Assumption made that Gideon kills the 77 officials/elders.	77
Judges 8:8-9 and 17	Gideon makes same request for food from people of Penuel. People refuse, and Gideon promises to come back and break down their tower. When Gideon returns, he kills the men of the city.	[See Chapter 4 discussion]	not known Massacre?
Judges 9:1-5	Abimelech, son of Gideon, goes to his father's house at Ophrah and kills his half-brothers, all except the youngest, who hides and survives.	[See Chapter 4 discussion] Abimelech kills all potential rivals and takes throne of Shechem.	69
Judges 9:22-45	In reprisal for a failed uprising by Gaal, son of Ebed, and his kinsfolk, Abimelech and his troops kill the people of Shechem in the city and those who go out into fields.		not known Massacre?

EXHIBIT E — Settling the Promised Land - Continued

SCRIPTURE	OCCURRENCE	COMMENT	#Killed
Judges 9:46-49	When lords of Shechem hear that Abimelech has killed the people, the lords enter the stronghold of a temple. Abimelech and his troops set fire to temple, so that all the people die — about 1,000 men and women.		1,000
Judges 9:50-57	Abimelech goes to Thebez and takes it, but people of city flee to a tower. Abimelech comes to burn tower, but woman throws a millstone on Abimelech, crushing his skull. Abimelech has one of his men kill him with a sword so that people will not think that a woman killed him.[13]	[See Chapter 4 discussion] Thus God repaid Abimelech for the crime he committed against his father in killing his brothers.	1
Judges 11:29-39	Jephthah bargains with God that if God delivers the Ammonites into his hands, he will sacrifice whoever first greets him. Jephthah has to sacrifice his daughter.	[See Chapter 4 discussion]	1

EXHIBIT E — Settling the Promised Land - Continued

SCRIPTURE	OCCURRENCE	COMMENT	#Killed
Judges 12:1-6	Men of Ephraim, angry that Jephthah does not enlist them to fight Ammonites, threaten to burn Jephthah's house. Jephthah and men of Gilead fight against men of Ephraim. 42,000 Ephramites fall.	[See Chapter 4 discussion]	42,000
Judges 14:1-19	Samson, from tribe of Dan, marries a Philistine woman and proposes riddle to Philistines, with loser to provide clothing. Wife coaxes answer to riddle from Samson and tells her people so they solve riddle. Samson kills 30 men of Ashkelon to take their clothes and pay his debt.	[See Chapter 4 discussion]	30
Judges 15:1-8	Because father of Samson's wife gives the wife to someone else, Samson destroys Philistine grain crop. In retaliation for causing the destruction, Philistines burn Samson's wife and her father. Samson takes revenge, striking down the Philistines.	[See Chapter 4 discussion]	not known Massacre

EXHIBIT E – Settling the Promised Land - Continued

SCRIPTURE	OCCURRENCE	COMMENT	#Killed
Judges 15:9-17	When Samson is bound and handed over to Philistines by Israelites, Spirit of Lord rushes on Samson. Samson breaks free and kills 1000 men with the fresh jawbone of a donkey.	[See Chapter 4 discussion]	1,000
Judges 16:18-31	After being betrayed by Delilah, Samson is captured and eyes gouged out by Philistines. In the Philistines' temple, Samson calls on Lord and topples the pillars, killing himself and all the people within.	[See Chapter 4 discussion] 3,000 people alone were on roof of temple.	not known Massacre
Judges 19:16-28 and 20:3-5	Israelites from tribe of Benjamin rape and abuse Levite priest's concubine until she dies.	[See Preface and Chapter 4]	1
Judges 20:1-32	In retaliation for Benjaminites' rape, 400,000 Israelite warriors fight against 26,000 Benjaminites. Benjaminites slay 40,030 of Israelites on first three days of battle.	[See Preface and Chapter 4]	40,030

EXHIBIT E – Settling the Promised Land - Continued

SCRIPTURE	OCCURRENCE	COMMENT	#Killed
Judges 20:27-48	On third day of battle, Israelites kill 25,100 Benjaminites, as well as all their wives (Judges 21:16). Only 600 Benjaminites survive.	[See Preface and Chapter 4] Verse 35: 25,100 slain Verse 46: 25,000 slain	25,100
Judges 21:1-23	In order to repopulate Benjamin tribe, Israelites kill every male and non-virgin female in Jabesh-gilead, giving the 400 virgins to the Benjaminites. Israelites also abduct women from town of Shiloh.	[See Preface and Chapter 4] Order is to "put the inhabitants of Jabesh-gilead to the sword, including the women and the little ones."	not known Massacre

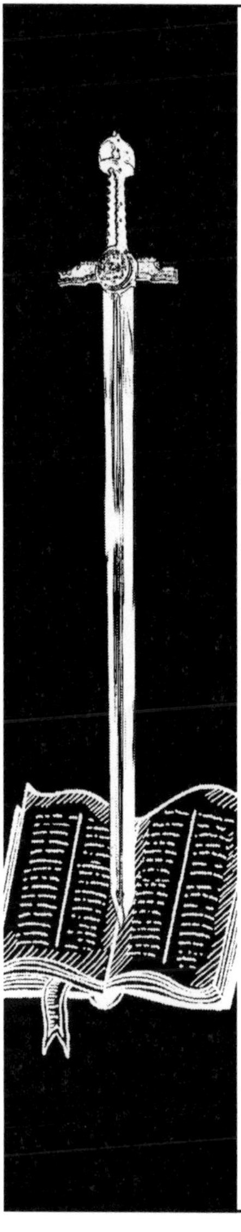

Exhibit F

Murderous Reign of King David

EXHIBIT F — Murderous Reign of King David

SCRIPTURE	OCCURRENCE	COMMENT	#Killed
1 Sam. 5:6-12	When Philistines have possession of Ark of the Covenant, Lords strikes some dead in punishment and sends others into panic.	[see Chapter 5 discussion] "Hand of the Lord was heavy."	not known
1 Sam. 6:19-20	When descendants of Jeconiah do not rejoice when Ark of the Covenant returned to Israelites, Lord kills 70 of them.	[see Chapter 5 discussion] "Lord has made a great slaughter."	70
1 Sam. 7:5-11	Israelites fight with the Philistines. Lord throws the Philistines into confusion, and they are struck down as far as beyond Beth-car.	Assumption made that Philistines killed by the use of term "struck down."	not known Massacre
1 Sam. 11:1-11	Nahash besieges Jabesh-gilead and Israelites bargain for time. Saul musters 370,000 Israelites to deliver Jabesh-gilead. Starting in the morning, Israelites cut down Ammonites until heat of day.	Nahash, king of the Ammonites, had been greatly oppressing the Gadites and Reubenites.	not known Massacre

EXHIBIT F – Murderous Reign of King David - Continued

SCRIPTURE	OCCURRENCE	COMMENT	#Killed
1 Sam. 14:1-15	Jonathon, son of Saul, and his armor-bearer cross over to the Philistines. The Philistines fall before Jonathon, and his armor-bearer, coming after him, kills them.	"In that first slaughter," about 20 Philistines killed.	20
1 Sam. 14:16-23, 31	Saul, with 10,000 men, defeats the Philistines. The Lord gives Israel the victory, and they strike down Philistines from Michmash to Aijalon.	Verse 30: slaughter among Philistines	not known Massacre
1 Sam. 14:24-27, 43-45	In a rash act, Saul orders fast before he avenges his enemies. Jonathon, not hearing his father, tastes some honey. Saul is ready to kill his son until the people ransom Jonathon.	Case of averted murder.[14]	0
1 Sam. 14:47-49	When Saul has taken kingship over Israel, he fights against his enemies on every side – against Moab, Ammonites, Edom, kings of Zobah, and Philistines. Wherever he turns, Saul routes them.	Verse 48: Saul strikes down the Amalekites.	not known Massacre

EXHIBIT F — Murderous Reign of King David - Continued

SCRIPTURE	OCCURRENCE	COMMENT	#Killed
1 Sam. 15:1-9	Saul and 210,000 Israelites soldiers go up against the Amalekites and destroy all the people by the edge of the sword. All that was despised and worthless they utterly destroyed. King Agag taken alive.	Lord's order: "utterly destroy all that they have; do not spare them, but kill man and woman, child and infant. . ."	not known Massacre
1 Sam. 15:32-33	King Agag of the Amalekites is brought before Samuel. Samuel hews Agag into pieces before the Lord.		1
1 Sam. 17:4-51	Ten-foot tall Goliath, a champion of the Philistines, challenges the Israelites. David kills Goliath with a sling and a stone.	[see Chapter 5 discussion] Israelites chase Philistines and plunder their camp.	1
1 Sam. 17:52-53 and 18:6-7	After David kills Goliath, the Israelites pursue Philistines. The wounded Philistines fall on the way.	[see Chapter 5 discussion]	not known Massacre
1 Sam. 18:6-11 and 19:9-10	After women extol David's fighting prowess over Saul's, Saul throws spear, hoping to pin David to the wall. In 19:1, Saul speaks to his son and servants about killing David.	[see Chapter 5 discussion]	0

EXHIBIT F — Murderous Reign of King David - Continued

SCRIPTURE	OCCURRENCE	COMMENT	#Killed
1 Sam. 18:20-27	David kills 100 Philistines for their foreskins.	[see Chapter 5 discussion]	100
1 Sam. 22:1-19	Doeg the Edomite tells Saul that Ahimelech in Nob helped David. Saul sends for Ahimelech and all the priests of Nob. Ahimelech protests his innocence, but Saul has 85 priests and all of Nob put to death, including men, women, children, infants, and animals.	The soldiers of Saul refuse to commit this atrocious deed against fellow Israelites, and Saul does not have authority to compel them. Doeg, the Edomite foreigner, with loyalty only to Saul, willingly does the deed.[15]	85 priests not known Massacre
1 Sam. 25:2-38	The Lord strikes Nabal dead after he refuses hospitality to David and his men.	[see Chapter 5 discussion]	1
1 Sam. 27:8-11	While living in Gath, David and his men raid Geshurites, Girzites, and Amalekites. David leaves neither man nor woman alive, but takes animals and clothing.	Scripture states that David left neither man nor woman alive to be brought to Gath so that no one could say anything about him.	not known Massacre
2 Sam. 1:1-16	Amalekite escapes from Israelite camp and informs David of death of Jonathon and Saul. Amalekite brings David the crown of Saul but then lies and says that he killed Saul after finding him mortally wounded. David kills Amalekite for killing Saul.[16]	[see Chapter 5 discussion] David did not know that the Amalekite was lying.	1

EXHIBIT F – Murderous Reign of King David - Continued

SCRIPTURE	OCCURRENCE	COMMENT	#Killed
2 Sam. 2:18-23	Asahel (a supporter of David) pursues Abner (a supporter of Saul). Abner tries to convince Asahel to back away, but Asahel refuses. So Abner strikes Asahel in the stomach with the butt of his spear, so that the spear comes out of Asahel's back and he dies.	This is arguably a case of self-defense by Abner.	1
2 Sam. 2:24-31	Fighting breaks out between David's supporters and Abner's men. Text relates 379 Israelite deaths: 360 of Abner's men and 19 of David's servants.	2 Samuel 3:1 states there is a long war between house of Saul and house of David. Abner and Ishbaal (two of Saul's men) are later at odds when Ishbaal accuses Abner of having sex with Rizpah, one of Saul's concubines.	379
2 Sam. 3:12, 27-29	After falling out with Ishbaal, Abner negotiates with David. But Joab, one of David's men, kills Abner without David's knowledge to avenge the death of his brother, Asahel (whom Abner killed). Joab stabs Abner in the stomach.	Joab had two motives:[17] 1. avenge death of brother 2. eliminate rival for post of commander-in-chief of army. David maintains his innocence and mourns Abner.	1

EXHIBIT F – Murderous Reign of King David - Continued

SCRIPTURE	OCCURRENCE	COMMENT	#Killed
2 Sam. 4:1-8	Seeking to curry David's favor, two captains of Ishbaal's raiding bands, Baanah and Rechab, kill Ishbaal and bring this head to David. They say to David, "Here is head of Ishbaal, son of Saul, your enemy."	[see Chapter 5 discussion] Baanah and Rechab are from the tribe of Benjamin.	1
2 Sam. 4:9-12	David has Baanah and Rechab murdered, saying they are wicked men who have killed a righteous man (Ishbaal) on his bed in his own room.	[see Chapter 5 discussion]	2
2 Sam. 5:17-25 1 Chr. 14:13-16	Philistines hear that David is appointed king over Israel. In a battle, David strikes down the Philistines from Geba all the way to Gerer.	Lord promises to go out before David and strike down Philistine army.	not known Massacre
2 Sam. 6:1-8	David and 30,000 men are moving Ark of the Covenant on a cart. When oxen shake ark, Uzzah reaches out to presumably steady the ark. The Lord, angered, kills Uzzah.	[see Chapter 5 discussion]	1

EXHIBIT F — Murderous Reign of King David - Continued

SCRIPTURE	OCCURRENCE	COMMENT	#Killed
2 Sam. 8:2	David defeats the Moabites and, making them lie down on the ground, measures them off with a cord: two lengths of cord for those to die and one length for those to be spared. The 1/3 spared become David' servants.	[see Chapter 5 discussion] In verse 1, David attacks the Philistines and subdues them, but no mention of death or striking down.	not known Massacre
2 Sam. 8:3-4 1 Chr. 18:3-4	David strikes down King Hadadezer and takes 1700 horsemen and 20,000 foot soldiers.	Scripture in 2 Samuel indicates only king killed, but 1 Kings 11:24 references a "slaughter by David."	1 Massacre?
2 Sam. 8:5	When Arameans of Damascus come to help King Hadadezer, David kills 22,000 of their men. Arameans also become servants of David.		22,000
2 Sam. 8:13-14 1 Chr. 18:12	David kills 18,000 Edomites in the Valley of Salt. Note: the 1 Chronicles version has Abisha as the slayer.	1 Kings 11:16-17: Joab stayed in Edom six months until he had eliminated every male.	18,000

EXHIBIT F – Murderous Reign of King David - Continued

SCRIPTURE	OCCURRENCE	COMMENT	#Killed
2 Sam. 10:1-18	When David sends envoys of condolence to Ammonite king, the envoys are rebuffed and humiliated. David goes to war against Ammonites, who hire soldiers from other cities. David's army kills 700 chariot teams, 40,000 horsemen, and the army commander.	Scripture informs that Arameans hired 33,000 fighting men.	at least 40,701
2 Sam. 11:14-17	David connives to have Uriah killed in battle by directing Joab, the army commander, to send Uriah to front lines and then not protect him.	[see Chapter 5 discussion]	1
2 Sam. 12:15-19	In punishment for David's adultery with Bathsheba and murder of Uriah, the Lord strikes down the first child of David and Bathsheba. The child dies on the 7th day.	[see Chapter 5 discussion	1
2 Sam. 13:1-30	David's son Absalom has beautiful sister named Tamar. David's son Amnon falls in love with her, rapes her, but then loathes her. Absalom has Amnon killed.	[see Chapter 5 discussion]	1

EXHIBIT F – Murderous Reign of King David - Continued

SCRIPTURE	OCCURRENCE	COMMENT	#Killed
2 Sam. 18:1-6	David's army battles forces of Absalom, and Absalom's men are defeated. The battle spreads over face of all the country, and the forest claims more victims than the sword.	Verse 6: The slaughter was great on that day. Great numbers were driven into the forest, a trackless jungle, from which there was no escape.[18]	20,000
2 Sam. 18:9-17	David tells his men to deal gently with Absalom. But Joab never withheld a fatal blow when in David's interest. Joab murders Absalom when he is caught in tree.	[see Chapter 5 discussion] Absalom's body taken and thrown into great pit in the forest, with a great heap of stones piled on top.	1
2 Sam. 20:7-10	David replaces Joab by appointing Amasa commander-in-chief of army. During an offensive attack to quell a revolt, Joab murders Amasa.	[see Chapter 5 discussion]	1
2 Sam. 20:1-2, 14-22	Joab's forces corner Sheba and his men in a remote city. A wise woman from city bargains for city's sparing in exchange for head of Sheba. Joab agrees, and head of Sheba is cut off and thrown out to Joab.	Sheba and his men are from a disaffected tribe of Israelites.[19]	1

EXHIBIT F – Murderous Reign of King David - Continued

SCRIPTURE	OCCURRENCE	COMMENT	#Killed
2 Sam. 21:1-9	Lord tells David that a three-year famine on land is because of bloodguilt of Saul when he put Gibeonites to death. David asks Gibeonites how he can atone. Gibeonites demand seven sons of Saul to be impaled on mountain of the Lord. David hands over two sons and five grandsons.	[see Chapter 5 discussion] There is no prior record in the Old Testament of Saul putting Gibeonites to death.[20]	7
2 Sam. 21:15-22 1 Chr. 20:4-8	Israelites war against Philistines, and David's men kill four giants.	One giant has six fingers on each hand and six toes on each foot.	4
2 Sam. 23:8	Josheb-basshebeth, one of David's warriors, wields a spear and kills 800.	Scripture gives no further information.	800
2 Sam. 23:9-10 1 Chr. 11:12	Eleazer, one of David's warriors, stands his ground while other Israelites withdraw from a battle with the Philistines. Eleazer strikes down Philistines until his arm grows weary.	The Lord brings about a great victory, and the others return to strip the dead.	not known Massacre
2 Sam. 23:11-12	Shammah, a mighty warrior, stands alone to fight Philistines after Israelite army flees. Shammah kills the Philistines.	The Lord brings about a great victory.	not known Massacre

EXHIBIT F – Murderous Reign of King David - Continued

SCRIPTURE	OCCURRENCE	COMMENT	#Killed
2 Sam. 23:18-19	Abishai, son of Zeruiah and brother of Joab, kills 300 men with his spear.		300
2 Sam. 23:20-21	Benaiah, a valiant warrior for David, strikes down two sons of Moab and also kills an Egyptian. Benaiah, with only a staff, fights the Egyptian who has a spear. Benaiah snatches the Egyptian's spear and kills him with it.	Verse 20: Benaiah also killed lion on a day when snow had fallen.	3
2 Sam. 24:1-24	Anger of Lord kindled against Israel, and David told to count the people. After census, David repents of his sin and chooses between three penances offered by the Lord.	[see Chapter 5 discussion]	70,000

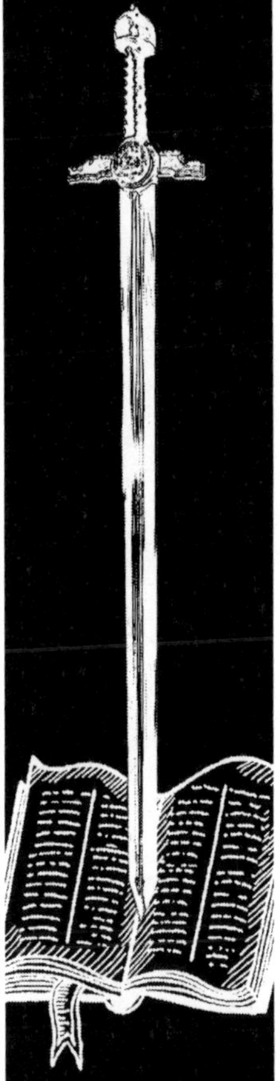

Exhibit G

Assassinations, Child Sacrifice, and Prophets

EXHIBIT G – Assassinations, Child Sacrifice, and Prophets

SCRIPTURE	OCCURRENCE	COMMENT	#Killed
1 Kings 2:13-25	Adonijah asks Bathsheba, mother of Solomon, to request that Solomon give him Abishag (part of David's harem) for a wife. Solomon sends Benaiah to kill Adonijah. David bypassed Adonijah in favor of Solomon for throne.	Solomon finds an excuse to eliminate Adonijah. Members of a king's harem were considered royal property to be passed on to next king. By his request, Adonijah made himself vulnerable.[21]	1
1 Kings 2:28-35	Solomon has Benaiah kill Joab because without David's knowledge, Joab had killed Abner and Amasa, two of David's commanders-in-chief.	In verses 5-6, David asks Solomon not to let Joab's grey head go down to Sheol in peace.	1
1 Kings 2:36-46	Solomon has Benaiah kill Shimei for leaving Jerusalem.	Solomon had forbidden Shimei to leave Jerusalem.	1
1 Kings 12:1-18	King Rehoboam succeeds Solomon and refuses to acknowledge followers of Jeroboam. When Rehoboam sends Adoram to enforce policy in the north, all Israel stone Adoram to death.	Rehoboam is Solomon's son.	1
1 Kings 13:11-25	Old prophet deceives man of God re: God's instruction not to eat or drink. Man of God eats and then is killed by lion.	[See Chapter 6 discussion] Assumption made that lion is God's instrument of death.	1

EXHIBIT G — Assassinations, Child Sacrifice, and Prophets - Continued

SCRIPTURE	OCCURRENCE	COMMENT	#Killed
1 Kings 14:1-18	The prophet Ahijah predicts the death of Jeroboam's child because Jeroboam has not kept the Lord's commandments. The child dies, presumably by the hand of God because of Jeroboam's apostasy.		1
1 Kings 15:25-28	Baasha, son of Ahijah, assassinates King Nadab of Israel.	This assassination begins a series of assassinations of kings of Israel.[22]	1
1 Kings 15:29	King Baasha kills all the house of Jeroboam; not one was left who breathed.		not known
1 Kings 16:1-7	Lord, angered over King Baasha's sins, destroys and consumes Baasha and his house.		1 (the king) not known
1 Kings 16:8-10	Elah, son of Baasha, rules over Israel two years. Zimri, a commander-in-chief, conspires against Elah. Zimri murders Elah while Elah drinking himself drunk.		1

EXHIBIT G – Assassinations, Child Sacrifice, and Prophets - Continued

SCRIPTURE	OCCURRENCE	COMMENT	#Killed
1 Kings 16:11-13	When seated on throne, Zimri kills all the house of Baasha because of the evil they had done.	Verse 11: Zimri did not leave a single male of Baasha's kindred or his friends.	not known
1 Kings 16:15-19	Zimri reigns seven days in Israel. Israel decides, however, to make Omri, an army commander, the king. Zimri commits suicide by burning house he is in.	Case of suicide combined with arson.	1
1 Kings 16:21-22	Omri overcomes a portion of Israel devoted to his rival, Tibni. So Tibni dies.	Assumption made that Tibni killed by Omri's supporters.	1
1 Kings 16:34	Israelite named Hiel lays foundation of Jericho at cost of his firstborn and sets up its gate at cost of youngest son.	[see Chapter 6 discussion] Assumption made that Hiel killed his firstborn and youngest sons.	2
1 Kings 18:17-40	Prophet Elijah challenges the prophets of Baal and Asherab to see whose God can put fire to animal offering. Only the Lord God consumes the offering with fire, and Elijah orders the Israelites to seize and kill the 850 false prophets.	[see Chapter 6 discussion] The slaughter of prophets of Baal is sometimes interpreted as a vast human sacrifice to the Lord.[23]	850

EXHIBIT G — Assassinations, Child Sacrifice, and Prophets - Continued

SCRIPTURE	OCCURRENCE	COMMENT	#Killed
1 Kings 19:10	The prophet Elijah states that Israelites have forsaken God's covenant, thrown down His altars, and killed Lord's prophets with the sword.	Assumption made that the Israelites have killed some of the Lord's prophets.	not known
1 Kings 20:1-21	King Ahab and 7,232 Israelites battle King Beh-hadad of Aram and 32 kings allied with him. Each Israelite kills his man, the Arameans flee, and Israel pursues them.	Israel defeats Arameans "with a great slaughter." King Ben-hadad escapes on his horse with the cavalry.	not known Massacre
1 Kings 20:26-30	King Ben-hadad musters Arameans to fight Israel. Battle begins on 7th day, and Israelites kill 100,000 Aramean foot soldiers in one day. The rest flee into city, and wall falls on 27,000 remaining men. Ahab spares life of King Ben-hadad.	Text does not indicate whether 27,000 killed by falling wall. Verse 42: Lord criticizes Ahab for sparing life of Ben-hadad.	100,000
1 Kings 20:35-36	At command of Lord, one prophet says to another, "Strike me!" Second prophet refuses, and first prophet predicts his death because of disobedience. Second prophet killed by lion.	[see Chapter 6 discussion] Assumption made that lion is God's instrument of death.	1

EXHIBIT G — Assassinations, Child Sacrifice, and Prophets - Continued

SCRIPTURE	OCCURRENCE	COMMENT	#Killed
1 Kings 21:1-13	Jezebel, wife of King Ahab of Israel, gets two Israelite scoundrels to bring false charges against Naboth and have him stoned to death in order to acquire Naboth's vineyard for Ahab.	Naboth charged with cursing God and the king. Two witnesses needed for death by stoning. Deut. 17:5-6; 19:15	1
1 Kings 22:46	King Jehoshaphat of Judah exterminates the remnant of male temple prostitutes.		not known
2 Kings 1:2-12	Ahaziah falls and is injured, so he sends two envoys to inquire of prophet Elijah whether he will recover. Elijah has fire of God consume each envoy.	[see Chapter 6 discussion]	102
2 Kings 6:25-29	King Ben-hadad of Aram lays siege to Israel and famine results. Two mothers agree to eat each other's sons for food. Mother complains to king of Israel that other mother has hidden her son.	[see Chapter 6 discussion]	1

EXHIBIT G – Assassinations, Child Sacrifice, and Prophets - Continued

SCRIPTURE	OCCURRENCE	COMMENT	#Killed
2 Kings 7:1-2, 17-20	Prophet Elisha predicts to king of Israel that famine will end tomorrow. An Israelite captain expresses doubt, and Elisha predicts his doom. The next day, captain is appointed charge of the gate and is trampled to death by people.	[see Chapter 6 discussion]	1
2 Kings 9:1-27	Elisha anoints Jehu the king of Israel. Jehu assassinates King Joram of Israel and King Ahaziah of Judah.	[see Chapter 6 discussion]	2
2 Kings 9:30-37	Jehu has Jezebel thrown out a window, her blood spatters on wall, and horses trample her.	[see Chapter 6 discussion]	1
2 Kings 10:1-8	Jehu challenges sons of Ahab for control of Samaria. Samarian leaders say they'll serve Jehu. Jehu demands heads of Ahab's sons. So leaders kill 70 sons and send their heads to Jehu.	[see Chapter 6 discussion] The 70 sons probably includes grandsons.[24]	70
2 Kings 10:11	Jehu kills all the leaders, close friends, and priests of Ahab until no one survives.	[see Chapter 6 discussion]	not known

EXHIBIT G – Assassinations, Child Sacrifice, and Prophets - Continued

SCRIPTURE	OCCURRENCE	COMMENT	#Killed
2 Kings 10:12-14	Traveling to Samaria, Jehu meets 42 relatives of King Ahaziah of Judah. Jehu has all 42 relatives slaughtered in pit.	[see Chapter 6 discussion]	42
2 Kings 10:15-17	Arriving in Samaria, Jehu murders all remaining persons with connections to Ahab.	[see Chapter 6 discussion]	not known Massacre
2 Kings 10:18-28	Jehu uses deception to assemble all prophets, priests, and worshippers of Baal from throughout Israel into temple of Baal. Jehu's 80 guards put them all to the sword.	[see Chapter 6 discussion]	not known Massacre
2 Kings 11:1-16	Throne of Judah temporarily seized by Athaliah, mother of Ahaziah. Jehoiada has king's house surrounded, and Athaliah is put to death.	Text states that Athaliah set about to destroy royal family, but does not indicate if any actually killed.	1
2 Kings 11:17-18	After murdering Athaliah, people tear down house of Baal and kill Mattan, the priest of Baal, before the altars.		1

EXHIBIT G – Assassinations, Child Sacrifice, and Prophets - Continued

SCRIPTURE	OCCURRENCE	COMMENT	#Killed
2 Kings 12:20-21	Joash reigns for 40 years until two of his servants assassinate him. 2 Chr. 2:23-27 relates a different version regarding death of Joash.	Assumption made that the two servants are Israelites.	1
2 Kings 14:1-6 and 2 Chr. 25:1-4	King Amaziah, son of Joash of Judah, kills the servants who murdered his father.		2
2 Kings 14:7 and 2 Chr. 25:11-13	King Amaziah and people of Judah kill 10,000 Edomites in Valley of Salt. Another 10,000 are captured alive but then thrown down from top of Sela, dashing them to pieces.	Recall 2 Sam. 8:13-14 and David's murder of 18,000 Edomites in the Valley of Salt.	20,000
2 Chr. 25:7-13	Continuation of 2 Kings 14:7 – Israelites, angry at being sent away from battle, fall on cities of Judah from Samaria to Bethlehem, killing 3,000.	[see Chapter 6 discussion]	3,000
2 Kings 14:19-20	Amaziah is captured by Joash after they go to war. Upon learning of a conspiracy, Amaziah flees to Lachish, but he is still assassinated. 2 Chr. 25:14-16 indicates that Lord had hand in Amaziah's death due to his apostasy.	Amaziah was perhaps murdered by those resentful of punishment he had meted out to his father's assassins.[25]	1

EXHIBIT G — Assassinations, Child Sacrifice, and Prophets - Continued

SCRIPTURE	OCCURRENCE	COMMENT	#Killed
2 Kings 15:8-10	Shallum assassinates King Zechariah.		1
2 Kings 15:13-14	King Shallum is assassinated by Menahem.		1
2 Kings 15:16	Because Tipshah would not open up its town to Menahem, Menahem sacks city and rips open all the pregnant women.	Assumption made that pregnant women and/or their fetuses die.	not known
2 Kings 15:23-25	Pekahiah, son of Menahem, is assassinated by Pekah, his captain, and 50 people of Gilead.		1
2 Kings 15:30	Hoshea, son of Elah, assassinates King Pekah.		1
2 Kings 16:3 and 2 Chr. 28:3	Ahaz makes his son pass through fire according to the abominable practices of other nations.	[see Chapter 6 discussion] See Ezekiel 16:20-21	1
2 Kings 17:25-26	King of Assyria, upon fall of Israel, brings in foreigners. Because the foreigners do not worship God, God sends lions among them and some die.		not known

EXHIBIT G — Assassinations, Child Sacrifice, and Prophets - Continued

SCRIPTURE	OCCURRENCE	COMMENT	#Killed
2 Kings 19:32-35	King of Assyria, after capturing Israel, goes against King Hezekiah. The Lord says that Assyrian king will not enter the city, and that night, angel of Lord strikes down 185,000 Assyrians.	2 Chr. 32:21: And Lord sent angel who cut off all the mighty warriors and commanders and officers in camp of king of Assyria.	185,000
2 Kings 21:6	King Manasseh of Judah makes his son pass through fire.	[see Chapter 6 discussion]	1
2 Kings 21:16	King Manasseh sheds much innocent blood until he has filled Jerusalem from one end to another.		not known Massacre
2 Kings 21:19-23 and 2 Chr. 33:24	Servants of King Amon of Judah conspire against him and assassinate king in his house.	Assumption made that the servants were Israelites.	1
2 Kings 21:24 and 2 Chr. 33:25	People of Judah kill all the servants who had conspired against King Amon. People make Josiah, son of Amon, king.		not known

EXHIBIT G – Assassinations, Child Sacrifice, and Prophets - Continued

SCRIPTURE	OCCURRENCE	COMMENT	#Killed
2 Kings 22:1-2, 23:20	Josiah returns the people to the true worship of the Lord. As part of his reformation, he slaughters all the priests of the high places and then burns human bones on them.	Besides David, Josiah is the favorite king for following Moses' laws.[26] Pharaoh Neco of Egypt kills Josiah (23:29)	not known Massacre?
2 Kings 25:22-25	Nebuchadnezzar appoints Gedaliah as governor over the remnant of Judah. Ishmael of the royal family, along with 10 men, kills Gedaliah.		1
2 Kings 25:25 and Jeremiah 41:1-3	Ishmael and his men also murder the Judeans and Chaldeans that are with Gedaliah at Mizpah.		not known Massacre?
Jeremiah 41:4-9	On the day after Gedaliah's murder, Ishmael intercepts a group on a pilgrimage to Jerusalem. Ishmael and his men slaughter 70, while another 10 barter for their lives. The dead bodies are thrown into a cistern.	This excerpt from the book of Jeremiah is included here as it is a continuation of the story in the second book of Kings.	70

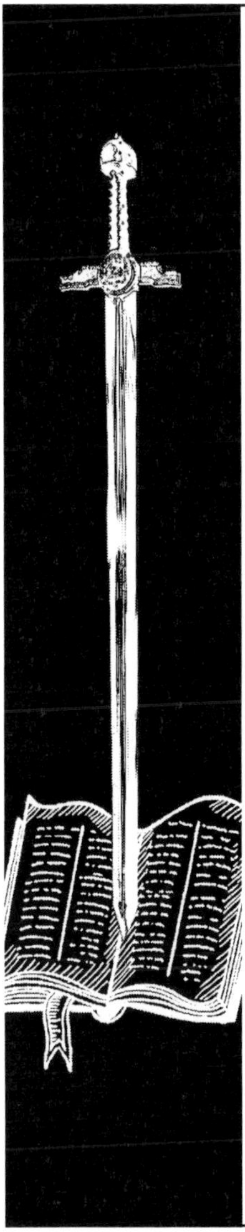

Exhibit H

Chronicles and Esther

EXHIBIT H — Chronicles and Esther

SCRIPTURE	OCCURRENCE	COMMENT	#Killed
1 Chr. 2:3	An Israelite named Er is wicked in the sight of the Lord, and God puts him to death.	Er is the firstborn son of Judah and his Canaanite wife.	1
1 Chr. 4:39-41	In the days of King Hezekiah of Judah, Israelites attack the Meunim at Gedor and exterminate them.		not known Massacre
1 Chr. 4:42-43	Five hundred Israelites from tribe of Simeon go to Mount Seir and destroy the remnant of the Amalekites that has escaped.		not known Massacre?
1 Chr. 5:10	In the days of Saul, members of the tribe of Reuben make war on the Hagrites, who fall by the sword.		not known Massacre
1 Chr. 5:18-22	Reubenites, Gadites, and half-tribe of Manasseh have 44,760 warriors. They war against the Hagrites in Jetur, Naphish, and Nodab. Many fall slain, and 100,000 are captured.	This could be a restatement of the war in 1 Chronicles 5:10. Scripture states that the war is one of God.	not known Massacre

EXHIBIT H – Chronicles and Esther - Continued

SCRIPTURE	OCCURRENCE	COMMENT	#Killed
2 Chr. 13:1-20	Jeroboam goes to battle with King Abijah. Abijah and his army defeat Israel with a great slaughter – 500,000 picked men of Israel fall slain.	[see Chapter 7 discussion]	500,000
2 Chr. 13:20	The Lord strikes down King Jeroboam of Israel.	[see Chapter 7 discussion]	1
2 Chr. 14:1-13	King Asa of Judah has army of 300,000 from Judah and 280,000 from Benjamin. Asa wars against Ethiopian army of 1,000,000 men and 300 chariots. The Lord defeats the Ethiopians before Asa, and the Ethiopians fall until no one remains alive.	[see Chapter 7 discussion] There is no hint of this battle elsewhere in the Bible.[27]	1,000,000
2 Chr. 20:1-24	People from Moab, Ammon, and Mount Seir go against King Jehoshaphat. Lord ambushes them, and they are routed. Moabites and Ammonites utterly destroy people from Mount Seir, and then Moabites and Ammonites destroy one another.	Text indicates that Lord caused the three peoples to destroy one another. Verse 24: Judah looked toward the multitude; they were corpses lying on the ground; no one escaped.	not known Massacre
2 Chr. 21:2-4	When King Jehoram of Judah ascends the throne, he puts his brothers to the sword as well as some Israelite officials.	Verse 2 indicates six brothers.	at least 6

EXHIBIT H — Chronicles and Esther - Continued

SCRIPTURE	OCCURRENCE	COMMENT	#Killed
2 Chr. 24:20-22	Zechariah reprimands people of Judah for not following the Lord. The people conspire against him, and by order of King Joash, Zechariah is stoned to death.	[see Chapter 7 discussion]	1
2 Chr. 28:1-7	Because of the apostasy of King Ahaz of Judah, Lord gives him into hands of Israel, who defeats him with a great slaughter. Pekah kills 120,000.	[see Chapter 7 discussion]	120,000
2 Chr. 28:7	Zichri, a mighty Ephramite warrior, kills king's son, the commander of the palace, and the next in authority to the king.	[see Chapter 7 discussion]	3
Esther 9:5-15	In citadel of Susa, Jews kill 500 of their enemies and 10 sons of Haman. On the second day, Jews kill another 300 in Susa.	[see Chapter 7 discussion]	810
Esther 9:16	The Jews who are in Persia gather to defend their lives and kill 75,000 of their enemies.	[see Chapter 7 discussion]	75,000

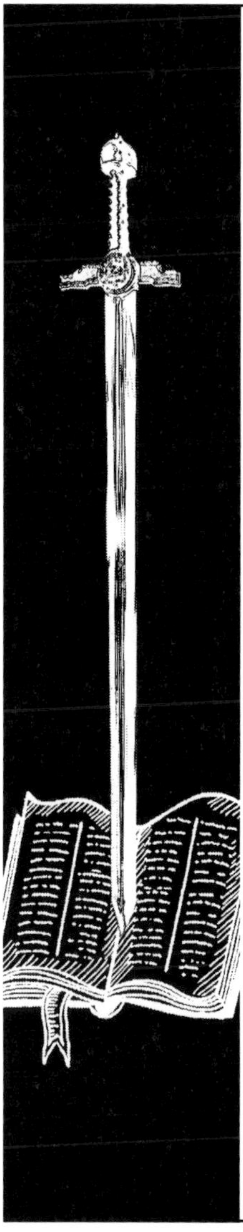

Exhibit I

Prophetic Murder

EXHIBIT I – Prophetic Murder

SCRIPTURE	OCCURRENCE	COMMENT	#Killed
Isaiah 22:15-19	An Israelite named Shebna presumably arrogates improper status to himself. Isaiah relays the Lord's sentence of death for Shebna.	[see Chapter 8 discussion]	??
Isaiah 53:4, 10	Suffering servant is struck down by God. It is the will of God to crush servant with pain, and servant's life is made an offering for sin.	[see Chapter 8 discussion]	??
Jeremiah 11:21-23	Jer. 11:18-12:6 indicates plot against Jeremiah's life. The Lord announces his judgment on those who seek the prophet's life.	[see Chapter 8 discussion] Lord issues death threat.	??
Jeremiah 26:20-23	Uriah prophesies in name of Lord about destruction of Jerusalem. Upon hearing of death threat by King Jehoiakim, Uriah flees to Egypt, but is captured and brought back. King Jehoiakim kills Uriah and throws his dead body into burial place of common people.	[see Chapter 8 discussion]	1

EXHIBIT I — Prophetic Murder - Continued

SCRIPTURE	OCCURRENCE	COMMENT	#Killed
Jeremiah 28:1-17	Hananiah claims he is a prophet, but Jeremiah states that Lord did not send Hananiah. Jeremiah predicts that Lord will send Hananiah off face of earth within the year, and Hananiah dies in seventh month.	[see Chapter 8 discussion]	1
Jeremiah 29:21-23	Jeremiah states that Ahab and Zedekiah are lying prophets. Jeremiah predicts that Lord will deliver the deceivers to king of Babylon. The Babylonian king roasts Ahab and Zedekiah.	[see Chapter 8 discussion]	2
Ezekiel 9:1-7	Six divine executioners are directed by Lord to pass through Jerusalem and kill everyone without mark on forehead.	[see Chapter 8 discussion]	not known

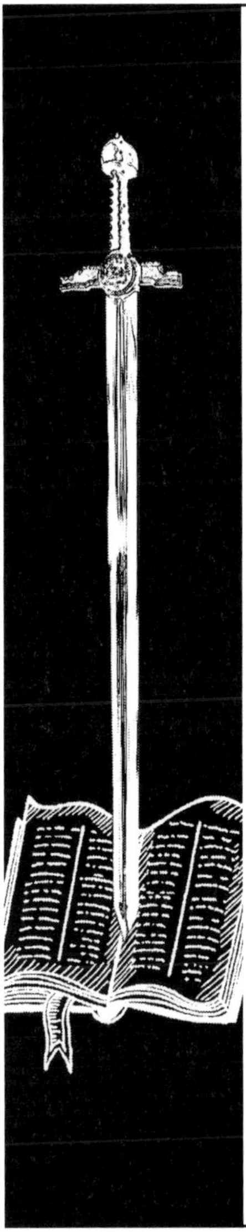

Exhibit J

Final Numbers

EXHIBIT J – Final Numbers

Exhibit	#Murders	#Massacres	#Possible Massacres
A	606	5	0
C	41,972	4	0
D	12,024	14	0
E	239,916	4	4
F	172,486	12	1
G	309,168	2	4
H	1,695,822	4	1
I	4	0	0
TOTALS	**2,471,998**	**45**	**10**

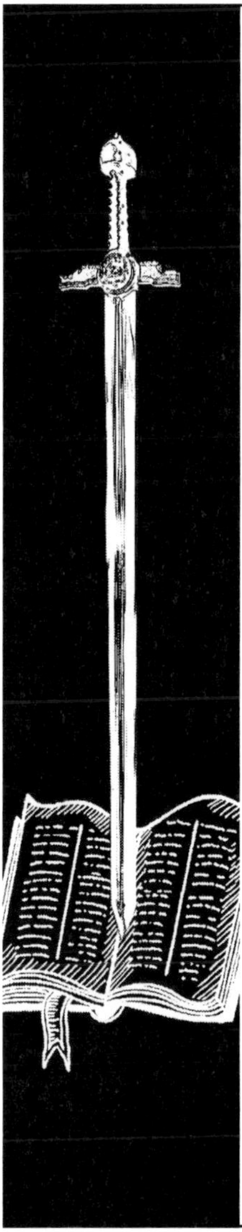

Bibliography

The New Oxford Annotated Bible, ed. Bruce M. Metzger and Roland E. Murphy, New York: Oxford University Press, 1994.

The Jewish Study Bible, ed. Adele Berlin and Marc Zvi Brettler, New York: Oxford University Press, 1999.

Where To Find It in the Bible, Ken Anderson, Nashville, TN: Thomas Nelson Publishers, 1996.

The New Strong's Compact Bible Concordance, James Strong, Nashville, TN: Thomas Nelson Publishers, 2004.

Don't Know Much About the Bible, Kenneth C. Davis, New York: Avon Books Inc., 1988.

Whose Bible Is It? Jaroslav Pelikan, New York: Penguin Books, 2005.

101 Myths of the Bible, Gary Greenberg, New York: Barnes & Noble, Inc., (Sourcebooks, Inc.) 2000.

Unsettled: An Anthropology of the Jews, Melvin Konner, New York: Penguin Books, 2003.

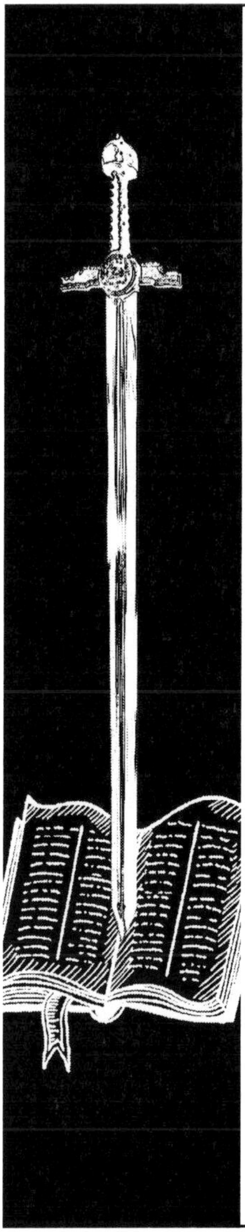

Annotations

Note: All Old Testament Scripture references are from the *New Revised Standard Version of The New Oxford Annotated Bible*, editors Bruce M. Metzger and Roland E. Murphy [New York: Oxford University Press, 1994]. Tanakh references are from the *Jewish Study Bible*, editors Adele Berlin and Marc Zvi Brettler [New York: Oxford University Press, 1999]

Preface

1. The name Shem [Noah's son] is the source of the word "Semite," which applies to all the groups who were descended from Shem, Jew and Arab alike. *Don't Know Much About the Bible*, Kenneth C. Davis [New York: Avon Books, Inc. 1988], p. 66.

2. ["Thou Shalt Not Kill"] is another critical King James Version mistranslation of the original Hebrew. The correct reading is "You shall not murder" (NRSV, JPS, and others). As the rest of the Hebrew scriptures clearly indicate, God had no problem with certain forms of killing: the death penalty was invoked for a wide variety of offenses, including house burglary, striking one's parents, adultery, bestiality, and homosexuality. God also gave very unambiguous directions that Israel's enemies were to be killed in the conquest of Canaan and in the later battles with the Philistines. God not only sanctioned killing Israel's enemies but often acted as an accomplice.... It all falls on your definition of "murder." *Don't Know Much About the Bible,* p. 121.

3. This study does not include the murders and killings in the *Apocrypha*, which is considered by Catholics and others to be part of the Bible, but is not recognized by most Protestants or Jews as canonical Scripture.

4. Judges, chapters 19-21.

Chapter One

1. God issues the first death threat in the Bible at Genesis 2:16-17: And the Lord God commanded the man, "You may freely eat of every tree of the garden, but of the tree of the knowledge of good and evil you shall not eat, for in the day that you eat of it you shall die."

2. Exodus 5:1.

3. Exodus 11:5.

4. *Oxford Annotated Bible*, p. 86-87, note 14.2: The sea, known in Hebrew as the "Sea of Reeds," was not the Red Sea itself, but a shallow body of water farther north, perhaps in the area of Lake Timsah.

5. Moses goes up and down Sinai like a yo-yo, making eight trips that take several months to complete. *Don't Know Much About the Bible*, p. 125.

6. The notion of Jews as a studious, mild, ethical people who do not fight is a myth. Ancient Israel was born in violence.... The great Jewish gifts to the world – monotheism, the Ten Commandments, resistance against tyranny – were born in weakness in a group of tribes, then a kingdom, buffeted between great empires; nurtured in a series of bitter exiles; and annealed in genocide. This produced allegiance to a single all-powerful God who could protect them, a code of laws that maintained decency in the face of perversions of power, and a searing sense of injustice. *Unsettled: An Anthropology of the Jews*, Melvin Konner [New York: Penguin Books 2003] p.xvi.

7. *Jewish Study Bible*, p. 148, note 20.1.

8. See also Ecclesiastes 7:13: Consider the work of God; who can make straight what he has made crooked?

Chapter Two

1. Ambiguous killings are also not included. For example, in Daniel 5:24-30, Daniel predicts divinely-caused disaster to befall Belshazzar, the Chaldean king. Verse 30 states that that very night, Belshazzar was killed. As Scripture does not clearly indicate whether God or someone else killed Belshazzar, this death is not included.

2. Genesis gives two different explanations for God's wrath against humanity and the reason for bringing on the flood. In Genesis 6:5-7, God's anger initially arose from the wickedness and evil present in humanity, but for some unexplained reason he chose to destroy not just humans but beasts, creeping things, and fowl....Genesis 6:11-13 is concerned with corruption and violence rather than wickedness and evil, and it imputes such behavior to all creatures, not just humans, saying all the earth was corrupt and all flesh (not just humanity's flesh) had corrupted God's ways. *101 Myths of the Bible*, Gary Greenberg [New York: Barnes & Noble, Inc. (Sourcebooks, Inc.) 2000] p. 84.

3. *Oxford Annotated Bible*, p. 50, note 38.8.

4. The aborted sacrifice of Isaac has been interpreted as a symbolic moment in which human sacrifice was rejected by God. Unfortunately, the practice didn't stop with Abraham. As the later history of ancient Israel shows, human sacrifice continued in Jerusalem for centuries. *Don't Know Much About the Bible*, p. 78.

5. *Jewish Study Bible*, p. 113, notes 4.24-26.

6. *Oxford Annotated Bible*, p. 74, note 4.25.

Chapter Three

1. This is arguably another instance of averted murder when Moses convinces the Lord not to consume the Israelites.

2. *Oxford Annotated Bible*, p.136, note 10.1; *Jewish Study Bible*, p. 227, note 10.1.

3. *Oxford Annotated Bible*, p.49, note 37.35.

4. Deuteronomy 7:1-5.

Interlude I

1. There are two stories in Genesis regarding the renaming of Jacob to Israel. In Genesis 32:24-31, Jacob wrestles with a stranger, who renames him Israel at a place called Peniel. In Genesis 35:9-10, at a place called Bethel, God himself tells Jacob that he will now be known as Israel.

Chapter Four

1. Evidence in the following book of Judges, as well as archeological discoveries during the twentieth century, have shown that the Israelite conquest of Canaan was not the grand holy war it was cracked up to be in Joshua. *Don't Know Much About the Bible*, p.147 But the sojourn in Egypt, the generations in the wilderness, the conquest against all odds – these are legends. They may

be true, but all we know about them is what we read in the Bible. It isn't necessarily wrong, but neither is it necessarily right. Scientifically, it is unproven. *Unsettled: An Anthropology of the Jews*, p.5 Archeologists now agree that there was no major war of conquest in Canaan in which the conquerors were Israelites, no replacement of Canaanite culture but rather the gradual growth of a new, Israelite culture in towns in the central highlands, p. 15.

2. The Jews came onto the stage of history as a group of warlike tribes centered in the hill country of Judea. They were indigenous to the Jordan River region, and slowly developed from a collection of tribes into a kingdom. Like everything else in the ancient world, this involved great violence. What we call civilization was nourished by rivers of blood. *Unsettled: An Anthropology of the Jews*, p.xvii The roots of the Jews are lost in the deep, blood-soaked mud of ancient empire. p.4 With Joshua at the helm, Israel crossed the Jordan and marched into Canaan, where they waged numerous campaigns of mass slaughter and physical destruction. *101 Myths of the Bible*, p. 189.

3. Ironically, recent research into this period seems to be chipping away at the biblical version of the Conquest, so the worst of the killing done by the Israelites seems to have been embellished with retelling. More likely, in current scholarly opinions, the Israelites gradually took over Canaan in a much longer process of "Settlement," combining emigration and negotiations, while scattered conflicts between localized groups went on for a much longer time. *Don't Know Much About the Bible*, p. 153.

4. Particularly in the Kethuvim, the Writings and Historical Books, the Tanakh describes the way of life of a peo-

ple in a perpetual state of war. *Whose Bible Is It?* Jaroslav Pelikan [New York: Penguin Books 2005] p. 239.

5. In Exodus 33:19, the Lord had said to Moses: "I will be gracious to whom I will be gracious, and will show mercy on whom I will show mercy."

6. But see Joshua 16:10, where the Israelites did not drive out the native Canaanites who lived in Gezer. These incidences, however, appear few in the Old Testament. Moreover, the remaining native peoples were often subject to forced labor.

7. Recent archeology has tempered the biblical account of the Conquest. In the thirteenth century BCE, the likely date of the entry of the Israelites into Canaan, Jericho was an unfortified village. *Don't Know Much About the Bible*, p.151 Joshua's destruction of Jericho stands as one of the most famous battle stories in all history.... As trumpets blared, Joshua commanded the Israelites to shout loudly and the powerful reverberations caused the walls to collapse. Joshua's troops marched into the city and utterly destroyed what remained, putting to the sword all the men and women, young and old, oxen, sheep, and asses. It's a pretty gruesome picture and quite a testament to the power of Israel's god. Despite the obvious fantasy nature of the battle, many people determined to preserve the Bible's integrity argue that the continuous noise created enough vibrations to weaken the walls and that the story has some scientific plausibility. Even if we wanted to stretch our imagination to allow for such an unlikely possibility, archaeological evidence shows that at the time of Joshua, Jericho had neither walls nor residents. The city had been vacated centuries earlier. *101 Myths of the Bible*, p. 239.

8. After the traditional stoning and immolation, Joshua buried Achan (henceforth known as "The Troubler of Israel") under a pile of rocks. This sacred execution brought about the necessary purification and on God's word Joshua renewed plans for an attack on Ai. *101 Myths of the Bible*, p. 243.

9. Note that the Song of Deborah states that Jael drives a tent peg into the temple of Sisera. The second version indicates that Jael shatters Sisera's skull with a mallet.

10. Scripture appears unclear as to the actual number of sons killed. Judges 9:2 states there are 70 sons, and 9:5 indicates that 70 were killed. However, verse five also states that the youngest son survived, so perhaps only 69 sons were killed. This study takes the conservative approach and records only 69 deaths.

11. This is arguably a case of assisted suicide. The assumption is made that the young man was an Israelite.

12. *Oxford Annotated Bible*, p. 318, notes 11.30-37.

Chapter Five

1. Goliath was only four cubits and a span, according to another version of the story found in the Dead Sea Scrolls, making him about six feet nine. . . . Then there is Elhanan, a soldier who kills Goliath in 2 Samuel 21. . . . The King James translators of 1611 tried to cover up the discrepancy by inserting the words "brother of" before the second mention of Goliath, but older texts don't bear that version out. *Don't Know Much About the Bible*, p. 177 The real killer of Goliath was Elhanan, who belonged to "The Thirty," King David's elite fighting cadre. *101 Myths of the Bible*, p. 276.

2. In some versions of the Hebrew text, David actually goes Saul one better and delivers two hundred foreskins. *Don't Know Much About the Bible*, p. 178.

3. The death of Uriah, although killed in battle against the Ammonites, is included in the final tally as a proxy murder by David. In 2 Samuel 12:9, the prophet Nathan says to David, "You have struck down Uriah the Hittite with the sword, and have taken his wife to be your wife, and have him killed with the sword of the Ammonites."

4. Although Absalom's servants murdered Amnon, the murder is included in the final tally as a proxy murder by Absalom.

5. *Oxford Annotated Bible*, p. 409, note 18.5.

6. *Oxford Annotated Bible*, p. 415, note 21.1: There is no record of the occasion upon which Saul . . . put the Gibeonites to death.

7. *Oxford Annotated Bible*, p. 415, note 21.10 states that the law of Deuteronomy 21:22-23 was not yet in effect.

8. *Oxford Annotated Bible*, p.415, note 21.10 states that the long exposure was an added insult to the deceased.

9. *Oxford Annotated Bible*, p.420, note 24.1.

10. Jewish Study Bible, p.665, note 24.1.

11. Jewish Study Bible, 1 Samuel 6:19.

12. *Jewish Study Bible*, p. 572, note 6.19: The number fifty thousand is far too big for a little town like Beth-sh-

emesh. Read only seventy, as in Antiquities of the Jews by Josephus.

13. *Oxford Annotated Bible*, p. 392, note 6.7. From the Exodus of Moses to the rise of David and Solomon, one of the key icons in biblical history was the Ark of the Covenant. Surmounted by two golden cherubim and built to hold the Ten Commandments, it served as a throne for God. This ark had magic powers and served to aid Israel against its enemies as long as Israel remained righteous. When Israel abandoned the Lord, the Ark failed to protect them. After the fall of the united monarchy, the Bible no longer mentions its presence. No passages say that it had disappeared or had been destroyed or had been captured by enemies. It simply vanishes from biblical history. Ethiopian tradition holds that a son of Solomon by the Queen of Sheba took the Ark to Ethiopia. *101 Myths of the Bible*, p. 191.

14. *Jewish Study Bible*, p. 630, note 6.6-8.

Chapter Six

1. Ulphilas, the fourth-century "apostle to the Goths," was reported to have omitted the Books of Kings from his translation of the Bible, on the grounds that the Goths were already warlike enough and did not need any more encouragement in that direction from the bloody battles described in the Scriptures of their new religion. *Whose Bible Is It?*, p. 214.

2. *Oxford Annotated Bible*, p. 318, note 11.35: While human sacrifice was not usually acceptable in ancient Israelite religion, neither was it unknown (2 Kings 16:3; Ezekiel 20:25-26, 31).

3. Ezekiel mentions the continuing practice of human sacrifice as well. His description of life during the siege before Jerusalem's capture suggests that the people in the city were probably forced to resort to cannibalism. *Don't Know Much About the Bible*, p. 248-249 See Ezekiel 16:20-21, 36.

4. *Oxford Annotated Bible*, p. 451, note 16.34.

Interlude II

1. Numbers 21:14 refers to a Book of the Wars of the Lord, which no longer exists. Joshua 10:13 and 2 Samuel 1:18 refer to the Book of Jashar. The *Oxford Annotated Bible* (note 10.13 on p. 282) states that the Book of Jashar, no longer extant, appears to have been a collection of poetry that extolled Israel's military victories and heroes.

Chapter Seven

1. The Book of Esther has the distinction of being the only book in the Bible that doesn't include the name of God. Its adoption into the biblical canon was a matter of great controversy and debate among both Jews and Christians. *101 Myths of the Bible*, p. 291.

Chapter Eight

1. *Oxford Annotated Bible*, p. 894, note 22.15-25.

2. *Oxford Annotated Bible*, p. 922, note 42.1-4.

Chapter Nine

1. In 2 Kings 18:25, King Sennacherib of Assyria claims

that the Lord told him to "Go up against this land (Judah), and destroy it." See also Isaiah 36:10.

2. Although an argument can be made that the deaths of any Israelites are proxy murders by God through his agents, Assyria and Babylon (see annotation #1), any such deaths are not included in the tally of killings. The Israelites do sometimes blame God for their misfortunes. For example, in Psalm 44:22, the Israelites lament that "Because of you (Lord God) we are being killed all day long, and accounted as sheep for the slaughter." In Lamentations 3:43, the Israelites cry out that "You (Lord God) have wrapped yourself with anger and pursued us, killing without pity."

Chapter Eleven

1. *Oxford Annotated Bible*, p. 214, note 35.9-15.

2. *Oxford Annotated Bible*, p. 214, note 35.9-15.

3. Numbers 35:16-18.

4. Numbers 35:20-21.

5. *Oxford Annotated Bible*, p. 214, note 35.9-15.

6. *Oxford Annotated Bible*, p. 133, note 7.20: Cut off from their kin is a reference to the death penalty.

Exhibits

1. This tale attempts to explain the presence of salt in the desolate southern shore of the Dead Sea. *101 Myths of the Bible*, p. 127.

2. In Exodus 15, considered the oldest original poem in the Bible (perhaps twelfth to tenth centuries BCE), and which follows right after the story of the drowning of the pharaoh's army, we have the Song of Moses, a recap of the pharaoh's defeat. In it there is no mention of the splitting of the sea, just the drowning of the soldiers. . ..The biblical poem depicts the pharaoh's army as rebelling against God, a slightly different image than that generally presented in the rest of Exodus, and God sent down his wrath to destroy them. *101 Myths of the Bible*, p. 210.

3. In *Don't Know Much About the Bible* (p. 108), Kenneth C. Davis states that Pharaoh sent out 600 chariots, which three men to each chariot. This would make the number killed at least 1,800. However, because the Bible does not specifically state that three men were in each chariot, only 600 deaths are recorded.

4. The Bible doesn't explicitly say the pharaoh drowned with them, but it is implied, as the pharaoh would have been at the head of his troops. *101 Myths of the Bible*, p. 188.

5. But see Numbers 23:19 – God is not a human being, that he should lie, or a mortal, that he should change his mind. Has he promised, and will he not do it? Has he spoken, and will he not fulfill it?

6. If God wanted Jacob to be the principle heir, why didn't he just arrange for Jacob to be born first? And why should God consign his hope that Jacob would succeed to a plan of outright dishonesty?....Jacob, instead of sharing the food with his brother, as any humane family member would do, took advantage of the situation and offered to sell the food to Esau in exchange for the birthright. Is

this Jacob the role model for a God who supposedly gave a commandment not to covet another's property? *101 Myths of the Bible*, p. 139.

7. *Oxford Annotated Bible*, p. 183, note 13.1-33.

8. With regard to remembering the Sabbath, Deuteronomy states that the purpose of the commandment is to remind Israel that God liberated the Hebrews from servitude in Egypt. The Exodus version says that the purpose of the Sabbath is to remind Israel that God rested on the seventh day of Creation. *101 Myths of the Bible*, p. 217.

9. *Oxford Annotated Bible*, p. 189, note 16.31-33.

10. Jericho was one of the earliest and most ancient cities of the world. Archaeological data suggests an inhabitation going back to the eighth millennium BCE. Evidence for a destruction of the walls dates to about 2300 BCE, but inhabitants rebuilt the town and erected new fortifications. Jericho appears to have been thoroughly destroyed by fire during the sixteenth century BCE, and, at best, only sparsely populated thereafter. Prior to 1300 BCE, the fortifications already had been destroyed, leaving no walls to tumble down before Joshua. At the time of the biblical battle, the city had been completely abandoned for at least a century or two. *101 Myths of the Bible*, p. 239-240.

11. The vivid biblical description of the cruel treatment of the Canaanites in Ai and other cities comes wrapped in the cloak of divine approval, pointing up one of the great ethical contradictions of the Bible. When a supposedly "evil" people are eradicated at God's direction, does that justify it? Remember, God's own commandment said

not to "murder," leaving some "wiggle room" for cases of killing that could be justified. *Don't Know Much About the Bible*, p. 152.

12. To the biblical scribes who wrote this story, the solar miracle demonstrated the awesome powers of God to alter natural phenomenon, and it showed that the victory of Joshua over the kings came as a gift from God. *101 Myths of the Bible*, p. 246.

13. This is a case of assisted suicide. See also 1 Samuel 31:3-5, where Saul, mortally wounded in battle, requests his armor-bearer to finish him off before his enemies are able to.

14. Other interesting cases of averted murder are a talking donkey saving a man named Balaam from death at the hands of an angel of God (Numbers 22:21-35); Abram pretending that Sarai is his sister so as not to be killed by the Egyptians (Genesis 12:10-13); Isaac pretending that Rebekah is his sister so as not to be killed by the men of Gerar (Genesis 26:6-7); the real mother saving her son from being divided in two by King Solomon (1 Kings 3:16-27).

15. *Oxford Annotated Bible*, p. 372, note 22.17-18.

16. In *101 Myths of the Bible* (p. 280-281), author Gary Greenberg submits that the second story of Saul's death – the one involving the Amalekite – is a less noble death than the purported suicide. He states that the suicide account appears to be an attempt to cover up the fact that Saul died at the hands of an enemy soldier.

17. *Oxford Annotated Bible*, p. 389, note 3.32-39.

18. *Oxford Annotated Bible*, p. 409, note 18.6-8.

19. *Oxford Annotated Bible*, p. 413, note 20.1-2.

20. *Oxford Annotated Bible*, p. 415, note 21.1-14.

21. *Oxford Annotated Bible*, p. 427, note 2.13-25.

22. *Oxford Annotated Bible*, p. 450, note 15.25-32.

23. *Oxford Annotated Bible*, p. 454, note 18.40.

24. *Oxford Annotated Bible*, p. 477, note 10.1-36.

25. *Oxford Anotated Bible*, p. 483, note 14.19.

26. *Oxford Annotated Bible*, p. 496, note 22.1-2.

27. *Oxford Annotated Bible*, p.552, note 14.9-15.